salt matters

a consumer guide

Dr Trevor C Beard

Lothian
BOOKS

GW00467477

The Menzies Research Institute is a World Health Organisation Collaborating Centre for Population Based Cardiovascular Disease Prevention Programmes.

Technical Editors

Associate Professor Michael Stowasser, MB BS, PhD, FRACP
Director, Hypertension Unit and Senior Lecturer, University Department of Medicine, Princess Alexandra Hospital, Woolloongabba, Brisbane, QLD 4102; Member of the Blood Pressure Advisory Committee, National Heart Foundation.

Associate Professor Malcolm Riley, PhD
Head of the Nutrition & Dietetics Section, Department of Medicine, Monash University, Melbourne, VIC 3168

Disclaimer

The author has made every effort to ensure that the information and advice in this book is complete and accurate. However, the information, ideas, suggestions and dietary advice contained in this book are not intended as a substitute for consulting your doctor and obtaining medical supervision regarding any action that may affect your well-being. Consulting your doctor before changing your salt intake is especially relevant if you are pregnant, ill, taking prescription medication or have suffered from any kidney disease. Individual readers must assume responsibility for their own actions, safety and health. Neither the author nor the publisher shall be liable or responsible for any loss, injury or damage allegedly arising from any information or suggestion in this book.

Brand or product names mentioned in this book that are trademarks or registered trademarks of their respective companies have been capitalised.

Thomas C. Lothian Pty Ltd
132 Albert Road, South Melbourne, 3205
www.lothian.com.au

Copyright © Trevor C Beard 2004

First published 2004
All rights reserved. No part of this publication may be reproduced, stored in a retrieval system or transmitted in any form by any means without the prior permission of the copyright owner. Enquiries should be made to the publisher.

National Library of Australia
Cataloguing-in-Publication data:

Beard, Trevor C. (Trevor Cory).

Salt matters : for your health's sake.

ISBN 0 7344 0610 X.

1. Salt-free diet. 2. Salt – Physiological effect. I.

Title.

613.285

Cover and text design by Black Widow Graphic Design
Typeset by Amanda Griffin
Index by Clodagh Jones
Printed in Australia by Griffin Press
Cover photograph courtesy of National Geographic Image Collection
Printed in Australia by Griffin Press

Foreword

Between 5000 and 6000 years ago salt was found to have the magic ability to preserve food. This allowed the development of settled communities and civilisation. Salt became the most traded and taxed substance in the world, analogous to oil currently. As it was pure and white, it also became an item of religious significance. However, with the invention of the deep-freeze and refrigerator its preservative role was no longer necessary. Unfortunately, this gift to civilisation came at a great price because our bodies are not designed to eat all this salt; indeed they are designed to cope in environments where there is virtually no salt in the diet. Salt is a toxic chemical in the amounts that we now consume — it increases our blood pressure and this kills and maims many hundreds of thousands of people worldwide from stroke and heart attacks, as well as having many other harmful effects on our bodies.

This excellent book outlines all the problems that salt causes, and shows, in a clear and informative way, how easy it is to give up this added chemical in our food. Trevor Beard was an early pioneer in pointing out the dangers of salt. Many years ago he developed a unique Salt Skip Program, and has become one of the leading world authorities on helping individuals to reduce their salt intake. This is not easy because more than three-quarters of our salt intake is now hidden in processed, fast, restaurant and canteen foods. At the same time, Trevor has been responsible for pressuring the food industry to make reductions in the very high and unnecessary salt content of their products.

This outstanding book represents a distillation of all Trevor's work and combines his expert knowledge in this area with a very practical approach. The book is written in an attractive and easily understood style. If everyone took notice of this book and changed their salt intake, there would be huge improvements in the health of the world with large reductions in strokes, heart attacks and heart failure.

Professor Graham A MacGregor
Professor of Cardiovascular Medicine
Blood Pressure Unit
St George's Hospital Medical School
Cranmer Terrace, London, SW17 0RE

Contents

Preface

I was staggered when I first discovered how much salt we eat in processed foods. I was looking at salt and sodium because I had developed 'high normal' blood pressure (now known as prehypertension) — my blood pressure was rising with age. I knew this affected my whole future, compromising any dream of a long and healthy retirement. Both my parents had died of strokes.

A fatalistic friend may tell you we all have to die of something, and a stroke is a 'nice way to go'. As a medical practitioner I can also tell you that only a minority succumb to their first stroke, and the remainder find a stroke a very unpleasant way to linger. In 1994 strokes accounted for nearly 25 per cent of all the chronic disability recorded in Australia. A stroke leaves some people lying paralysed in bed in an institution, unable to speak. They are only waiting for another stroke and hoping it will be their last — the one described as a 'nice way to go'.

There is strong evidence today that high blood pressure and stroke are almost completely preventable. If you would like to know how, this book will tell you. It starts with an overview of why salt matters more than you thought — and its link with high blood pressure and about a dozen other serious health problems. It reveals how processed foods (not salt shakers) are the central problem.

The next section introduces you to the Salt Skip Program. This dates from 1981, when a group of volunteers joined group discussions at a low salt cookery class at Woden TAFE in Canberra. The Salt Skip Program is all about choosing foods low in salt, then eating them like any other good food and forgetting about sodium and serving sizes. In the Salt Skip Program you don't go on a diet, you come off a diet — the high salt diet common to industrialised societies — and just choose better food (which is easy when you know how).

We are almost addicted to salt — highly dependent at least — but the basic practicalities of the Salt Skip Program help you to break free from salt dependency and turn instead to the hundreds of alternative food flavours that are more interesting and safer to eat. It describes the cooking methods that conserve flavour. It has a chapter on bread, another with recipes to get you started on low salt foods, and a chapter dealing with special situations like dining out and special occasions like Christmas, as well as a chapter on replacing iodised salt with safer iodine supplements.

The next section explains how and why salt is linked with high blood pressure and with other serious health problems, while the last deals with the host of questions frequently asked about salt, such as its connections with sport, hot weather and cramp. There is an important chapter on recognising how those with vested interests manipulate us with their own commercial agenda and create the daunting problem of what to believe. The final chapter canvasses the feasibility of salt skipping societies with healthy diets and lifestyles that give their members little, if any, increase in blood pressure with age and virtually abolish high blood pressure.

Dr Trevor C Beard
Hobart

Read this before you start

Don't play games with your salt intake — it matters.
It can alter the course of diseases and it can change
the way drugs work.

- *Are you pregnant?*
- *Are you ill?*
- *Do you take prescribed medication?*
- *Have you ever suffered kidney damage?*

**If so, read Appendix 1 carefully and discuss it
with your doctor before making any changes to
your salt intake.**

I   Introduction

Abbreviations

EBM	evidence-based medicine
FDA	Food and Drug Administration (USA)
MSG	monosodium glutamate
NHMRC	National Health and Medical Research Council
QHA	Queensland Hypertension Association
RDI	recommended dietary intake
WHO	World Health Organization

1
Why salt matters

Common salt, or sodium chloride, is a natural ingredient of nearly all foods. We can also add salt artificially as dry crystals of sodium chloride, or in solution in seawater or brine. We have been doing this rather liberally, and modern medical science is blaming an excess of salt for several serious health problems. I have written this book to tell you why salt matters, and what you can do about it.

Look at the huge amount of extra salt you eat. A cob of sweet corn has a natural sodium content of 3 milligrams of sodium in 100 grams of corn (3 mg/100 g), but the manufacturer of a packet of cornflakes states on the label that this brand of cornflakes gives you about 800 mg/100 g of sodium. A carton of fresh milk shows a sodium content of 56 mg/100 g, yet a packet of butter shows a sodium content of 800 mg/100 g. Food processing raises the natural sodium content of these foods artificially by about fourteen times for butter and more than one hundred times for cornflakes. We have been taking it for granted that we were all amazingly tolerant to all this extra sodium.

Some people can indeed handle a heavy load of sodium better than others, but in industrialised societies nearly every single inhabitant shows an increase in blood pressure by the time they reach middle age, and there is an international scientific consensus that our high sodium intakes are largely and directly responsible for this. By middle age most people no longer tolerate extra sodium as well as they once did. An increase in blood pressure is only one of about a dozen health problems that are now firmly linked with extra sodium and known to be both treatable and preventable by cutting the added sodium right down. Sodium chloride (common salt) is one of over forty sodium compounds approved as food additives in Australia, but about 90 per cent of all the sodium added to food is in sodium chloride.[1]

Salt is giving you a heavy burden of extra sodium. A noticeable difference to your health requires a big reduction in the salt you eat. In this book reducing your salt intake is called 'skipping salt' and the advice I have put together to make that process easier has become known as the Salt Skip Program.

Do we need salt?

Food writers often stress our need for salt. An attractive spice book tells us (correctly): *'We like salt, we need it and we cannot survive without it'*.[2] The sodium in sodium chloride is indeed vital for transmitting electrical impulses through nerves and assisting muscle contraction, and sodium also controls the distribution of water in the body. These functions need a little salt, plus a host of other essential elements that food writers ignore (since they are mostly tasteless, like calcium in the form of calcium carbonate, or bitter, like the calcium in calcium chloride), but we can survive without additional salt from a salt shaker — not only survive, but live well.

'Salt-free' societies

Humans acquired the technology for bulk manufacture of sodium chloride as a food additive about 5000 years ago, which is very recent against the timescale of human evolution. Today the world still has about twenty 'salt-free' societies that enjoy robust health without adding a grain of salt or a drop of seawater to their food.[3] Societies that depend entirely on the natural salt content of their food have been found on every inhabited continent, and include tribal Australian Aborigines, the bushmen of the Kalahari in Africa and the Tukisenta in the Papua New Guinea Highlands. Although some of these groups have access to salt in seawater, salt deposits or brine springs, they make no use of added salt at all. In 1973, at a time when the Tukisenta people had seen very little of the outside world, an Australian medical expedition measured their stamina with the Harvard Pack Fitness Test. The salt-free locals produced higher scores than the fit young men in an Australian air force unit posted to the same district.[4]

Thus the question about the need for salt is where to draw the line between adding no salt at all (which would be perfectly safe) and adding amounts that are being blamed for giving almost everybody an increase in blood pressure by the time they reach middle age. The government answers this question in the Dietary Guidelines for Australian Adults, which were updated in 2003 to conform with the latest international scientific consensus.[5]

Dietary Guidelines for Australian Adults

Health-conscious Australians who want to eat good food should try to follow the Dietary Guidelines for Australian Adults (2003). The dietary guidelines are set out in Chapter 10, which also shows readers how to use food labels to help them follow the guidelines. The Salt Skip Program takes full notice of all the dietary guidelines, and in particular, the salt guideline: *Choose foods low in salt*. Most foods in their natural state (and a few processed foods) are low in salt. It is easy to recognise low salt processed foods because 'low salt' is defined by the Australian and New Zealand food regulations. They must contain no more than *120 milligrams of sodium in 100 grams of food (120 mg/100 g)*. This international definition of 120 mg/100 g (set in Geneva by the United Nations) is the official yardstick in most countries.

Salt and high blood pressure

An early warning that adding salt to food could cause harm came from two French doctors in 1904. They found that six hospital patients with high blood pressure made a substantial recovery when they stopped eating food containing added salt.[6] Their blood pressure rose again when they were served soup with the usual salt content, but improved once more when the salty soup was taken off the menu. All the patients improved when skipping salt. We now know that a low salt intake will not *always* reverse high blood pressure — a point we will return to — but it will always reduce the average blood pressure of a group. This is because the majority of people show some benefit from skipping salt, and some do very well, so the net result is positive.

High blood pressure is often called 'the silent killer' because there are usually no symptoms before the onset of one of its complications — coronary heart disease, heart failure, stroke or kidney failure. Heart disease and stroke, between them, are the most common cause of death in both sexes, especially in men, and a coronary heart attack is still the most common cause of sudden death in fathers of young children.

High blood pressure is also a far more universal problem than most people realise. About one adult Australian in six has high blood pressure. This doesn't make it safe for the other five to eat as much salt as they like. Blood pressure increases with age and high blood pressure afflicts most people if they live long enough. A fifty-year follow-up of the population of Framingham, Massachusetts, found that the middle-aged and elderly had a 90 per cent lifetime risk of high blood pressure.[7]

Many people with a raised blood pressure find they can control their blood pressure without drugs — sometimes indefinitely — by adopting a healthier diet and lifestyle. They eat low salt foods, and in addition can increase the benefits of this action by controlling their weight, taking regular exercise, eating more fruit and vegetables than is usual in industrialised societies, limiting alcohol and managing stress.[8]

In Finland the government withholds the subsidy for drugs for high blood pressure unless the doctor certifies that the patient has made all the above changes of diet and lifestyle for at least six months, and agrees to continue them if medication is prescribed.[9] Even if drugs are prescribed, a healthier diet and lifestyle is important because it usually allows better control of blood pressure with lower doses of drugs, at lower cost and with fewer side-effects — thus the law in Finland provides both a financial bonus to the government and taxpayers and a health bonus to patients.

Why do we like salt if it can cause serious problems?

There is a popular theory that a liking for salt helped our ancestors to survive in salt-poor environments. However, explorers and anthropologists have reported the exact opposite — they find that salt-free societies *dislike* salt, often very strongly. The explorer C von Ditmar used to enjoy sharing his food with the salt-free nomadic tribes of Siberia just to watch their grimaces of revulsion.[10] The explorer Stefansson lived among Eskimos who disliked salt so intensely that he could put it to practical use — he could make his food unpalatable to them by adding a pinch of salt.[11] Australian anthropologist Janice Reid, who spent periods in Arnhem Land gathering food with the women of a local Aboriginal tribe, always needed to dip her cooked crabmeat in the sea to salt it, while her Aboriginal companions felt no such need.[12]

The Yanomama Indians of South America are the most salt-free humans in the world with a total sodium intake of no more than 160–180 mg *per person per day*.[13,14] Nevertheless, the Yanomama dislike salt intensely when they first taste it.[15] These salt-free societies have never acquired the taste for salt. The rest of us acquire the taste when we are young.

Is it always safe to skip salt?

The salt-free societies provide unequivocal proof that it is safe for healthy adults to skip added salt completely, and all human societies (including our own) prove that it is safe for healthy newborn babies too. In proportion to their size, babies need more salt than adults because they need an extra allowance for growth. Even though they can double their birth weight in six months they get all the salt they need from breast milk, which has a sodium content of 14 milligrams in 100 grams of milk (14 mg/100 g). This is constant, regardless of the mother's own salt intake. As growing babies are able to thrive on food with a sodium content of 14 mg/100 g, the dietary guideline allowing up to 120 mg/100 g obviously provides a generous surplus for adults who no longer need a special sodium allowance for growth.

Is this enough when sweating?

The amount of salt lost in sweat is variable. Ironically, a salty sweat is one of the results of eating salty food (a vicious circle). Aboriginal Australians in their tribal state used no added salt, yet were well adapted to strenuous exercise in very hot climates. Paradoxically it is better for athletes and travellers to the tropics to skip salt, so that they lose less salt through sweating.[16] Athletes will find a fuller discussion of sport and hot weather in Chapter 14.

Salt in special situations

If you are pregnant, ill or taking prescribed medication — or even if you just have a past history of kidney disease — you may have special needs that should be discussed with the doctor who is looking after you. Appendix 1 explains why this is so, and provides important information that will help you to understand the medical advice you are given.

Salt's rich but erroneous folklore

The discovery that salt was an edible food preservative gave it immense importance, and in addition human ingenuity has found countless further uses for it. There is a common belief, for example, that extra salt is essential to prevent muscle cramp, and to keep well in hot weather.

Muscle cramp

The possible connection between salt and muscle cramp is poorly understood, and few people have questioned it until recently. Before prescribing a low salt diet it was traditional to warn the patient to expect occasional muscle cramp at first, and yet several controlled trials of low salt diets have been unable to confirm a link. When patients were randomly allocated either to a diet group with a low salt intake or a control group that made no change, there was no significant difference between the two groups in the amount or severity of muscle cramp they reported, even after the diet group in each trial had been warned to expect more cramp.[17–19] Chapter 14 provides a fuller discussion of cramp and the other questions people ask about sport and hot weather.

Military dependence on salt

In the past, the Australian armed forces used to issue salt tablets to personnel travelling to hot climates, in the belief that extra salt would be needed to replace the salt lost in sweat. Despite the fact that the salt in military rations increases the salt content of the sweat, the loss in sweat is still small enough to be compensated by the next meal. Modern armies thus regard salt tablets as unnecessary, even in the tropics. Also salt tablets tended to cause vomiting if taken on an empty stomach, and increased the need for water, a significant liability in combat conditions, when water transport may be critical.

Until recently salt-preserved foods were valued in warfare because fresh foods were often unavailable on the march, whereas salt-preserved foods were portable and always ready to eat. A shortage of salt for this purpose delayed one of Napoleon's campaigns and interrupted Mao Zedong's Long March. Modern armies use foods preserved by methods that make no extra demand on fluid intake.

Animal salt hunger

It is often asserted that 'animals love salt' and 'obviously need it' because cattle and wildlife will trek vast distances in search of a salt lick. This salt hunger is peculiar to a few species of plant-eating animals. It can also affect a human individual who is deprived of salt for some special reason, but is not generally seen in whole populations that eat only natural (unsalted) foods — these populations *dislike* salt.

The cattle and wildlife that display salt hunger feed on plants that are virtually salt-free in some habitats — the sodium content of grass is below 1 mg/100 g in some continental pastures remote from the coast.[20] Animals without this problem include mice, which can multiply in plague numbers in the Australian wheat harvest, without access to any added salt. Unlike cattle and browsing wildlife, mice can thrive spectacularly on an exclusive diet of unsalted wheat grains with a sodium content of only 3 mg/100 g.

Salt in gastronomy

Chefs argue that 'good cuisine needs salt'. However, chefs and their clientele need salt added to their food because their palates are so completely adapted to salty food. Salt skippers discover that the sense of taste recovers, with substantial improvement within four weeks of changing to a low salt intake.[21] Within three to six months of skipping salt palates recover enough to be described as truly *normal* (that is, no longer subdued by salt) for the first time since infancy. Normal palates can detect and enjoy the real and subtle flavours of well-cooked food. Normal palates have no objection to any of the harmless food additives such as the wonderful range of flavours offered by the many herbs and spices available.

Medical conditions connected with salt intake

High blood pressure is by no means the only health problem linked with high levels of salt intake. Fluid retention, seen in swollen ankles in hot weather, in travel oedema and in carpal tunnel syndrome, is directly associated with a high salt intake and relieved by a low salt intake. Salt is the main trigger for the serious vertigo that occurs in Meniere's syndrome. Women with severe symptoms of premenstrual syndrome (PMS), such as bloating, mood swings and swollen ankles, can reduce or eliminate these symptoms with a lower salt intake. Salt cannot be excreted in the urine without an accompanying loss of calcium and this has a direct effect on osteoporosis and the development of kidney and bladder stones. Cancer societies worldwide warn of the link between stomach cancer and frequent consumption of salt-preserved foods such as salamis, salted fish, bacon and ham. These and other salt-related health problems are discussed in more detail in Chapter 13.

Salt matters because a massive international consensus blames it for many serious health problems. High blood pressure is by far the most important of these — it has become the greatest epidemic of non-infectious disease ever to afflict the human race — and the other problems are by no means negligible.

We could either eliminate or effectively control all the health problems associated with salt simply by consuming a lot less of it. This means shopping for better food, and adapting some of our favourite recipes. The next chapters will help you to do this well and to enjoy doing it.

2
The salt shaker is not the problem

Many people agree that salt can be a health hazard and happily proclaim, 'Since I heard that, I haven't touched the stuff'. How wrong they are! When they learn to read food labels they will discover that many common processed foods provide a huge load of added salt.

Cooking salt and table salt

In the 1995 Hobart Salt Study a research team invited every tenth person from a subsection of the Hobart electoral roll to talk about food and answer questions about their shopping and eating habits.[1] Over half the people (54 per cent of men and 61 per cent of women) stated that they never or rarely cooked with salt and more than half said they never or rarely added salt at the table (51 per cent of men and 73 per cent of women). These people believed they were avoiding salt, and wondered what more they could do. They were not aware how much salt they were already eating each day in processed foods, many of which (like cornflakes and many other breakfast cereals) are not even salty to taste.

A landmark study in Scotland in 1987 drew attention to the high salt level of many processed foods. The study found that people who completely cut out salt in cooking and at the table make only about a 15 per cent reduction in their salt intake, unless they also change their shopping habits and choose low salt foods.[2] Fresh food supplies about 10 per cent of the salt we eat, and cooking and table salt supply only 15 per cent. The remaining 75 per cent of the salt we eat comes from processed foods.[2]

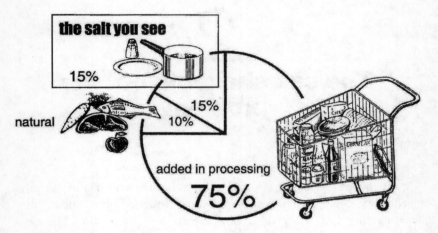

Figure 2.1 The findings of a 1987 Scottish study of the main sources of salt in the diet of industrialised societies

The Hobart Salt Study, 1995

Before the Hobart study made any mention of salt, participants were asked to make a 24-hour urine collection, which was analysed for salt content. The figure overleaf shows the amount of sodium excreted in the urine per day plotted against age. Men's results are shown by black dots and women's results by open circles.

The range of these results was impressive, with one man excreting 337 mmol of sodium per day (337 mmol/day) — twelve times more than a woman who excreted only 26 mmol.* Men always have a higher average sodium excretion, and in the Hobart data the increase was in proportion to their larger body size, muscle development and likely meal size.[3]

The average sodium excretion rate was 170 mmol/day for men and 118 mmol/day for women. Sodium excretion above 250 mmol/day was confined to younger men (perhaps by chance, given the small number of subjects in the sample). Apart from that and the gender difference, the ages and sodium excretion rates seem to be quite random. Young or old, the individual results may be high or low, or anywhere in between.

*Medical laboratories measure sodium excretion in millimoles (mmol), while food labels use milligrams (mg). See Appendix 3 for further explanation.

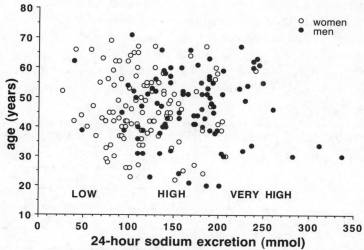

Figure 2.2 24–hour sodium excretion of 194 Hobart people, aged 18–70 years, plotted by sex and age

Statistical analysis was unable to predict which people had reported that they cooked with salt or added salt at the table. A few who thought they were doing everything possible to avoid salt had surprisingly high sodium excretion rates. Again, this seemed to be quite random.

Because all surveys of sodium excretion show this wide variation, the Hobart study tried to find other possible explanations, and failed. One woman said she avoided salt as she followed the Pritikin diet, but the data showed no statistical association between sodium excretion and age, education or any of a range of standard psychological measures selected for their likely relevance.[1] In practice, a surprisingly high urine result may be the result of a take-away meal, or a visit to a restaurant, often an Asian restaurant. People who take no notice of the salt content of the foods they buy must expect a wide and unpredictable variation in their daily sodium excretion.

Salt added in food processing

The robust health and vigour of the world's salt-free societies provides abundant evidence that fresh foods provide all the salt we need for perfect health.[4] When natural foods are processed, salt is added as a preservative, a flavour, or, in the case of bread, a dough improver as well as a flavour. This means that processing often makes a huge difference to the sodium content of our food. Look at the table below comparing fresh and processed foods and notice the large change in chemical composition that takes place between the natural food and the processed food. Sodium content is shown in milligrams per 100 grams (mg/100 g):

Fresh food	(mg/100 g)	Processed food	(mg/100 g)
Cow's milk	56	Butter	800
		Cheese	1500 (up to)
Wheat	3	Bread	750 (up to)
Lean pork	65	Lean ham	1580
		Fried bacon	2000
Lean beef	76	Corned beef	1200
Green olives	3	Stuffed olives	2070
Fresh fish (bream)	84	Salted anchovies	5480

Reading food labels

When you start reading food labels, however, you will notice that a few processed foods are surprisingly low in salt. Examples include most of the mueslis, up to 30 per cent of the other breakfast cereals, and all of the Coles range of no-added-salt groceries. Variations in different brands of the same food will also surprise you if you have not read food labels before.

For example, one supermarket brand of sun-dried tomatoes may have a sodium content of 1580 mg/100 g while another brand with no salt shown in the ingredient list contains only 29 mg/100 g, as would be expected. A tandoori curry paste that received a top taste rating from a Melbourne food writer has only 4 mg/100 g and yet another brand has 3326 mg/100 g — a difference of 3322 mg in the one food item.

Reading food labels for salt content

Since December 2002, Australian food regulations have required manufacturers of processed food to present a panel of 'Nutrition information' in a standardised format somewhere on the label of the food item and since December 2003 it has been mandatory and enforceable. To find out how much salt there is in a particular food, there are two main steps. First look at the top of each column and select the column with the heading 100 grams (100 g). Then look for 'Sodium' on the left-hand side of the label and read across to check the sodium figure in the 100 g column. This tells you how much sodium the food contains in milligrams of sodium per 100 grams of food (mg/100 g). With a little practice you will soon be able to read the sodium content of different foods reliably. (Chapter 10 explains how to use nutrition information panels to check the fat content and other details.)

The food labels on page 14 show the difference between two breakfast cereals on sale at the time of the Hobart Salt Study in 1995. Cereal A had a sodium content of 1093 mg/100 g, while Cereal B had only 3 mg/100 g — a difference of 1090 mg.

Identifying high salt foods

A cereal with a sodium content of 1093 mg/100 g is saltier than sea-water — which has 1068 mg/100 g — yet the taste of salt was hard to recognise in Cereal A's combination of sugar and cereal. Without reading the label very few people would guess that this cereal contained any salt at all. By 2003 the sodium content of this particular cereal had been by reduced by 34 per cent to 720 mg/100 g, making it even more difficult to identify the presence of salt by taste alone. This means you can't always trust your taste buds to identify high salt foods. You have to check the labels.

The taste of salt is usually unmistakable in foods pickled with salt. Pickling brine can be made with 100 grams of salt in a litre of water, which gives it a sodium content of about 4000 mg/100 g (about four times more salty than seawater). Brine-preserved foods like olives and capers seldom have less than 2000 mg/100 g. Dry salting gives even higher levels in foods such as fish. For example, the sodium content of the salted anchovies served on top of a pizza is over 5000 mg/100 g.

In an ancient world without refrigeration technology the discovery that salt preserved food was extremely valuable. Any food is better than starvation, and the palates of hungry people can adapt to

CEREAL A

NUTRITION INFORMATION

Servings per package – 9
Serving size – 30 g (1 cup)

	PER 30 g SERVE	PER 30 g WITH ½ CUP WHOLE MILK	PER 100 g
ENERGY	461 kJ (110 Cal)	823 kJ (197 Cal)	1537 kJ (367 Cal)
PROTEIN	1.7 g	6.0 g	5.6 g
FAT	0.4 g	5.3 g	1.3 g
CARBOHYDRATE			
–TOTAL	26.1 g	32.0 g	87.1 g
–SUGARS	3.0 g	8.9 g	10.0 g
DIETARY FIBRE	1.0 g	1.0 g	3.3 g
SODIUM	328 mg	401 mg	1093 mg
POTASSIUM	37 mg	230 mg	123 mg

CEREAL B

NUTRITION INFORMATION

Servings per packet - 12
Serving size - 30 g (1 cup)

	PER 30 g SERVE	Per 30 g WITH ½ CUP SKIM MILK	PER 100 g
ENERGY	457 kJ (109 Cal)	635 kJ (152 Cal)	1523 kJ (363 Cal)
PROTEIN	3.2 g	7.6 g	10.5 g
FAT	0.8 g	1.0 g	2.6 g
CARBOHYDRATE			
-TOTAL	23.4 g	29.4 g	78.0 g
-SUGARS	0.3 g	6.3 g	0.9 g
DIETARY FIBRE	2.8 g	2.8 g	9.3 g
SODIUM	1 mg	65 mg	3 mg
POTASSIUM	97 mg	280 mg	322 mg
CHOLESTEROL	0 mg	2.5 mg	0 mg

Figure 2.3 Two breakfast cereal labels illustrating the range on sale in 1995

very high concentrations of salt and readily tolerate salt–preserved foods. Salt removed the spectre of seasonal famine, and rapidly became one of the most valuable items of international trade. Wars were fought over access to salt.

Apart from causing thirst and a demand for more water, the main drawback to eating food containing additional salt was that every other food tasted very bland unless salt was added as a condiment. We are very lucky that this effect is reversible. Once people start eating at a lower salt intake, their sense of taste recovers substantially within a few weeks, even after years of suppression by eating excess salt.

Choosing low salt foods

Shopping for low salt foods and thus eating for health and longevity has never been easier.
• Buy fresh foods and eat them without added cooking or table salt.
• Buy only those processed foods that comply with the Australian dietary guidelines and Food Standards Code (that is, foods with a sodium content up to 120 mg/100 g).
• Choose low salt — not reduced salt — foods.
You will soon be able to read the sodium content reliably with the

new standardised format shown below, which has been mandatory since 31 December 2003.

Reading the nutrition information panel shows that this is a low salt food (sodium at 60 mg/100 g is under the 120 mg/100 g guideline).

You can see that the precaution of cutting out the salt used in cooking and at the table has been totally inadequate when we eat so much salt in processed foods. Even if you no longer buy salt or keep any in the house you have made no more than a token reduction of at most 15 per cent. You and your doctor are unlikely to notice any measurable health benefit until you reduce the 75 per cent of salt that is coming from processed foods. This means checking every food label and choosing low salt foods. In the 100 g column, check the sodium. Double-check that you are looking at the 100 g column and not at the amount per serving (some labels switch the positions round and put the 100 g column on the left). If sodium is no more than 120 mg/100 g, you have a low salt food.

NUTRITION INFORMATION		
Servings per package: 3		
Serving size: 150 g		
	Quantity per serving	Quantity per 100 g
Energy	608 kJ	405 kJ
Protein	4.2 g	2.8 g
Fat, total	7.4 g	4.9 g
– saturated	4.5 g	3.0 g
Carbohydrate, total	18.6 g	12.4 g
– sugars	18.6 g	12.4 g
Sodium	90 mg	60 mg
Calcium	300 mg (38%)*	200 mg
* Percentage of recommended dietary intake		
Ingredients: Whole milk, concentrated skim milk sugar, strawberries (9%), gelatine, culture, thickener (1442).		

Figure 2.4 The nutrition information panel mandatory on processed foods throughout Australia and New Zealand since 2003

II   The Salt Skip Program

Abbreviations

tsp	level metric teaspoon (5 mL)
tbs	level metric tablespoon (20 mL)
LS	low salt
NAS	no added salt

3
Achieving independence from salt

Achieving independence from salt is the major aim of the Salt Skip Program. The first step in understanding this program is to recognise one of the modern world's important problems. Most people believe they eat normal food, with a 'normal' salt intake. Their view is that sick people sometimes have to adopt a 'restricted diet', for example to treat high blood pressure, by restricting their salt intake. The evidence today, however, is that our food is the exact opposite of normal.

Medical science now attributes a large share of our chronic disease and disability to the *artificial diet* of our sick society.[1] We saw in the previous chapter that some of the processed foods in our so-called 'normal diet' contain over 100 times more sodium than the same food in the fresh, natural state in which nature provides it. The huge overload of added salt (sodium chloride) and other sodium compounds available nowadays as food additives has been converting our food into an artificial diet that gives us a sodium problem. Some people no longer tolerate excess sodium as well as they once did, and they need the more natural food that would have kept them well if they had been eating it earlier.

Healthy people don't need a doctor to help them skip salt or to give them permission to skip salt. If they can read the nutrition information panels on food labels they should be able to follow the salt guideline of the Dietary Guidelines for Australian Adults. It is a pity that so many healthy people lack both the knowledge and the motivation to do this. If they let their blind spot about 'normal food' go on misleading them they will continue to jeopardise their health with the artificial diet that is now linked with a high risk of chronic disease.[2,3] The Salt Skip Program can give that knowledge to all the healthy people who have the motivation to read this book.

Sick people are in a different position — they are already under medical care. Skipping salt may alter the course of many diseases (for the better), make a number of drugs more effective at a lower dose, and replace the need for diuretics with their long-term side-effects. To get well and stay well, patients need to collaborate with their doctors in every detail of their treatment, including their salt intake. This means the sick must always talk to their doctors about the pros and cons of skipping salt.

Until now everybody has found it difficult to skip salt properly without help. Today we have the nutrition information panel on food labels, and help from the Salt Skip Program on how to use the panels.

The Salt Skip Program

The Salt Skip Program dates from 1981, when a group of volunteers took part in a low salt cookery class at Woden TAFE College in Canberra held in conjunction with a trial of low salt foods as a treatment for high blood pressure.[4] Many in the class disliked the negative connotations of 'avoiding' salt and wanted a better word to describe what they were trying to do. Janet Coburn, the class teacher, found one. She suggested that the class was 'skipping' salt. Skipping — positive, happy and healthy — said it all. 'Salt skippers' were born.

This Canberra group of salt skippers, NoSal Incorporated, later became Salt Skip Incorporated when its base moved to Hobart. Today the Queensland Hypertension Association (QHA) supports people with high blood pressure in all states and territories and acts as the contact business address for the Salt Skip Program.

The Salt Skip Program's goal is to make it easier for people to skip salt in their daily food. It identifies low salt foods by checking how many milligrams of sodium there are per 100 grams of food. (The dietary guidelines suggest that everybody should be choosing foods low in salt, and a program designed for everybody has to be easy.) The Salt Skip Program has four distinguishing features:

1 It takes people off the high salt diet of industrialised societies and gives them better (healthier) food.

2 It uses food labels to identify better food. There is no need to add up the kilojoules of energy or the milligrams of sodium eaten in a day.
3 It offers the whole family better food (some of the family will carry the same genes, and catering is easier if everyone gets better food). In other words, the program caters for prevention as well as treatment, and offers prevention to the families who need it most.
4 It tells serious salt skippers how to check progress and measure their salt intake by 24-hour urine collections.

Choosing healthy foods

When you skip salt and choose better foods it is worth the effort to follow *all* the Dietary Guidelines for Australian Adults. Not only do better foods have less salt; they also contain less fat, less sugar, more potassium and more fibre. The Salt Skip Program concentrates almost exclusively on salt because the other dietary guidelines are covered in detail elsewhere.*

The Salt Skip Program identifies a range of ways to remove salt from the diet without creating a diet that is uninteresting or boring. Following chapters will look at alternative ways of flavouring food without using salt (using herbs, spices and sauces) and methods of cooking that conserve flavour in foods. As bread is a staple food for most people and one that normally relies on salt, there are recipes for making low salt bread, as well as a collection of other handy low salt recipes. There are ways to manage special occasions such as dining out and celebratory times such as Christmas. The program also shows you how to get enough iodine to prevent thyroid problems without depending on iodised salt.

Checking food labels

As mentioned earlier, taste alone cannot be relied upon to identify high salt foods. It is essential to check food labels of processed foods for their sodium content. The nutrition information panel makes this

* The National Health and Medical Research Council (NHMRC) will send a free 30-page booklet called *Eat Well for Life* in response to a toll-free call to 1800 020 103 or an email to <phd.publications@health.gov.au>. Although addressed to older Australians it is equally useful for all adults. It can also be down-loaded from the NHMRC website <www.nhmrc.health,gov.au>.

easy, as explained in detail in Chapter 11. As you are not trying to follow a prescribed diet there is no need to worry about serving sizes. Simply check whether a food is safe to eat, that is, whether the sodium level is at or below 120 mg/100 g. If it is, *you can eat as much or as little of the food as you like*, within the limits of appetite and common sense, and the need for a trim waistline.

Offering the whole family better food

One of the important aims of the Salt Skip Program is to offer the whole family better and healthier food. If you have discovered that salt is causing a health problem, such as high blood pressure or fluid retention, it would be wise to let your close relatives improve their diets at the same time as you do (as already indicated above). It is also easier to cater for a family when everybody eats the same food. Don't forget your older relatives, especially as the benefits of skipping salt are often more rapidly obvious in old age than in youth. The rest of your family has a choice — to continue the unhealthy diet and lifestyle of industrialised societies with its known hazards ('diseases of civilisation') or to eat food that helps to prevent these problems.[3]

Checking progress

Those who follow the Salt Skip Program for medical reasons can ask their doctors to measure their progress with a 24-hour urine collection when they think they are doing everything right. The amount of sodium excreted will indicate whether your intake is low enough. This test is not done routinely in all medical practices, but both doctors and patients will find the essentials in Appendix 2.

In the Salt Skip Program everybody who *tries* to skip salt properly is called a *salt skipper*, and everybody who *succeeds* (has a good result with a 24-hour urine test) is called a *serious salt skipper*. A good 24-hour urine result is a sodium excretion rate below 50 mmol/day for a man and below 40 mmol/day for a woman.

Professional dietitians normally suggest introducing a change of diet gradually (it is easy and painless, with a cumulative effect) but many recruits to the Salt Skip Program want immediate results. If salt has been making them ill they want to get rid of it as soon as possible. The rate of adjustment is entirely your choice. 'Cold turkey' has been the unanimous choice of the patients with Meniere's syndrome seen at the Menzies Clinic since 1991 and no one has reported any side-effects from the rapid changeover. Good motivation usually makes adaptation to the Salt Skip Program surprisingly easy. In addition, the suggestions and recipes offered in this book should help.

The importance of bread

In the Australian food tables the sodium content of various breads ranges from 400 to 725 mg/100g, and a single slice of ordinary bread would add about 8 mmol to your 24-hour urine result. Most supermarkets sell no suitable bread except the Indian flat bread mentioned in Chapter 11. This is excellent but unsuitable for toast, so most salt skippers make their own bread without salt.

Low salt and salt-free bread have a very different taste at first, but the rapid adaptation of the palate described below enables the majority of salt skippers to enjoy it and gradually begin to dislike ordinary bread.

Adaptation of the palate

When you adopt the Salt Skip Program and start to skip salt, you will find that your palate restores itself. Nature will help to repair the damage that salt has done to your tastebuds, and their recovery will create a lower level of salt preference.[5]

Within four weeks of adopting the Salt Skip Program most people find they can no longer tolerate salty foods like olives or anchovies, even when they have enjoyed these foods previously. An adapted palate is the cheapest and best salt substitute, introducing the connoisseur to the real flavours of food, and the subtle and wonderful nuances previously masked by salt.

Like salt, cigarette smoking is an enemy to an adapted palate. As well as making a huge contribution to your health and longevity, quitting smoking will improve your palate's ability to appreciate the natural flavours of food.

Foods preserved with salt

When food is preserved by prolonged exposure to high concentrations of a food additive with the powerful chemical and electrical properties of sodium chloride, there is a health hazard involved. A pinch of salt is not sufficient to preserve food. The sodium content of brine used for pickling onions or olives is about 4000 mg/100 g, while the sodium content of salt-pickled food is usually 2000 mg/100 g or more. Preserved foods like bacon and salami contain very large amounts of salt.

A higher salt intake leads to a greater preference for salt.[6] In restaurants and homes, many people sprinkle salt on their meal before they have even tasted it. Foods like bacon, ham, corned beef, olives and anchovies are preserved with salt and need salt-tolerant palates. Nobody can tolerate foods preserved in salt until they have trained their palates to accept them. This makes other foods seem insipid, so palates adjusted to salt in preservative concentration need salt as a condiment. Eating salt-preserved foods keeps you in the fast lane for salt consumption.

Salt is only one of the problems of delicatessen foods. Their exotic and powerful flavours come from the chemical changes that surviving bacteria and fungi can produce when salt inhibits normal putrefaction. These new foods in the timeframe of human evolution are common causes of migraine and other symptoms of food allergy and intolerance. Thus the health benefits of a lower salt intake sometimes include the relief of symptoms of previously unsuspected food intolerance. Some people who have been complaining of chronic indigestion report welcome relief when the sensitive lining of the stomach is no longer in regular contact with foods preserved with salt.

While very salty food such as olives can be overpowering after skipping salt for a while, some people find it easier to tolerate less salty flavours such as ham. Unfortunately, ham is a food that violates both the fat and the salt guidelines. Ham smoked without salt is palatable, but unsafe. Traditional recipes that use no salt are responsible for a few cases of botulism in Europe each year when food is home smoked without salt in violation of the food regulations. Botulism is a rare but dangerous form of food poisoning, and is usually fatal. In the Balkans, sauerkraut has traditionally been made without using salt. In this case, the acid fermentation removes any danger of botulism, so salt-free homemade sauerkraut is safe.[7]

Revising some culinary traditions

Traditionally salt has been used in cooking to remove moisture from eggplants. With eggplant, the ancient ritual varied, but one version was to cover slices or cubes of eggplant liberally with salt. After half an hour some recipes recommended rinsing off the salt before cooking the eggplant, but rinsing still left an unacceptable residue of salt. Salt was said to 'remove the bitterness'. However, bitterness is seldom noticeable in Australian eggplants, and one simple precaution is to avoid buying an old eggplant. If a dip made of eggplant purée tastes bitter, an alternative is to add half a teaspoon of sugar and blend it again. This tip comes from Gabriel Gaté's book *Smart Food*, written for the Anti-Cancer Council of Victoria — a reduced-salt cookbook because of the link between a high salt intake and stomach cancer.

Salt was also said to 'remove excess moisture', but slices of eggplant can be fried after simply patting them dry on kitchen paper. One salt skipper believes slices of eggplant absorb less oil during frying if they are dried briefly in the microwave first. For people who watch their weight, an alternative is to dab the eggplant slices very lightly with olive oil and bake them on the grill or barbecue.

Before roasting a leg of pork it was traditional to rub the surface with salt and then plain flour to make the crackling crisp when roasted. People who still eat crackling will find that plain flour works just as well without salt if the oven is hot enough in the initial period (230–250°C for the first half hour, then 150°C until cooked). However, the saturated animal fat in pork crackling doesn't fit the Dietary Guidelines for Australian Adults that relate to heart disease, raised blood cholesterol and overweight. To cook a leg of pork in a healthier way, trim off all visible fat and roast it in an oven bag or in foil, adding herbs to bring out the flavour.

Recipes may suggest salting cucumbers or gherkins when making pickles. An alternative is to use calcium chloride, available from a pharmacy. Chemical food additives (other than sodium chloride) have numbers, and calcium chloride (509) keeps vegetables firm (non-mushy) when canned or bottled. It works without salt. The taste — bitter rather than salty — is not noticeable in the amount used for pickling (see the recipe in Chapter 7).

Adapting recipes

You can nearly always adapt favourite recipes just by leaving out the salt and increasing the amount of herbs and spices. This works equally well with new recipes you may find in cookbooks and magazines. There are also low salt cookbooks available (see Chapter 5).

Thus the Salt Skip Program has the same target audience as the Dietary Guidelines for Australian Adults — every healthy Australian adult (the *prevention* audience). However, the target audience that can expect measurable (often substantial) benefit within a few weeks of becoming serious salt skippers will be several million Australians with the health problems outlined in Chapter 1 and described more fully in Chapters 12 and 13, together with over 3 million others who have prehypertension — blood pressure above 120/80 (the *treatment* audience).[8]

While helping people to observe all of the Australian dietary guidelines, the Salt Skip Program's sharpest focus is on the salt guideline — the one guideline that has been so poorly understood and so badly neglected. For the first two decades of its gradual evolution the Salt Skip Program has consisted of leaflets and booklets, and now this book updates and consolidates them in one publication.

4
Flavouring food without salt

When a dish seems to need something to give it a lift, chefs and home cooks have about three hundred flavours they can add. Salt skippers have full access to all but two of these — salt and monosodium glutamate (MSG). The herbs that are available fresh in season can also be bought in dried form all year round, while supermarkets carry a wide range of spices. For a choice of up to three hundred flavours, you will need to find a specialty shop selling an even wider range of herbs and spices. These spice shops often sell salt substitutes and low sodium versions of 'flavour boosters', proprietary mixtures that are designed to bring out other flavours in foods.

This chapter shows you how to increase flavour in cooking without using salt, by using salt substitutes, flavour boosters, herbs and spices. (Chapter 11 and Appendix 5 give details of suppliers for some of these items.) It also looks at an alternative method of smoking fish and examines some misleading claims made about salt substitutes.

Salt substitutes

Fruit juices, vinegars and spices with acid flavours

Experienced salt skippers are able to entertain without using salt; they can provide salt shakers on the table and have the satisfaction of seeing no one use them. At least two authors have had that satisfaction.[1,2] Although these publications are both out of print, modern salt skippers report the same achievement with methods outlined here and in Chapter 5.

One basic principle of cooking without salt is to use acid flavours such as lemon juice and all the other fruit juices, especially plum and the more exotic tamarind. Then there are the vinegars, particularly balsamic vinegar.

One spice with an acid flavour is sumac, used in ancient Greece and Rome when lemons were apparently unknown in Europe. Sumac has a flavour in the same family as lemon, but with a most agreeable astringency. It is a dark red powder, readily available from shops that specialise in selling herbs and spices. It is perfect for sprinkling on fish or on a white sauce or dip. It can be sprinkled in the same density you would use for decorating a dip with paprika, and the visual effect is similar, but with attractive dark red grains. It can be sprinkled through a salt shaker or sprinkler bottle that has larger holes.

Some people find the Indian spice amchur (unripe mango, dried and powdered) a bit too much like lemon to be worth buying, but sometimes it may be convenient to have 'lemon' available as a dry powder.

Potassium chloride (additive 508)

Potassium chloride is a very satisfactory salt substitute in bread and cheese making. With table use it has a bitter or metallic taste unless used sparingly. When used in small amounts, it tastes like salt. However, a small minority of people find even small amounts unpleasant.

The two brands of potassium chloride on sale in Australian supermarkets are both called 'No Salt'. Both carry the following warning on the label which puzzles many prospective purchasers:

> Not suitable for diets requiring low or restricted sodium or potassium intake without medical advice. Not suitable for use with certain diuretics.

Food regulations require this warning on the label because potassium chloride must be avoided by patients in kidney failure, and by those who take certain medications. Heavy users of table salt who take prescription drugs should not buy No Salt without medical advice that the drugs they are taking are compatible with potassium chloride.

There is no warning when food labels list additive 508, because measured amounts seldom compensate fully for the potassium lost in processing (see below). Similarly — in the absence of severe kidney failure — measured amounts should be safe in homemade bread.

The value of potassium to most of the population

As explained more fully in Appendix 6, natural foods contain more potassium than sodium and the vast majority of the population — everyone except a small proportion of the sick and those on medication — would benefit from a return to the higher potassium and lower sodium intake of our ancestors.[3] Food processing tends to waste potassium, for example canned peas not only have more sodium than fresh peas (from added salt) but processing spoils them still further by also removing potassium. The Australian tables of food composition show that the potassium content of fresh peas drops from 420 mg/100 g to 380 mg/100 g when they are boiled (if the water is discarded), and to 120 mg/100 g when they are canned — about a 70 per cent loss with canning. Whole wheat and brown rice also lose about 70 per cent of their potassium when milled to make white flour and white rice.

Since thirty-three potassium compounds are permitted as food additives, the low potassium content of processed foods may seem surprising. The net wastage of potassium leaves the food industry with no excuse for continuing to ignore a specific recommendation to make greater use of potassium chloride as a salt substitute in food processing.[4]

Freezing has the great advantage of preserving the natural potassium content of foods. When you can't buy fresh vegetables, buy frozen vegetables, which have all the potassium content of fresh ones and the double bonus of preservation without the loss of flavour that is the usual pretext for adding salt to processed foods. If frozen vegetables are *processed*, for example minted peas, take care to read the label. Manufacturers like to add salt to make a 'value-added' product.

Children often make heavy use of the salt shaker when their mother or father stops cooking with salt. Three Canberra mothers independently hit on the idea of filling the salt shaker with potassium chloride. None of the children noticed the difference. All the children gave up using the potassium chloride salt shakers within a month (unlike their behaviour with salt). The explanation that adults give for giving up potassium chloride so quickly is that it paradoxically loses its charm — it still tastes like salt at a time when their salt preference is steadily declining.

Flavour boosters

Stock cubes have been the downfall of many people who thought they were 'cooking without salt'. Beef cubes and chicken cubes are really brown salt and yellow salt with additives known as food flavours (they contain no beef or chicken). At present, there are no low salt stock cubes, but powders are available. No-added-salt stock powders are retailed in health food shops in several states as Salt Skip Stock Powder in three flavours (see Appendix 5 for a mail order address).

A dried yeast flavour booster is available in bulk to the food industry under the trade name Zyest. A version of Zyest containing no added salt is also available in a retail pack by mail order as Salt Skip Flavour Booster.

Asian food shops and some spice shops sell MSG. Although it is an effective flavour booster, a few people report a food intolerance to MSG.[5] Many others object to it on principle. Another reason not to use MSG is because MSG crystals are 12 per cent sodium, which is quite a lot (even salt is only 39 per cent sodium). The equally effective flavour boosters — disodium guanylate and disodium inosinate — also contain sodium. While not being sold retail at present, these are commonly found in many ingredient lists for soups and other savoury processed foods, either by name or number (they are additives 627 and 631 respectively). MSG, disodium guanylate and disodium inosinate all have a savoury flavour called *umami* by the Japanese.

There are several sodium-free glutamates, including monopotassium glutamate and calcium diglutamate.[6] Like MSG, they may be retailed in pure form before long. Meanwhile you can already see them on food labels for low sodium foods, especially soups.

Herbs

There are many herbs that can be used to flavour foods. Some perennial favourites not listed here include ginger, horseradish, celery seeds and mint.

Basil

For those who cling to the belief that they 'can't possibly eat a tomato without salt', the answer is basil. There is no happier marriage in the plant kingdom than tomato with basil — fresh or dried. Cherry tomatoes can be sliced in half and served, each with a sliver of fresh basil leaf, to go with drinks before a dinner party. Basil is one of the basic herbs in Italian dishes, including pizzas. It is another of the few herbs that increase in flavour when cooked, and can be used in soups, stews and sauces.

Dried basil is sold on the spice shelves in every supermarket. In the spring you can grow fresh basil from seed. Seedlings don't transplant well, however, and need minimum root disturbance. Basil needs moist, well-drained soil and a sunny but sheltered position. It needs regular watering but does not like to have 'wet feet'. The slightest whiff of frost kills it — the basil may be dead even when tomato plants escape. Fresh basil flown from Queensland, however, is available in fruit and vegetable shops in winter throughout Australia.

Other accompaniments for tomato include oregano, a little powdered garlic, or freshly ground black pepper. Another companion flavour is clove, much used in commercial tomato sauce and ketchup.

Celeriac

Celeriac, also called turnip rooted celery, is another plant of special value to salt skippers. Only the root is used since, although the stems and leaves resemble celery, they may taste rather bitter. Celeriac can be grown from seed, and in winter you can usually find it at vegetable markets. Choose a root that is heavy for its size, as some of the others are hollow and spongy when cut. Scrub the root and peel it like a turnip. Cook it in pieces, or serve it shredded and blanched in a salad.

Diced or shredded celeriac is very useful in gravy. It can be frozen in ice-cube trays and the blocks transferred to plastic bags for storage in the freezer. One block can transform gravy, even though the sodium content is only 21 mg/100 g.

Fennel and dill

What basil and oregano are to tomato, fennel is to fish. Dill is equally suitable, with a similar but more subtle flavour. The two plants look alike, and will even cross-pollinate (and should not be grown together). The fine feathery fronds are ready for use as a garnish without slicing or chopping.

Supermarkets sell whole fennel seeds and powdered fennel seeds. Garden fennel is a hardy perennial and a roadside weed in southern Tasmania, but Mediterranean fennel is a separate species, bulbous at the base of the stem, and is earthed up like celery to blanch it. The bulbous portion can be chopped and eaten in salads like celery, or cooked as a vegetable. Fresh fennel fronds are served with fish as a garnish (but are ideal to eat with the fish). The leaves and seeds go well in sauces and soups, especially celery soup and pumpkin soup.

Dill is an annual, but in season fresh dill leaves have the same uses as fennel leaves. The dried leaves and seeds are available from the supermarkets. The seeds are fairly pungent and important in some pickles, especially with cucumber and gherkins.

Of all the herbs, fennel and dill (with a flavour like aniseed or liquorice) are perhaps the least attractive to people who like to nibble a leaf, but this is not the way to judge herbs. Pungent volatile oils protect these plants against grazing and browsing animals — a goat that would destroy a hawthorn hedge gives rosemary a wide berth — and the secret with herbs is to use small amounts with the appropriate foods. Few people object to the dill in dill pickles, which can be made without salt.

Lovage

Many Australians of Dutch extraction living in Hobart grow lovage, a member of the celery family. Because it has the flavour of Maggi soup cubes (without the surplus salt, of course), they call it the 'Maggi herb'. Lovage is often difficult to buy, fresh or dried, so you have to grow your own.

It's not worth buying lovage seed, because you will need only one plant, which can be bought in spring as a seedling from most nurseries. A friend who has one can give you self-sown seedlings. Lovage is a hardy perennial but dies back to the taproot in winter, so mark its position with a stake to protect it from damage by spades and forks. It likes a damp position and will tolerate frost and most soils except heavy clay. Each spring there is a vigorous new growth and by late summer the flowering heads bring it to a final height of 2 metres or more, and a single plant has enough fresh leaves for the largest family.

Chopped lovage leaves can be added to soups, broths and

casseroles. Use a little at first, then more if necessary. Lovage doesn't have to be added at the last minute — cook it with the food. The leaves can be used sparingly in fresh salads, including coleslaw. Some people just rub the salad bowl with the crushed leaves. It can be finely chopped and used like parsley, for example one tablespoon can be added to a cupful of white sauce for fish. It can be part of a tasty pesto made by blending lovage, garlic, walnuts, ground almonds and olive oil.

One salt skipper who forgot she had planted a lovage seedling noticed a vigorous new plant in the garden, about twice the height of the rhubarb. Recognising the leaf, she tried it in a soup that needed more flavour. The result was dramatic, and that household has grown and used lovage ever since.

Mixtures of dried herbs

There are several mixtures of dried herbs that can be used in small amounts to bring out the flavour of savoury dishes. Packets of all the ingredients are expensive and make too much mixture for one family, but a mixture prescribed by the National Health and Medical Research Council is available in small packets by mail order (see Chapter 11 and Appendix 5). Commercial packets of 'Mixed Herbs' hardly ever have salt added, but it may be a good habit to check the ingredient list if it is a brand you have not bought before.

Oregano and marjoram

Oregano grows wild in the Mediterranean region, and is sometimes called wild marjoram. It has the flavour of marjoram, but stronger, and these remarks apply to both plants. Like dried basil, dried oregano is also sold in the herbs and spices section of supermarkets. Basil and oregano are the lusty pizza herbs that make a pizza taste authentic, regardless of its sodium content.

Fresh oregano is very pungent and powerful and should be used carefully. A few leaves of fresh oregano greatly improve a chicken and salad sandwich or a sandwich of no-added-salt sardines.

Fresh or dried oregano is interchangeable with basil for all kinds of tomato dishes, grilled tomatoes, tomato soup and unsalted tomato juice cocktails. It is also at home in all pasta dishes, and adds flavour to meat loaves, rissoles, meat sauces, stews and stuffings. Baked and grilled fish go well with oregano.

Fresh oregano can be bought in the vegetable market, but is also very easy to grow at home, being a hardy perennial that thrives outdoors in winter in most parts of Australia, so fresh sprigs can be cut from the garden throughout most of the year. It can be grown from seed or seedlings bought from nurseries. It likes light, well-drained soil and a sunny position. In its second year it may behave almost like a weed, and people who grow oregano often have plenty of healthy young plants to give away.

Rosemary

This hardy evergreen shrub is a perennial that grows best in a light, sandy and fairly dry soil in a sunny position. It prefers some shelter, and does well against a wall. Apart from watering in dry weather it needs practically no attention, growing to a height of about 1.5 metres and spreading widely if unchecked.

The spiky leaves have many uses in cooking. The intense flavour must be used with care. If you have a large rosemary bush, a good way of cooking a lot of scrubbed new potatoes on a barbecue is to wrap them in foil with a whole branch of rosemary. Drizzle a little oil over them before closing the foil, and leave them for about an hour in moderate heat at the side of the barbecue.

A few young leaves (cut or chopped) can be added to a green salad or potato salad, and salads can be strewn with the pretty small blue flowers of the rosemary. Instead of mint, use a few rosemary leaves in pea soup or when boiling green peas, marrow, broad beans or turnips. Italians include a sprig of rosemary when roasting lamb, and it also goes well with veal, duck and chicken.

Rosemary scones can be made by adding 1 tbs of chopped rosemary leaves to 2 cups of flour, without the usual added salt, and with sodium-free baking powder.

Tarragon

The variety of tarragon sold in Australia is usually French tarragon, propagated from cuttings or root division, and available from plant nurseries. It grows well in poor soil but needs a sunny, well-drained position. Although a perennial, it is cut by frost in the southern states and disappears. You may need to mark its position with a stake, to protect the roots from accidental disturbance in winter.

Many people who nibble a leaf are reminded of fennel, but tarragon finishes with a bite. Dried tarragon is not always easy to buy, but tarragon vinegar is readily available. Tarragon is one of the few herbs that can compete with the powerful flavour of vinegar, although a salad flavoured with fresh tarragon leaves is quite different from a salad dressed with tarragon vinegar. Fresh lemon juice gives a less assertive companion flavour.

The chopped fresh leaves can be used freely in salads and salad dressings, in main dishes such as steaks and fish, and on all vegetables. This is another herb that can be added at the beginning of cooking. Tarragon is an important flavouring for soups, stews and sauces, and makes a subtle difference to marinades, shellfish, crayfish and stuffing for fish and poultry. It is often combined with other herbs, and is one of the ingredients of *fines herbes*. Combined with celeriac it can make a powerful replacement for salt.

Winter savory

Winter savory is a perennial in all Australian states, unlike summer savory, and has a stronger flavour. The prostrate form is easy to grow in a sunny position. Let it take over its own patch of the garden and provide enough self-sown seedlings for all your friends. The small leaves are only a little larger than thyme, and need no chopping after stripping from the stem. A salad or salad sandwich is delicious with a good sprinkling of winter savory, and it gives the perfect 'herbal' flavour for chicken dishes.

Winter savory is uniquely suitable for beans, and in Germany and Holland is even called the 'bean herb'. No-added-salt baked beans are transformed with a generous sprinkling of winter savory leaves stirred into them, hot or cold.

Spices

Read this section even if you 'dislike spices'. Chillies and peppers — the main offenders — are only a handful of the hundreds of different spices and spice mixtures that are available. People who avoid hot spices are generally avoiding less than a dozen out of the hundreds that are sold in a specialist herb and spice shop.

Many people can accept a mild curry made without chilli, and several of the individual curry spices are mild and delicious when used alone, two good examples being cumin and turmeric. Herbs like winter savory and basil (especially dried basil) have some of the agreeable overtones of pepper without any of the irritation. All the spices for sweet foods are delicious without salt — just think how many people enjoy cinnamon or nutmeg in apple strudel or hot cross buns.

Cinnamon

Cinnamon can be bought as cinnamon powder, or as a mixture called cinnamon sugar. Salt-free porridge can be flavoured with cinnamon. Stewed apple goes well with cinnamon, either alone or with nutmeg and cloves. Cinnamon is also used in 'mixed spice' (allspice [pimento], cinnamon, cloves, nutmeg and ginger), which is excellent for chutneys, as well as cakes and puddings.

Mexican spice mixture

Mexicans make extensive use of beans, flavoured with generous amounts of chilli and cumin in mixtures known to the rest of the world as 'Mexican Spices'. These mixtures are an alternative to winter savory as a flavour for no-added-salt baked beans. With beans you can also use cumin by itself, or any of the numerous curry powders, after checking its sodium content.

Pepper

Peppers come in many varieties, each suited to its own ethnic cuisine. Ground pepper, paprika, cayenne pepper and special brands of mild pepper mixtures are normally salt-free. Peppercorns are suitable only if they are dried (peppercorns stored in liquid in a bottle are usually very salty, although vinegar alone would preserve them). The unique flavour of native Tasmanian pepper is available by mail order from Spice World.

Although peppers have so many uses, they sometimes have a fatal attraction for the restaurant chef who takes an order for a meal without salt. Experienced salt skippers who prefer to retain full control of the pepper ask for 'no salt or pepper' when they place their order.

Single spices versus spice mixtures

Spice lovers can indulge freely without consuming salt unless they buy ready-made mixtures. Such mixtures, especially curry powders, may contain added salt. Most spice bottles are small enough to be exempt from the regulation requiring a nutrition information panel, so they may lack sodium data. However, the ingredient list is mandatory on all food labels, so if any salt or MSG (additive 621) is added, the ingredient list must declare it. The best rule is to avoid all foods with salt in the ingredient list, even when it comes last on the list, which usually implies the smallest quantity. (Sometimes salt may come last in the ingredient list on a label that declares a sodium content of 1000 mg/100 g.) If your supermarket doesn't carry a curry powder without added salt, you may need to buy some from a spice shop, either directly or by mail order (see Appendix 5). Indian cooks like to blend their own curry powder from the single ingredients, which is another option for spice enthusiasts.

Worcestershire sauce

The spice mixture in Worcestershire sauce is the answer for the person who insists that a boiled egg 'needs salt'. One metric teaspoonful (5 mL) of the original brand of Worcestershire sauce (Lea & Perrins) supplies enough sodium to augment a 24-hour urine result by 2 mmol (rather a lot). If you wish, you can make your own Worcestershire sauce without salt at home and consume it freely. Two recipes are given in Chapter 7.

Smoked foods

Many people enjoy smoked foods. Smoking without salt is well worth considering. The smoke flavour makes any fish a new delicacy that can be enjoyed on its own or in dishes such as kedgeree. There are two ways of smoking fish — hot smoking and cold smoking. Cold smoking will not sterilise the flesh, and is not recommended without the conventional salting. Fish can be smoked without salt if the method used is hot smoking (which cooks the fish). Hot-smoked fish will not slice thinly like cold-smoked salmon, but is equally renowned as a delicacy. It has plenty of flavour after smoking without salt, and is well worthwhile.

Two conditions must be met when food is smoked without using salt:

- smoking must be done commercially under well-controlled factory conditions, to abolish any risk of food poisoning
- deep-freezing is needed after smoking.

Technically the fish must be stored below 4°C. Commercial refrigeration plants comply with the national standard (at or below 4°C), but domestic refrigeration is often unsafe for perfect temperature control, and only the deep-freeze should be trusted for storing smoked fish at home. Don't store it anywhere else (even for twenty-four hours). All imported smoked salmon is deep-frozen, so there is no problem for the gourmet.

In theory if you catch a fish you could ask for it to be smoked without salt. In practice a well-run commercial smokehouse usually insists on supplying the fish rather than risk contaminating the premises with raw material over which it has had no control. You should ask for the fish to be smoked and then deep-frozen. Thawing and refreezing should be avoided, so it is a good idea to have the whole batch packed in small quantities such as two servings, so that packs of two servings can be removed from the deep-freeze at home without any risk of thawing the rest of the batch. Thawed fish must be consumed the same day.

There is likely to be considerable scope for smoking of other foods if the demand increases for food processing that complies with the Dietary Guidelines for Australian Adults (producing an end product that is low in salt). A Queensland company launched excellent unsalted lean bacon in 1998 using potassium instead of sodium chloride, with remarkable success. It was naturally more expensive than ordinary bacon, and unfortunately failed to secure the expected niche market. All the participating supermarkets discontinued it within twelve months.

Misleading claims about salt substitutes

Health food shops carry many so-called 'salt substitutes' that would add flavour to your diet, but they do this mainly by adding salt. Most of them are imported foods with foreign labels, and shoppers need a pocket calculator to work out the amount of sodium in 100 grams of the food. Consumers can be caught at various times by labels that provide the data in a misleading and confusing format.

'Reduced salt' Asian sauces (liquids)

Soy, teriyaki and tamari sauces are bottles of strong brine, wrongly labelled. The 'low salt' (or 'low sodium') soy, teriyaki or tamari sauces cited in many cookbooks do not exist. The terms 'low salt' and 'reduced salt' are legally defined in Australia, limiting the sodium content to 120 and 600 mg/100 g respectively. These sauces declare a sodium content of about 3000 mg/100 g (full-strength soy sauces vary from about 6000 to about 9000 mg/100 g). Kikkoman soy sauce with a sodium content of 3574 mg/100 g is now labelled Kikkoman *Less Salt* Soy Sauce in Australia and New Zealand.

Women who look for soy and linseed for phytoestrogens (plant hormones helpful at the menopause) should note that soy sauce has none whatsoever.[7]

New Vegit All-Purpose Seasoning (powder)

One part of the label on New Vegit All-Purpose Seasoning powder says to sprinkle the powder liberally on everything, while another part defines one serving as *one-thirteenth of a teaspoonful*. According to the label the sodium content is 4.95 g/100 g ('less than 5 per cent'), which is 4950 mg/100 g. This means that New Vegit has about 80 per cent of the sodium content of standard soy sauce, and yet the label calls it a 'natural low-sodium vegetable seasoning', adding 'Gaylord Hauser recommends New Vegit as the zesty flavourful way to end the low-sodium "blahs" and add taste excitement to all your meals'. It does this by simply adding a high sodium powder to your low sodium diet.

Dr Bronner's Balanced Mineral Bouillon (liquid)

The label on Dr Bronner's Balanced Mineral Bouillon states that the salty flavour comes from 'natural complete soya–amino-acid–protein, mineralised with balanced potassium–calcium–phosphorus–iron–magnesium–chloride–mineral–salts'. In a report made available to the Menzies Institute, the Tasmanian government analyst found a sodium content of 3400 mg/100 g and potassium of 2000 mg/100 g, revealing that the sodium and potassium are completely unbalanced and the wrong way round.[3]

Bernard Jensen's Broth or Seasoning (powder)

The label says 'make it into a broth to taste, or *as a substitute for salt* [author italics]. Sprinkle on baked potatoes, salads, etc.' Again in a report made available to the Menzies Institute, the Tasmanian government analyst found a sodium content of 8530 mg/100 g — higher than many brands of soy sauce. According to the chloride analysis most of the sodium content was due to salt.

Krio Krush Vegetable Booster (powder)

This 'all natural seasoning' is made from 'tasty raw vegetables reduced to a fine powder'. The main ingredient is hydrolysed vegetable protein (usually made by boiling vegetables with caustic soda) and analysis showed a sodium content of 3300 mg/100 g.

Vecon Vegetable Stock (paste)

The UK label gives the sodium content in grams as 10.5 g/100 g, which is 10 500 mg/100 g, ten times more salty than seawater and around a hundred times too high. The first item in the ingredient list is hydrolysed vegetable protein (high in sodium if vegetables are processed with caustic soda).

Vogel Herbamare and Trocomare (powders)

The labels say that both products can be used as a 'flavourful preference to table salt'. In small letters the labels state that one serving is 'one-eighth of a teaspoon (1 gram)' — not enough to follow their advice to use them on salads, vegetables, beans, rice, pasta, meats or pizza. The imported American labels say one serving contains 340 mg of sodium, which comes to 34 000 mg/100 g. This makes it about 85 per cent salt; moreover sea salt[8] — the worst kind of salt — tops the list of fifteen ingredients.

Bragg's All Purpose Seasoning (liquid)

This All Purpose Seasoning, or 'Liquid Aminos from Soy Protein' has reached Australia with an American nutrition information panel that says it contains only 110 mg of sodium per serving, and claims that it is made only from soy beans and purified water:

> Bragg's formulated soy protein is from healthy non-GM certified soybeans and purified water only. Contains no alcohol, preservatives, additives, no colouring agents or chemicals. It's not fermented.

The label also states that 'Bragg's has a small amount of naturally occurring sodium. No table salt is added'. Most foods have some naturally occurring sodium. However, the nutrition information panel says the serving size is half a teaspoon (given as 2.4 mL) and if 110 mg is the sodium content of *one serving*, the amount per 100 mL (about the same as the amount per 100 g) is 4583 mg.

Fresh soy beans have a sodium content of about 8 mg/100 g, and purified water has none, so — if no salt is added — where does the sodium content of 4583 mg come from? Amino acids come from chemical digestion of protein, and one way of making this dark brown liquid from beans without fermentation would be to process them with caustic soda, making hydrolysed vegetable protein. An enquiry to the company asking about the sodium content was acknowledged, but no reply to the enquiry was given.

Common salt varieties

Substitutes for table salt and cooking salt that are at least 50 per cent common salt (and up to 98 per cent) include black salt, celery salt, 'Corrected Salt', garlic salt, 'Lite Salt', 'Malden Salt', 'New Salt', onion salt, 'Pan Salt', 'Saga Salt', rock salt and sea salt.

Black salt

Two large and attractive books about spices (published in the 1990s) make incorrect statements about black salt, a form of rock salt imported from India. One tells readers that 'black salt contains no sodium, so has no effect on blood pressure and is in fact considered an antidote to dehydration (it is even mixed into lemonade to counter the effect of the heat)'.[9]

A letter to the publisher was referred to the book's author, who named her source — another authoritative and attractive coffee-table-style book.[10] This second book devotes a page to Indian rock salt, black salt or *saindhav*, which is headed 'Sodium chloride, rock salt (*kala namak*)'. This book expressly describes black salt as sodium chloride, but claims it behaves differently from common salt and has medicinal uses: 'As it does not increase the sodium content of the blood, unlike ordinary salt, it is recommended for patients with high blood pressure or those on a low salt diet. It is also a sure cure for flatulence and heartburn.'

A colleague at Royal Hobart Hospital was interested in the first statement that black salt has no sodium, and we analysed a sample of Indian black salt supplied by a Hobart spice shop. The black lumps of rock salt exactly matched the colour photograph in the second book and the solution had the authentic sulphurous smell.[10] Chemical analysis showed it to be 98 per cent sodium chloride, with small amounts of calcium and magnesium and a small insoluble sediment.[11] As black salt is about as pure as table salt, it is unequivocally harmful for blood pressure in proportion to the amount consumed.[12]

Sea salt

Contrary to popular belief, the iodine content of sea salt is negligible, as most of the iodine in the ocean is in the marine plants and animals, which spend their lives extracting it from seawater. The salt in Herbamare and Trocomare (see above) is described as 'natural sea salt', pandering to the naïve belief that every natural product is by definition harmless.

Rats given sea salt for twelve months have higher blood pressure than rats given plain salt in amounts corresponding to the sodium chloride content of the sea salt.[8] This experiment cannot be repeated in humans for ethical reasons, but a study of six tribal societies in the Solomon Islands found these societies had high blood pressure in proportion to their salt intake, and the single group with especially high blood pressure was the only group cooking vegetables in seawater.[13]

Salt, nutrition and food safety

Nutritional adequacy of a low salt diet

Early allegations that skipping salt — even moderately — might lead to losses of essential nutrients were unfounded.[14] Salted foods arrived very late in human evolution, and some of the fittest humans live in salt-free societies that add no salt at all to their food. Their health and stamina is good evidence of adequate nutrition. These salt-free societies have never been offered salt or any other dietary supplement as a public health measure.

Nutritional analysis of 65 mmol and 85 mmol diets for hypertension has demonstrated that moderately reduced salt intakes in developed countries are also compatible with a well-balanced diet.[5,12,15]

Preserving vegetables in oil without using salt

Salting is not the only option for preserving foods. Depending on the food, alternative methods for preserving without salt include drying, pickling in vinegar or alcohol, or storing in strong syrup. Modern options include canning, refrigeration, freezing, freeze-drying, vacuum-packing and irradiating.

Although oil will not prevent putrefaction, a popular way of keeping garlic is to store it in olive oil in the fridge, as the oil can later be used as a flavoursome addition to salads. Food Science Australia, however, produces a fact sheet warning people to add acid, for example vinegar, lemon juice or citric acid, when storing vegetables in oil at home. See the CSIRO website at <http://www.csiro.au> for details of their fact sheet about this.

Tomatoes contain enough acid to be safe, especially when semi-dried, but all other vegetables and herbs need vinegar unless they are dried well enough to keep indefinitely in the dried form. Any residual moisture makes vinegar necessary. All the vegetables must be in contact with vinegar before any oil is used, and you must use enough vinegar. At least three parts of vinegar to four parts of vegetables (measured by weight) must be used, so 300 g of vinegar would do for 400 g of vegetables. At that dilution the food would still spoil unless properly refrigerated, but there would be no risk of botulism. Three hundred mL of vinegar weighs 300 g, but you must use kitchen scales for the vegetables. Store the vegetables in the whole of the vinegar without draining.

Many varieties of garlic behave normally, but some go green or blue-green in vinegar. This is harmless to health but looks unappetising. It is not possible to tell by looking at the garlic whether it will go green in vinegar; commercial producers prevent this by storing the garlic cloves at a temperature above 23°C for four weeks.

Commercial bottling in oil is normally safe, but two serious outbreaks of botulism (a rare but fatal illness) in the US and Canada in the 1980s were traced to chopped garlic that was preserved in oil. This had been produced commercially and depended on refrigeration alone to prevent botulism. Refrigeration below 4°C (the industry standard) would have been safe, but in practice food can warm up on the way home, and domestic fridges may allow temperatures higher than 4°C. Food regulations now require such foods to be acidified, in addition to refrigeration, so the commercial product is quite safe, and it would be safer for home bottlers to follow the same regulations.

A nutrient or a food additive?

Opinions differ on the question of whether salt is a nutrient or a food additive. Even some health professionals say a nutrient is not an additive (and additives have numbers). Chefs argue that salt is a condiment and one of the four flavour sensations — salty/sweet/sour/bitter — and thus essential to good cuisine. But MSG, while it may be anathema to many Australians, is 'essential to good cuisine' in China. The Chinese correctly call MSG a nutrient when it is found in natural foods such as breast milk, mushrooms, edible seaweed and tomatoes; the pure or synthetic crystalline glutamate added to soup as a flavour enhancer is surely an artificial chemical food additive (additive number 621).

Vitamin C (ascorbic acid) occurs naturally in fruit and vegetables as a nutrient. Like salt, it is not only a nutrient but an *essential nutrient*. Yet when added to foods as an antioxidant, pure ascorbic acid is an artificial chemical food additive with a number (300).

Salt is like that. Salt in breast milk and other natural foods is an essential nutrient, but crystalline sodium chloride added to flour as a dough improver or to soup as a flavour enhancer is an artificial chemical food additive. On food labels, while numbers save space, especially if several additives have long names, a four-letter word such as 'salt' is short enough not to need a number; in fact a number might hide the fact that salt was added.

Chefs who argue that salt can't be called an 'additive' when customers 'need' it, should understand that the amount of salt each customer 'needs' depends on their habitual intake. Heavy users want more, light users want less, and non-users want little if any. The palate can alter radically in as little as a month.[16,17]

The fact that light users want less salt, and non-users want little if any is a new problem for food writers as well as chefs. One reviewer's published comment on the meal served at a restaurant was: 'The salmon was heavily seasoned with salt, which doesn't suit my taste' and 'the food was well executed as well as presented, although I am not used to the strong use of salt in almost all the dishes we tried'.[18] The predicament now facing chefs and food writers is that there is no longer a 'right' amount of salt. They have to cope with a clientele with a wide range of preferences. Moreover, palates adapt rapidly to a change in habitual intake — so a level of saltiness a customer enjoyed last month may not please the same customer as much next month.

Thus salt is both a nutrient and an additive. The right amount confers the benefits of the nutrient and controlling the amount avoids the harm of the additive. To get the right amount choose foods low in salt.[18]

Choosing foods low in salt leaves a big gap in the cook's repertoire at first, but that should come as no surprise. Salt has been the second most commonly used food additive after sugar, and we are removing salt from a cuisine based on salt. After such heavy use you will miss it most during the initial period of adaptation, while your palate is still recovering from years of suppression by salt. Nevertheless, salt is only one of many, many food flavours, and a closer acquaintance with the host of others available will help to smooth the transition to healthier food.

5

Cooking to conserve flavour

Cooking adds heat to food in various ways that not only make it hot, but change its colour, texture and flavour. Poor cooking can destroy flavour, and salt has been the poor cook's easy remedy. Good cooking conserves flavour and removes the need to conceal the damage with salt.

Boiling, stewing, poaching and steaming

Eggs in their shells can be boiled without losing flavour, but peeled potatoes suffer a serious loss of flavour, along with potassium and other minerals, when they are boiled.

Ideally, cooking should conserve both minerals and flavour. Peeled potatoes boiled in plain water lose 21 per cent of their potassium, and 36 per cent when boiled in salted water.[1] Unpeeled, potatoes lose only 6 per cent of their potassium in plain water, and no potassium at all when steamed.[1] Many of the best restaurants steam their vegetables and serve them — full of their own flavour — without adding any salt, and we, too, can do that at home. While a potato boiled without salt seems tasteless to people who normally boil potatoes in salted water and add extra salt at the table, salt doesn't replace the original flavour of the potato or any of the other losses — it adds a *foreign flavour and a health risk*. Saltaholics can use potassium chloride at first instead of salt, while waiting for their sense of taste to recover.

New potatoes are not usually peeled. Jane Brown, home economist for the Salt Skip Program, doesn't peel old potatoes either. She stabs them with a fork and cooks them in a microwave oven with a piece of kitchen paper top and bottom. For 500 g of old potatoes this takes 5–10 minutes on high, depending on oven power. The potatoes can be wrapped afterwards in foil to keep them hot and allowed to stand for 2 minutes to cook through before serving.

Mutton and the less tender cuts of beef get tougher at higher cooking temperatures, but can be tenderised by stewing or poaching in water at a temperature just below boiling point, when the surface of the water starts to quiver and form a scum (around 90–95°C).[2] The joint that is most often boiled is salted or 'corned' silverside, but fresh silverside does equally well.

Meat is the muscle of the animal, and heat makes the muscle fibres contract, expelling the juices that contain most of the flavour. The meat itself loses flavour and the water gains flavour, becoming 'stock'. Meat nearest the bone has the most flavour, and bones can be browned in the oven (for more flavour) before adding water. The smaller the volume of water the stronger the stock, so use the smallest pan that will hold the joint and add only just enough water to cover it. Start with cold or tepid water, reduce the heat just before it boils and keep it there until the meat is cooked. A joint weighing 1 kilogram takes about 2 hours.

A flavourful alternative is to rub the meat all over with no–added-salt mustard (French or Dijon, see Chapter 7) before browning, and replace the water with a half-and-half mixture of water and white wine. Some of the stock can be served with the meat, and some can be saved for soup and other recipes that need stock. Stock without the meat can be boiled down to a smaller volume with more intense flavour, and needs no salt or salt substitute. Add carrots and onions to the stock for extra flavour.

Slow cooking

Meat begins to cook at about 65°C, and an oven that can be set at 75–85°C can be used to cook dishes for 8 hours or longer. This is another ideal treatment for the less tender cuts of meat, and for a large repertoire of other foods such as fish, soups, casseroles, stews, vegetables, savouries, sweets and preserves. Meat may be cooked in an oven bag or sealed casserole dish, or 'slow cooker'. Slow cooking retains the natural flavours of meats without overcooking, and meals can be left to cook all day — or all night — without attention. The oven can be filled to capacity with enough dishes to last several days.

When cooked in this way, the shrinkage of a leg of lamb is

negligible and the flesh is very tender and juicy, and slices well. Place the leg of lamb in an oven bag, with rosemary and slivers of garlic pushed into cuts in the meat (stabbed with a pointed knife), and cook at 75–85°C for 6–8 hours, depending on the size of the joint.

Baking, roasting, toasting, grilling and barbecuing

The heat from an oven, grill or barbecue seals the surface of the meat and conserves the flavour, as well as the potassium and other minerals. Baking, roasting, toasting, grilling and barbecuing do require the more tender and expensive cuts of meat, but have the advantage that the flavour is intensified. The meat shrinks as it cooks and expels the juices, which collect in the pan and dry off into a crust on the surface of the meat. Dry mustard powder can be rubbed on the surface of a joint of beef before roasting.

Vegetables such as potatoes, pumpkin, parsnips, carrots and onions cook to perfection in the oven with a joint of meat. Brush them with olive oil first, and then toss them in mixed dried herbs.

Baking potatoes in their jackets provides a fat-free alternative. Most restaurants will serve potatoes baked in their jackets as part of a low salt meal, but remember to ask for no sour cream — it's about 35 per cent fat by weight (mostly saturated fat). For a low fat lubricant there is low fat yoghurt (1 per cent fat), or ordinary yoghurt which is seldom more than 4 per cent fat. The stiffer Greek yoghurt is 6 per cent fat.

Making gravy

To make gravy, remove the roast from the roasting pan and pour off as much fat as possible, leaving only the meat juices. The best way to eliminate fat more thoroughly is to transfer the juices to a bowl, which is chilled in the refrigerator to solidify the fat, making it easy to remove, and leaving the juices for making gravy for the next roast.

Thicken the juices with wholemeal flour in the pan and cook the mixture. Thin the gravy to the desired consistency with a well-flavoured low salt stock and reheat, stirring constantly as the gravy thickens. A skinned and chopped tomato can be added and cooked in the gravy to help thicken and flavour it, and 1–2 drops of gravy browning (Parisian essence) can be added for colour. You will notice that the latter is salty if you taste it, but 1–2 drops will supply the colour you need with only a negligible amount of salt.

Red wine, sherry, mustard and (for beef) no-added-salt horserad-ish sauce will all contribute flavour.

Frying and stir-frying

Frying and stir-frying are both excellent ways of conserving flavour, but they do add fat. Deep-frying should be avoided altogether. To limit fat when frying and stir-frying use a non-stick pan or wok, and/or non-stick cooking spray. As an alternative to deep-frying for potato chips, you can buy frozen chips for oven baking at home. These are available in a no-added-salt form and have only about 3 per cent fat by weight.

Olive oil is favoured for frying, both for heat stability and for its health reputation in the Mediterranean diet, established over cen-turies. Its cost is not a problem when used sparingly. However, the identifiable flavour of olive oil does make it unsuitable in some recipes. Good fats like olive and canola oil reduce the risk of heart disease, but all fats are fattening (another reason for using olive oil sparingly). Sesame oil is an alternative for stir-frying that will add flavour, with only a few drops needed.

Stir-frying in a wok can be done with stock instead of oil. Chopped meat and vegetables take only about two minutes to cook in a wok, and stir-frying retains all the flavour, potassium and other minerals and most of the vitamins of fresh vegetables. The beginning salt skipper's dismay at losing soy sauce may give way to the satisfac-tion of enjoying the natural flavours of each vegetable without masking them with salt. Chapter 7 contains a recipe for a very good salt-free stir-fry sauce that is full of flavour.

Microwave cooking

Microwave ovens conserve flavours so well that even the general public can enjoy most microwave recipes without salt.[3] Short cook-ing times waste no heat, and running costs are cheaper. The elderly especially appreciate the ease of eating their meal from the plate or bowl it was cooked in. There is no tastier method for reheating a meal, and no oven is easier to clean. A few special peculiarities need to be noted, however.

In a microwave oven, the food heats unevenly. For example, a thick soup will be too hot in some parts and too cold in others unless it is stirred thoroughly. A revolving turntable helps, but doesn't eliminate the problem, so it is easier to sterilise food like a very thin soup that can be actively boiled. Foods like lasagne can't be stirred and must be *allowed to stand* in order to reach a uniform temperature before serving. Food Science Australia suggests dividing food into smaller portions, to avoid overcooking the edges while waiting for the centre to get hot. <www.csiro.au> Thaw frozen food first on the defrost cycle, and melt all the ice crystals.

Salt in microwave ovens

Salty food takes longer to cook than unsalted food. This is because ionised chemicals like sodium chloride have a shielding effect that reduces the penetration of microwaves and makes cold spots colder if the food is salty. This was reported in a leading scientific journal in 1990[4], but microwave instruction manuals and cookbooks tend to ignore this advice.

The study was prompted by an increase in cases of food poisoning with *Salmonella* and *Listeria* in Britain in the 1980s, when microwave ovens were becoming popular. For reasons understood by physicists, microwave energy may be dissipated as electricity instead of heat in the presence of salt. The effect is more serious in foods like mashed potato that have a very slow rate of heat transfer.

The study placed 200 g samples of mashed potato in the centre of the turntable of a 650 watt domestic microwave oven. Some had no added salt and others had various concentrations of either salt, MSG, ammonium chloride or potassium chloride. MSG had some shielding effect but the other ingredients had far more. When unsalted mashed potato with a sodium content of 3 mg/100 g was heated for 1 minute, the temperature rose by 30°C at the centre. With a sodium content of 213 mg/100 g the temperature rose by only 13°C and at 973 mg/100 g it rose by only 2°C.

Food Science Australia stresses the importance of the *standing time* to allow food to reach a uniform temperature when cooking food containing salt. For example, as the sodium content of a raw ham steak preserved with salt and sodium nitrite is 1090 mg/100 g, the cool spots should reach at least 75°C after allowing the full standing time. Cooking low salt foods means that this issue of standing time and uniform cooking should be less of a problem for salt skippers.

Warnings frequently forgotten

Handbooks that accompany microwave ovens usually mention basic techniques needed to cook eggs without an explosion, but omit many other useful warnings. For example, children should be taught that microwaves heat nothing but *the water* in the food and *the water* in the cup. This is why the baby's bottle may still feel tepid when the milk inside is hot enough to scald the baby's mouth. A hungry teenager was badly scalded when eating an American jelly-filled doughnut. He had taken it from the freezer and put it in the microwave for one minute. The outer crust was only comfortably warm, but after the first gulp he felt a searing pain inside his chest. This was due to a severe burn of the oesophagus (food pipe) which required hospital treatment.[5] The jelly in the centre was very much hotter than the outside crust.

A member of the Australian Consumers' Association followed an oven manufacturer's advice to clean the oven by heating a cup of water in it for three to four minutes, to steam the walls to make them easier to clean. She was badly scalded when she opened the oven door and the cup of water exploded in her face. Another woman had a mug of water explode suddenly after she added a teaspoonful of instant coffee to the liquid.

These explosions are due to a common laboratory problem called superheating. If the water is very pure and the vessel is extremely clean, the water temperature can climb above its normal boiling point without boiling. Boiling occurs late, with a sudden explosion. The solution for microwave ovens is to leave a plastic spoon or wooden skewer in the cup (although plastic spoons may bend). Workers who boil liquids in laboratory test tubes and glass beakers always put a fragment of broken crockery in the water. They use unglazed earthenware, but any fragment of broken crockery will do. Liquids bubble early, and boil in perfect safety. The same fragment of broken crockery can be used indefinitely.

Cookbooks

There is no need to discard old recipes or existing cookbooks when you begin cooking with low salt foods. Time and again you will find ways of modifying recipes very successfully. Recipes in some older low salt cookbooks often ignore the other dietary guidelines and use a lot of eggs, sugar, butter and cream, but are worth following if you allow for this. The best source to obtain some of the older books mentioned here may be your local library or a secondhand book-shop.

Imported cookbooks

The late Nathan Pritikin launched one of the first cookbooks to persuade Americans to eat less saturated fat, sugar and salt and more fruit and vegetables.[6] While the American Heart Association (AHA) advised small improvements thought to be feasible for everybody, Pritikin promoted the radical changes that were likely to work best, for both preventing and treating the diseases linked to bad diets. The Pritikin Program of Diet and Exercise also stressed the neglected problem of exercise. A tribute to Pritikin has been the gradual but steady closure of the gap between the AHA's advice and his.

In a Chinese restaurant Pritikin asked for food cooked without salt, soy sauce, MSG or sugar. He used 'a *little* soy sauce when the dish arrives, if necessary, using the soy-sauce shaker at the table', not recognising that soy sauce is six to nine times saltier than seawater.[7] He also allowed salt in bread at about half the standard amount.

The Pritikin program is very explicit about fat, but allows sodium up to 70 mmol/day (1600 mg) and still allows so-called 'low salt' or 'low sodium' soy sauce (although it is over three times saltier than seawater and as such can't be called '*reduced* salt or reduced sodium' in Australia). For a short time the Salt Skip Program allowed 'less salt' soy sauce to be used (as an experiment) provided it was accurately measured and limited to half a teaspoonful. In practice people so often guessed the amount that their 24-hour sodium excretion rates went above 100 mmol. Diets are too difficult. The Salt Skip Program returned to its original principle of cutting out salty ingredients that had to be measured.

The New Pritikin Program, Robert Pritikin

Pritikin's son Robert continues to permit reduced-salt bread, and 'less salt' soy sauce (sodium over 3000 mg/100 g) in the Pritikin diet program. The program expects people to count milligrams of sodium per serving, and recipes are presented with the sodium analysis, like diets for a medical prescription.

Low Salt Diet Book, Christiane and Graham MacGregor

Professor Graham MacGregor is one of the world's leading authorities on high blood pressure. He is the founder of CASH (Consensus Action on Salt and Hypertension), a group of hypertension specialists who are improving Britain's food supply through dialogue with the food industry (see Chapter 17). Christiane MacGregor is a Cordon Bleu graduate with a passion for good food. Their compact paperback is another gourmet guide. Using recipes from this book will give you a 24-hour urinary sodium excretion rate of about 25 mmol/day (about 600 mg/day).[8]

No-Salt, Lowest-Sodium Cookbook, Donald Gazzaniga

Don Gazzaniga collapsed while rowing at the age of sixty-three, developed severe congestive heart failure, and was considered for the waiting list for a heart transplant. His comprehensive cookbook is a monument to the radical change of diet that led to such a complete recovery that he has discontinued his diuretic.[9] His book fulfils the requirements for a medical prescription for a therapeutic diet limiting sodium to 500 mg/day (about 20 mmol/day). (*No-Salt, Lowest-Sodium Cookbook* can be ordered from <Amazon.com>, or through Don Gazzaniga's website <megaheart.com>, on which the Salt Skip Program is a guest.)

No-Salt, Lowest-Sodium Baking Book, Donald Gazzaniga

So many visitors to Don's web page asked for more bread recipes that he and his daughter Jeannie, a registered dietitian, produced a bread cookbook of about 200 pages full of ideas and recipes for breads, cakes, 'cookies', muffins and tea breads.[10] The recipes use a bread machine but also explain how to modify the recipes for kneading the dough by hand, and how to bake some recipes in the oven after the machine has kneaded the dough.

For details of his third cookbook on soups and sandwiches (2004) see his website.

No-Salt Cookbook, David and Thomas Anderson

These authors tell their readers how to eat well without using added salt.[11] Although it's another therapeutic diet book with the usual daunting task of counting milligrams of sodium, the reader can ignore that and measure progress with 24–hour urine collections, as in the Salt Skip Program.

Craig Claiborne's Gourmet Diet

Two of America's most famous food writers in the late 20th century were Craig Claiborne and James Beard (no relation to the present author), and both were put on strict low salt diets towards the end of their careers. Claiborne produced a low salt cookbook, which although now out of print, is interesting to read.[12]

Gourmet Cooking Without Salt, Eleanor Brenner

Eleanor Brenner's book is a comprehensive compendium of more than three hundred salt-free recipes suitable for using at dinner parties. The aim is to produce delicious meals that guests thoroughly enjoy without needing to add any salt at the table.[13] The author was a patient of Dr Walter Kempner, whose original diet of rice and apricots in the 1940s provided a sodium excretion rate below 10 mmol/day — the only non-drug measure that has ever been shown to reverse malignant hypertension.[14] Although this book has been out of print for a long time, copies are still held by some Australian libraries. A few recipes with butter, cream and eggs would be difficult to adapt, but this book's mastery of flavour makes it worth borrowing.

Australian cookbooks

All but one of several good Australian low salt cookbooks published in the last twenty years have gone out of print within two years of publication. The sole survivor was Julie Stafford's *Taste of Life*, which remained in print until 2003, having sold over 2 million copies between 1983 and 2003. (At the time of going to press, copies of the book are still available from Julie Stafford at email <juliestafford@ncable.com.au>.)

Taste of Life, Julie Stafford

Taste of Life is not a low salt cookbook as such. It resembles the
Pritikin program of diet and exercise, offering a healthier approach
to eating — recipes are low in saturated fat and high in fibre, and
emphasise fresh vegetables and fruits, mostly unrefined grains, and
low salt and sugar. This makes it an excellent book for following the
Dietary Guidelines for Australian Adults. The author's original reason
for improving her family's diet was to enable her husband to make
the best possible recovery from the effects of chemotherapy and radi-
ation for cancer.[15]

This book uses sodium-free baking powder. Salt is well controlled,
absent even from the bread recipes. The only departure that *Taste of
Life* makes from the dietary guidelines is the occasional use of Vecon,
a high sodium vegetable extract, and so-called 'low salt' soy sauce
(sodium over 3000 mg/100 g). Both are easily avoided, however, and
the book is otherwise excellent.

Simply Sensational, The Victor Chang Cardiac Research Institute Cookbook, Sally James

Cooking for Plenty — A Healthy Heart Recipe Guide for up to 50 People, National Heart Foundation of Australia

In both these books you will find a few recipes with a high salt
ingredient such as modified soy sauce or Thai fish sauce, and the dish
may not be low in salt unless you measure the high salt ingredient
very accurately. *Taste of Life*, *Simply Sensational* and *Cooking for Plenty*
all refer to modified soy sauce as 'low salt', 'low sodium' or 'reduced
salt', which is incorrect and misleading. The sodium content of ordinary soy sauce is between 6000 and 9000 mg/100 g. Modified soy
sauce still exceeds 3000 mg/100 g, whereas the upper limit for low
salt foods in the Food Standards Code is 120 mg/100 g and the limit
for reduced salt foods is 600 mg/100 g.

Mustards, Pickles and Chutneys, Margaret O'Sullivan

This is not a low salt cookbook, but has been included here because
so many of the recipes are ideal, containing no added salt at all.[16]

When you have been skipping salt for at least a month your palate is well on the road to recovery, and your rejuvenated tastebuds will confirm that good cooking needs no salt. The subtle flavours of well-cooked food — previously masked by salt — will speak for themselves, and can also make marvellous marriages with the hundreds of food flavours that are available, including all the herbs and spices.

6
The overriding importance of bread

The high salt content of ordinary bread comes as a great surprise to most people. In the food tables the sodium content of various Australian breads ranges from 400 to 725 mg/100 g.[1] Bread machine premixes commonly declare a sodium content of 600 mg/100 g in the finished loaf. Australian bakers get these figures by adding salt at 2 per cent of the flour weight, and sometimes ask why salt skippers need to worry about such a 'small amount'.

However, a loaf with a sodium content of 600 mg/100 g would give you 37 mmol from the bread alone if you just had two pieces of toast for breakfast and a sandwich for lunch, using standard bread slices weighing 30 g (toast thickness 40 g). The same amount of salt-free (unsalted) bread with a sodium content of 20 mg/100 g would add less than 2 mmol to your daily sodium excretion rate.

Patients who need a sodium excretion rate below 50 mmol/day will obviously have to avoid ordinary bread when such a moderate amount of bread contributes 37 mmol. If their family settles for a more moderate degree of salt skipping, the Australian recommended dietary intake of sodium for a useful preventive effect is 40–100 mmol/day.[2] Even at the upper limit of 100 mmol/day they would still be in some difficulty — the modest use of ordinary bread described above would limit their sodium intake from all other sources to 63 mmol/day.

Moreover, an official US government website proposes a daily sodium intake of 1500 mg (65 mmol) for the whole population of the United States.[3] The American government wants to prevent high blood pressure, and this proposal is based on an important study that used low salt bread with a sodium content of 36 mg/100 g.[4,5] What is now recommended for every American would be suitable for the salt skipper's family, and salt-free bread would make it much easier for them to achieve it.

What makes bread so important?

Bread is the central key to achieving independence from salt. No other single food adds as much to the huge sodium overload in the Western diet as bread, for two reasons: it is a staple food and it is far more salty than anybody realises. The dietary guidelines recommend eating more bread and cereals, preferably wholegrain. Most dietitians suggest at least four to five slices a day, and in 1995 the National Health and Medical Research Council recommended up to eight slices of bread a day.

When no salt is *added* to its natural salt content we should call bread 'unsalted' (but nobody does) and this book uses the common term 'salt-free'. Some bakers say it is impossible to make bread without added salt; in fact the American baking industry gave Nathan Pritikin that message. He was surprised to find salt-free 'Pritikin bread' on his first visit to Australia promoting his world-famous Pritikin program.[6]

The name 'Pritikin' was later registered as a trademark, and bakers who enter into a user agreement are allowed to add salt at about half the usual rate, a legacy of Pritikin's concession to the American baking industry. This gives the average Pritikin loaf a sodium content of up to about 240 mg/100 g, which is twice the upper limit for the Dietary Guidelines for Australian Adults.

The challenge of the different taste

The flavour of low salt bread (sodium up to 120 mg/100 g) and salt-free bread (about 20 mg/100 g) is quite unlike the taste of ordinary bread — it is as great a shock to some people as drinking tea for the first time without sugar. Although at first they can barely tolerate unsweetened tea, people do get used to it, and within three months it is sweet tea that is undrinkable. This also happens with salt in bread.

White bread has the greatest flavour problem, as white flour consists of little else but starch, after removing the wheat germ, bran, vitamins, minerals, and nearly all the flavour. White rolls are the most acceptable form of white bread, as they have more crust, which can be very tasty when fresh from the oven.

Responses to the taste of unsalted bread run the whole gamut. In the days before premixes were available for bread machines, some people were cooking without salt (on first principles) and disliked the idea of adding salt when they bought a bread machine. They proceeded to make salt-free bread with plain flour, no salt and no salt substitute. This usually makes a heavier loaf, but the remedy for that is to use one of the dough improvers available from supermarkets. These people insisted that they liked their salt-free bread, and obviously meant it. At the other extreme, people occasionally object to salt-free bread strongly enough to say that they would rather eat no bread at all.

In the 1980s, a Sydney bakery added potassium chloride to the salt-free wholemeal bread supplied to the Royal Prince Alfred Hospital, and the sandwiches supplied at meetings of the Australian Nutrition Foundation used this bread. About thirty or forty people (mostly professional dietitians) regularly ate these sandwiches, unaware of anything unusual about the bread.[7]

Packets of potassium chloride carry a warning, mentioned in Chapter 4, that this substance must be used only upon medical advice (patients in kidney failure, and those who take certain medications, must avoid it). It is worth repeating here that there is no warning when food labels include potassium chloride (additive 508) in the ingredient list, and that is because measured amounts seldom compensate fully for the potassium lost in processing. Similarly — in the absence of severe kidney failure — measured amounts should be safe in homemade bread.

The occasional person who refuses to accept the flavour of salt-free bread is usually very happy with potassium chloride as a salt substitute in a bread machine recipe (but remember that potassium chloride is not a dough improver, and a bread recipe needs another dough improver to replace salt). People seem to find the substitution with potassium chloride imperceptible, except for an occasional super-taster who can detect that something is 'wrong'.

There is another option for super-tasters. They generally find fruit bread (made without salt) highly acceptable. Even the most fastidious, salt-eating visitors will enjoy your raisin bread (fresh or toasted) without noticing that it has been made without salt. You can make it yourself by hand or in a bread machine, or find a local baker who will oblige.

Salt-free bread does have a bonus. Many people are surprised at its excellent keeping properties. An ordinary loaf kept in the refrigerator may go mouldy before a salt-free loaf, probably because the salt makes ordinary bread retain more moisture.

Veteran salt skippers with a strong preference for salt-free bread have reported an interesting effect on their favourite red wine if they forget to take their salt-free bread to a BYO restaurant. If they are tempted by some nice-looking bread rolls while waiting for the first course, the first nibble may be 'not too bad', but becomes unpleasantly salty by the time it is swallowed. The next sip of red wine is so unpleasant that they find they need several drinks of water to get rid of the taste. Appreciation of wine depends very much on the accompanying food, a point easily verified by anyone who tastes red wine with smoked oyster.[8] Veteran salt skippers find that this effect is hardly noticeable with white wine.

Acceptance of salt-free bread

Tuscany

Tuscan bread or *pane toscano* has been salt free for centuries, a legacy of a salt tax. When the tax was lifted and salt came back into general use, the Tuscans evidently had the same objection to salted bread that today's salt skippers have, and perhaps the same dismay when tasting it with a sip of their best *chianti*. In their judgement salty bread was not proper bread (and still isn't).

One of the attractions of village accommodation in Tuscany is that tourists can expect to eat well. In the words of gastronomic historian Michael Symons, tourists take home vivid memories of a 'sublime cuisine'.[9] Elizabeth Romer also fell in love with the cuisine of rural Tuscany when she was an art student, and gained an intimate knowledge of it during the years when her archaeologist husband was working in Egypt. The couple made Tuscany their base. Her book about rural Tuscan gastronomy warns readers of her unexpected discovery that the bread is salt free. She adds, 'This can be disconcerting at the first taste' but concedes that 'salt in fact is not a necessary addition'.[10] Don't expect 'Tuscan bread' sold in other countries to be salt free — elsewhere, it is probably Tuscan in name only, and usually as salty as the local bread. Shops sell what their customers will buy, and both Londoners and Tuscans buy what they like (which, in turn, is what they are accustomed to).

An Australian university

In 1984, the refectory at the Students' Union at the Australian National University in Canberra introduced a lunchtime 'Health Bar', where one table was set aside for salt-free food. Soon this table catered for about 25 per cent of the students. At that point the baker decided to leave salt out of the bread rolls — a bold move, because all customers ate the same rolls. After hearing no comment for a month, he announced that the bread rolls were being made without salt. Silence continued and the bread rolls were bought and eaten just as fast as before. Inevitably the experiment was abandoned when another caterer took over.

An Australian winery restaurant

A well-known Australian winery runs a restaurant where diners choose dishes from a gourmet menu, each dish being selected by the chef to accompany a glass of an appropriate wine. In 1999 two salt skippers who had pre-booked a low salt meal were delighted to find that the bread rolls, baked on the premises, were made without added salt. They checked if the baker had used a premix (premixes are pre-salted), but his sourdough recipe used plain flour and no salt. The excellent flavour confirmed the absence of salt.

Previous visitors had complained that salted butter with salted bread rolls spoilt a gourmet meal, so the restaurant started making its rolls with no added salt. For two years this generated no complaints. Sadly, the chef who made the salt-free bread rolls left, and the winery now buys rolls with the standard salt content from an outside supplier.

A Tasmanian bakery

Some traditional German recipes for pumpernickel bread use no salt. Bass Bakery in northern Tasmania successfully marketed salt-free pumpernickel bread throughout Tasmania in the 1990s. Although a little different in taste from German pumpernickel bread, this bread was found to be excellent, encouraging the bakery to invest in a much larger and more fully automated plant to cope with the increased demand. The new plant, however, would not work without salt being added to control the yeast, so production of the salt-free pumpernickel bread ceased.

Low salt bread

In 2000 a Hobart baker obtained an Australian patent for his recipe for low salt bread that has most of the salty flavour of ordinary bread, but a sodium content below 120 mg/100 g. Hobart salt skippers don't like it, pronouncing it 'too salty'. As salt skippers were the only customers, this recipe is not currently in production, but a low salt bread that tastes salty does have an advantage to the bread trade — a shorter proving time, making it cheaper to produce. It may also have great public health potential in future, as a highly acceptable prototype for the standard breads.

Buying salt-free bread

Both in Australia and overseas, it is generally possible to find a baker who is willing to make salt-free bread. The order must usually be placed a day ahead, and most bakers need an order for at least three to six loaves, which is more convenient if you have access to a deep-freeze (bread freezes well).

Look for a small bakery, because big companies cannot accept small orders. 'Hot bread' shops usually buy premixes, which are pre-salted. Some small family businesses with recipes requiring plain flour are called 'continental' bakeries. Some of the franchised bakery chains also keep plain flour for special recipes, and the owner of an individual business will sometimes accept an order for salt-free bread. The Bread Research Institute in Sydney gives free technical advice to the trade, and a baker who needs help (because bread dough behaves differently without salt) can apply to the Baking Division, Bread Research Institute, PO Box 7, North Ryde, NSW 2113 (Phone (02) 9888 9600, Fax (02) 9888 5821).

The salt-free bread you buy will usually have no nutrition information panel — not even an ingredient list. Bread is exempt from the labelling regulations when sold across the counter without a printed wrapper. This was a serious problem for one well-meaning Australian baker who made salt-free bread one day with a 'soda bread' recipe, using baking powder instead of yeast. The sodium bicarbonate in standard baking powder gave this baker's salt-free bread a high sodium content, making it especially unsuitable for people who skip salt and other sodium compounds very strictly for medical reasons.

Using a sodium-free baking powder such as Salt Skip Baking Powder (see Appendix 4) would have solved this problem and supplied a different kind of bread with a cake-like consistency that many people like for a change. Soda bread is popular in Ireland, and sometimes called 'Irish bread'.

Making salt-free bread

If you can't buy salt-free bread you can make your own, by hand or by machine.

Dough improvers

Salt was the world's first chemical dough improver. It strengthens the gluten in the flour, making a lighter and less crumbly loaf. It makes yeast rise slowly, so commercial bakeries can handle larger batches. Other dough improvers strengthen the gluten equally well, however, and need no salt.

To bake a light loaf without salt you will need an alternative dough improver. One alternative is vitamin C (ascorbic acid or calcium ascorbate), which you can buy in health food shops and pharmacies. Use $1/2$-1 teaspoonful of ascorbic acid powder per loaf. The chemical reaction destroys the vitamin, leaving no residual vitamin C. Some chemical flour treatment agents are exclusive to the baking industry, but several dough improvers are retailed in health food shops and in the health food or 'baking needs' sections of supermarkets, or by mail order (see Chapter 11 and Appendix 5). Follow the instruction book that comes with your bread machine, and be prepared to make a lot of experiments before you achieve the ideal loaf.

Bread machines

All breadmakers are an investment — *Choice* consumer magazine finds that even the most expensive pays for itself within twelve months if you bake daily. Some make large as well as small loaves, but the 680 g loaf supplies as much fresh bread as most families can use daily, and still cuts into full-size slices for the toaster.

Here are a few notes about using bread machines:

- Grains tend to scratch a Teflon bread pan, and only the factory (and one or two Teflon specialists) can recoat it.
- The loaf is lost if the power fails. Even if it's restored at once, most machines will probably begin a completely new cycle. Some (like the Panasonic 250) continue the cycle if power is restored within twenty minutes. Rural areas subject to power cuts need this feature.
- The recipes supplied with the machine give exact amounts for all ingredients, but each new batch of flour (especially wholemeal) may vary a little in water requirement — a good reason to buy 10 kilogram bags if you can use it all while it's still fresh. Open the lid during the first mix to check the dough and make sure it has enough water.
- When adapting other bread recipes to a small machine, be careful to limit the total quantity to an amount it can handle (maximum $2^1/2$ cups of flour or mixture of flour and other dry ingredients).

Bread premixes

Premixes for breadmakers are pre-salted to raise the sodium in a finished loaf to about 600 mg/100 g. For salt-free bread you need plain bread flour, white and/or wholemeal. Wholemeal bread has more flavour than white when made without salt, but recipes for white flour are included here because some people have a digestive tract that for various reasons cannot tolerate the extra fibre of wholemeal flour.

Recipes for salt-free bread using bread machines

These recipes are from past issues of *Salt Skip News*, the Salt Skip Program newsletter produced by the Menzies Institute for inclusion in *The BP Monitor*, newsletter of the QHA. Most of the recipes are based on many hours of patient trial and error. Factors that may prevent you from achieving similar results with the same recipe in the same model of the same machine include the exact nature of the flour, its freshness (very important) and the brand and freshness of the yeast. We get best results from Fermipan or Mauripan dried yeast in 500 g packs. Fridge storage enables you to ignore the use-by date.

Wholemeal loaf

(from Wendy Miles, Mount Wilson, NSW; using Breville Breadmaker 250)
 250 mL cold tap water
 1^1/$_4$ cups plain white bread flour
 1 cup plain wholemeal bread flour
 2 tsp brown sugar
 1 tbs skim milk powder
 ^{1}/$_2$ tsp ascorbic acid powder
 1 tbs Meadowlea NAS margarine
 1 tbs gluten flour
 1^1/$_2$ tsp dried yeast

Bake on the small wholemeal loaf setting. Dough improvers give a lighter loaf, but both the gluten and the ascorbic acid in this recipe are dough improvers.

White bread recipe

(from Dr Stephanie Whitmont; using Breville Baker's Oven Plus)
 290 mL water
 1 tbs oil
 1 tbs sugar
 3 cups (450 g) plain white bread flour
 1 tsp ascorbic acid
 1^1/$_2$ tsp dried yeast (Tandaco)
 ^{1}/$_3$ cup sunflower seeds (optional)

Use the basic light (A) setting. This makes a 750 g loaf.

Fruit loaf for Breville Ultimate Baker's Oven 400

(from Margaret Haynes, Kettering, Tas.; using Breville Ultimate Baker's Oven 400)

This recipe contains a slight modification of a recipe that came with the breadmaker.

270 mL water
3 cups white bread flour
1 tsp dough improver
1^1/$_2$ tbs brown sugar
1^1/$_2$ tbs milk powder
3 tsp ground mixed spice
1^1/$_2$ tbs canola oil
2 tsp dried yeast
1 tsp garam masala
1 cup dried fruit

The fruit is added to the Breville's dried fruit, nut and herb dispenser. The setting is Sweet or Basic, with the choice of light, medium, dark or rapid. Use the setting for the 750 g loaf.

White loaf

(Using Sunbeam Cool Touch Bakehouse Breadmaker BM4700)
This white loaf has a nice texture and makes good toast.
1 sachet Fermipan dried yeast
500 g (about 4 cups) white bread flour
1 tsp Lecimax dough improver
2 tbs gluten flour
1 tbs skim milk powder
1 tbs sugar
1 tbs olive oil
up to 1^2/$_3$ cups water

Use the standard setting for white bread.

Wholemeal loaf

(from Jean O'Connor, Cooloongup, WA; using Sanyo Breadmaker SBM–201)
1^2/$_3$ cups warm water
2 tbs oil
2 tbs molasses
3 cups white bread flour
^{1}/$_2$ cup plain wholemeal flour (not bread flour)
1^1/$_2$ cups rye flour
1 tbs gluten flour
2 tbs dried milk
2^1/$_4$ tsp dried yeast

Place ingredients in the machine in the above order and use Setting 5. On this setting there is no beep — the Sanyo signal for having a look at progress — but you can lift the lid and clean down the sides of the pan when the machine starts kneading. It cooks in just under 3 hours. Flavour comes from the rye flour and molasses.

You can get a bit more flavour by adding about $1/2$ cup of soy and linseed (mixed). Substituting 1 tsp sugar for half of the molasses reduces the molasses flavour. It is possible to vary the flours with equally good results, for example use 3 cups white bread flour with 2 cups rye flour, and 1 tbs gluten flour.

Potato bread

(Using Sanyo SBM–200)

The Sanyo SBM–200 supplies recipes for potato bread, for three sizes of loaf, using instant mashed potato. The largest (1 kg) uses $1/4$ cup dried potato flakes. Below is a Sanyo recipe for the smallest loaf. The changes that work well without salt in the Sanyo are shown in square brackets.

$3/4$ cup plus 2 tbs water (230 mL) [same as 1 cup minus 1 tbs]

$2^{1}/4$ cups bread flour [omit salt, and add optional $1/2$–1 tsp dough improver or calcium ascorbate]

1 tbs sugar
1 tbs [skim] milk powder [optional]
1 tbs olive oil or canola oil [not butter]
2 tbs dried potato flakes [Deb]
$1^{1}/4$ tsp dried yeast
Bake at Setting 1.

Commercial potato flakes are salted — too salty to use for mashed potato — but 2 tbs Deb leaves the sodium content of the whole loaf below 50 mg/100 g. Edgell Potato Whip works equally well but, being a powder (three times as heavy), you only need one-third of the volume (use 3 tsp).

Potato herb bread

(from Sandra Mercer, Hobart, Tas.; using Panasonic SD–200)

This recipe and the two below use fresh mashed potato instead of instant mashed potato powder. Users of other machines may need to experiment for best results. NAS breads made with mashed potato keep fresh much longer than ordinary loaves.

1 cup firmly packed mashed potato
400 g white bread flour
3 tbs dried milk powder
1 tbs sugar
1¹/₄ tsp dried yeast
2 tbs NAS poly/monounsaturated margarine
3 rounded tsp MasterFoods Italian Herb Mix
3 tbs gluten flour
350 mL water
Cook on Panasonic basic and bake settings for 4 hours.

White potato bread

For plain white bread, omit the herbs from the recipe above.

Wholemeal potato bread

Again, omit the herbs and use wholemeal flour. Use the same settings and baking times.

Instant mashed potato in other bread machines

Instant mashed potato flakes or powder may be worth trying in any bread machine. For a very small loaf try 2 tbs flakes or 3 tsp powder, as above. You would need to judge the amount of water by trial and error.

Soy and linseed bread

Soy grits and linseed can be added to your bread machine recipe. Weston Milling sell them as a salt-free mixture with kibbled wheat. The 360 g packet contains enough for adding to three loaf recipes, with instructions for four brands of bread machines. The mixture is available in all major supermarkets, or you can write to the address given in Appendix 5.

If you just want soy and linseed, buy the seeds in bulk from a health food shop when you see the quantity that suits your machine.

Iodine in bread

People who want an iodine supplement after giving up iodised salt can add it to homemade bread. Chapter 9 gives instructions for using kelp, or potassium iodide drops.

Gluten-free bread

Gluten-free bread is for people with coeliac disease or lesser degrees of gluten intolerance. Appendix 5 gives addresses for two organisations that provide special help with recipes and mail order ingredients for gluten-free bread (Carol Bates in Victoria and Basic Ingredients in Queensland). You can also buy FG Roberts's sodium- and gluten-free self-raising flour in health food shops and in the health food section of major supermarkets.

Gluten-free flour (plain)

$^1/_2$ cup soy flour
$^1/_2$ cup potato flour
$^1/_4$ cup rice flour
Sift all ingredients together three times. Use instead of plain white flour.

Gluten-free flour (self-raising)

$^1/_2$ cup maize corn flour
$^1/_3$ cup rice or soy flour
$^1/_2$ cup rice flour (sold as baby cereal)
2 tsp Salt Skip Baking Powder
Sift all ingredients together. Store in an airtight container.

7
Low salt recipes

While this is a book about salt, *all the Australian dietary guidelines* will contribute to your health and longevity if you follow them. Read about them in Chapter 10 and bear them in mind when you devise new recipes or adapt old ones to make them low in salt. Recipes in this chapter have been sent in at various times by salt skippers for *Salt Skip News*, and they may help you to make a few short cuts.

Low salt breakfasts

The Salt Skip Program recommends low salt cereals (sodium up to 120 mg/100 g) and for other healthy features it follows the Heart Foundation's criteria for breakfast cereals — dietary fibre 3 per cent or more, fat not more than 5 per cent, and sugar not more than 15 per cent. If the label carries the well-known Heart Foundation 'Tick' (see Chapter 17), it automatically means that the cereal complies with these three Heart Foundation criteria. However, you must still check the sodium, because the Heart Foundation allows the 'Tick' on some breakfast cereals and some other foods that are not low in salt.

The Australian dietary guidelines keep sugar, honey and syrup off the breakfast table as well as salt, and recommend reduced fat or low fat milk. You can add, or substitute, fresh or dried fruit, or fruit stewed without sugar. The combination of fruit and low salt cereal for breakfast is a good one and an easy one with which to create endless variety.

Fruit and cereal

Breakfast is a meal to enjoy with fruit and cereals rather than eating salted protein, such as bacon, fried in fat. The choice of fruit, fresh or stewed, is unlimited. Fresh fruit is free from preservatives, added sugar or artificial colours and is good for blood pressure.[1] Few people eat enough of it — a major fault in the diet of industrialised societies. Fruit makes a good start to the day because of its low fat and salt content. In their natural state cereals, such as rolled oats, have a very low sodium content, and make a sensible choice for breakfast.

Porridge

People accustomed to salt in porridge will miss it at first. A well-known dietitian and food writer found her family refused to eat porridge without salt. After gradually reducing salt in other foods throughout the summer, she made porridge without salt the following winter and no one noticed. Later the children stayed with their grandmother (who still salted her porridge) and told their mother afterwards they just couldn't eat grandma's porridge — they didn't know why, but it tasted awful.

The Scots are severe judges of salt-free porridge — they cook it with salt and add still more salt at the table. A Scotsman who joined one of the Salt Skip trials in Canberra said he couldn't face salt-free porridge, yet in middle age, after the habit of a lifetime, he frankly admitted that the cinnamon we suggested as an alternative to salt was much nicer.

Various forms of cinnamon can be used — cinnamon powder, cinnamon sugar, or apple stewed with cinnamon sticks. Cinnamon is the magic ingredient of apple strudel, and stewed apple is ideal to have with porridge or other cereals. The stewed apple suggested for breakfast cereals can be used in rotation with any other fruit with the changing seasons. When fresh fruit is scarce, use stewed dried fruit.

Muesli

Dr M Bircher-Benner of Zurich, Switzerland, chose oatmeal with fruit over a century ago for his Salt Free Nutrition Plan. Patients at his clinic in 1897 started the day with muesli. Instead of cooking the oatmeal, he softened it to a mush by soaking it overnight (his Salt Free Nutrition Plan promoted raw foods). In Swiss-German dialect the word for 'mush' is 'muesli', and muesli was Bircher-Benner's idea for making oatmeal delicious without adding salt.

The original recipe made enough for one invalid person, and was served fresh:

1 tbs rolled oats, soaked in 3 tbs water
1 tbs lemon juice
1 tbs sweetened condensed milk
200 g apples, washed and cored but not peeled
1–2 tbs extra water, depending on the type of apple
1 tbs grated hazelnuts or almonds

After soaking for 12 hours (overnight), the oats were blended into a mush, and then the other liquids were added. The apples were grated directly into the mush so that the flesh didn't turn brown. The grated nuts were sprinkled over the top just before serving.

Variations included apple muesli with almond purée, apple muesli with yoghurt, apple muesli with cream (an 1897 prescription for thin people), and muesli with berries, mixed fruit or dried fruit. Little could Bircher-Benner have guessed that a century later more than 100 000 tonnes of 'muesli' variations would be eaten every year around the world, at an estimated annual value of almost a billion US dollars. Some food companies defeat Bircher-Benner's whole intention by adding salt to their mixtures, although a sodium content of more than 120 mg/100 g is unusual.

Most toasted mueslis contain too much fat, and the high natural sugar content from dried fruit is often augmented needlessly with cane sugar and/or honey. The solid stick of material called a 'muesli bar' is usually salted, and sometimes over-salted, so read the label carefully.

Muesli can be mixed at home from any cereal, any fruit and any nut, in any proportions. Some people prefer their homemade mixture to anything they can buy. The original Bircher-Benner recipe used sweetened condensed milk with a high fat and added sugar content. To follow the dietary guidelines low fat yoghurt would be preferred nowadays, sweetened only with the natural sugar content of the fruit.

Raw rolled oats are not very easy to eat. Bircher-Benner softened them by soaking, but oats can be cooked instead, making a hot breakfast. Some muesli recipes cook better than others, but hot muesli can make a pleasant alternative to cold muesli. It can be served instead of soup as a snack at any time.

Ready-made cereals

The world's first ready-to-eat breakfast cereals had a very high salt content, as people in the 1860s thought that salt was harmless. In 1997, with a sodium content of over 1000 mg/100 g, Kellogg's Corn Flakes came second in Australia's ten top-selling ready-to-eat breakfast cereals according to the *Retail World* annual report. It would be wrong to give credit to the salt content; the overall market leader, Sanitarium Weet-Bix, had only 280 mg/100 g. Weet-Bix had less sodium than any of the rest of the top ten — the least salty cereal was the best-seller.

The Kellogg's cereal Just Right further contradicts any notion that salt sells cereals. After 1997 Kellogg (Australia) reduced the salt content substantially in most of their cereal range, with the biggest reduction in Just Right, from 284 mg/100 g to 49 mg/100 g. Kellogg (Australia) announced that this was achieved with no loss in palatability, and the market proved it — Just Right rose from sixth to fifth place in the retail food industry's list of the Top Ten best-selling ready-to-eat breakfast cereals, and remained there. It is hard to believe (but true) that Kellogg's Corn Flakes still have a salt level of about 800 mg/100 g.

By 2002 Kellogg (Australia) had twelve low salt ready-to-eat breakfast cereals, and all their major competitors had low salt brands on the supermarket shelves. Sanitarium Lite-Bix (Weet-Bix without salt, sodium 20 mg/100 g) has been on the market since 1990, and is usually very acceptable to people who have previously chosen Weet-Bix.

In 1998 the British press asked why Kellogg (UK) sold Just Right with a sodium content of 600 mg/100 g when Australians could buy it with 49 mg/100 g. Kellogg (UK) told the press it saw no reason for a lower salt content and didn't change it.

Cereals have replaced the high protein, high fat breakfasts of a bygone era. An Australian dietary survey found that cereal foods (including bread) supply over 20 per cent of the salt eaten in the whole day.[2] Cereals (the seeds of cultivated grasses) have an extremely low sodium content in their natural state, so the remedy is simple — eat suitable bread (see Chapter 6) and read the label to choose suitable breakfast cereals with low levels of sodium (see Chapter 11).

Homemade muesli *(Serves 2)*

$1/2$ cup rolled oats
4 tbs wheat germ
4 tbs unprocessed bran
2 tsp sunflower seeds
5–6 walnuts or almonds, chopped
2 tbs dried fruit, chopped

Combine all ingredients and serve with skim milk or low fat yoghurt. Fresh fruit may also be added when serving the muesli to make a complete breakfast. As a variation, store the muesli with a vanilla bean for added flavour.

Homemade toasted muesli *(Serves 2)*

Multiple batches of the muesli in the previous recipe may be toasted (as suggested by the National Heart Foundation) by adding 1 tbs olive oil, peanut or canola oil and 1 tbs water. These are added to the dry ingredients, which are then baked at 150°C for $1^1/2$ hours, stirring occasionally.

Walnut muesli *(Serves 6)*

100 g rolled oats
150 mL skim milk
50 g each of dates and walnuts, chopped
25 g each of raisins and wheat germ
1 apple, cored and chopped
200 g natural skim milk yoghurt
1 tbs lemon juice

Soak the oats overnight in the milk. Next day mix in the walnuts, raisins, wheat germ, dates and apple. Stir the yoghurt and lemon juice together and stir into the muesli.

Lunch

In addition to the salt-free breads you can buy or make at home, you may be able to find a low salt pita (pocket) bread. It's ideal for filling with salads, and is usually available in both wholemeal and white. Pita bread needs no spreads. Another alternative is a fruit loaf or bun.

Sandwich spreads

Low salt salad dressings and mayonnaises, low fat yoghurt, ricotta cheese, horseradish sauce, tomato sauce or low salt chutney, or a curry or chilli paste or sauce can be used as spreads for sandwiches and salt-free rolls. Tahini paste (sesame seed paste) also makes a change. It can be thickened if necessary by beating in a little lemon juice. Delicious sandwiches can also be made without using a spread, especially if a moist filling, such as tomato or avocado, is used.

Another alternative is to spread both pieces of bread with low salt tomato sauce liberally sprinkled with dried Italian herbs and filled with chicken pieces — the otherwise tell-tale flavour of tomato sauce is not recognisable.

The herb lovage, with a flavour reminiscent of Maggi soups, can be used to make lovage pesto as a sandwich spread.

Lovage pesto

(from salt skipper Elaine Speakman)

  3 cups fresh lovage leaves

  2 cloves garlic

  4 tbs of pine nuts (or 2 tbs each of skinned walnuts and ground almonds)

  1 tbs balsamic vinegar

  3/4 cup olive oil

Blend all the ingredients together. Some palates may require 1–2 tsp of sugar to balance the vinegar. The pesto can be stored in small jars in the fridge, where it will keep for a week or two. It is also excellent in salads, soups and gravies, and makes a tasty filling for potatoes baked in their jackets; some people like it spread on toast.

When basil pesto was made in the traditional pestle and mortar, the gritty salt in the recipe made it easier to pound the basil into a paste, but a blender works equally well without adding any salt. Food regulations now require commercial producers to use an acid such as vinegar or lemon juice when preserving vegetables in oil (see Chapter 4). Traditional basil pesto needs no vinegar because of its high salt content, derived from both added salt and Parmesan or Romano cheese, which have high sodium contents of 1440 and 1040 mg/100 g respectively.

Sandwich fillings

Low fat, low salt fillings for sandwiches and pita bread can include cold lean meat, poultry and fresh or low salt canned fish. Meat can be thinly sliced roast beef, lamb with mint sauce, or pork. Pieces of chicken or turkey with the fat and skin removed can be flavoured with low salt mustard or horseradish sauce, mint sauce, mint jelly or cranberry sauce.

Meat, poultry and fish go well with fresh salad. Use plenty of salad vegetables and/or fruit (anything from the usual lettuce, tomato, cucumber and grated carrot to bean, alfalfa or fenugreek sprouts, sliced radishes, Coles no-added-salt canned beetroot, asparagus, capsicum, shredded red or green cabbage, rocket, mushrooms, onion rings, pineapple or sliced kiwi fruit). No-added-salt sardines can be mashed with a little low salt, low fat ricotta to make a fish spread. Sprigs of fennel go well with fish, or use fresh or dried oregano, or mint leaves.

Sandwiches can be sweet as well as savoury — try low salt peanut butter with raisins or sultanas, preferably the unbleached dried fruit that is darker in colour and has a more intense flavour. You may have to look for these in health food shops. Chopped nuts or the flesh and seeds of passionfruit add interesting texture. A fresh apple or seedless grapes are delicious when eaten as an accompaniment to either sweet or savoury sandwiches, pita bread or filled rolls.

Instead of sandwiches, try filling the lunch box with meat, fish or chicken salad on its own. Small or partitioned containers ensure that separate salad ingredients look appetising after the box has been carried to work or school. If you have a microwave oven at work you can reheat a stew, casserole or curry for lunch.

Pizzas

Low salt pizzas must skip ingredients such as canned anchovies (sodium 5480 mg/100 g) and olives (2070 mg/100 g). This is easy after four weeks of salt skipping because the palate can no longer tolerate such high salt concentrations (even if you start eating the pizza you can't finish it). After four weeks you enjoy low salt pizzas.

Quick snack pizza (Serves 1)

 1 slice salt-free bread
 2 tsp NAS tomato sauce or paste
 2 slices green capsicum
 2 sliced mushrooms
 sprinkling of dried oregano or basil
 1–2 tbs grated Salt Skip Low Salt Cheddar Cheese
 Flatten bread slice thinly with a rolling pin. Toast under the grill, on one side only. Spread untoasted side with a layer of each remaining ingredient, ending with the cheese. Grill until cheese melts.

Additional filling ideas

Cottage cheese, thinly sliced onion, pineapple pieces, unsalted canned or fresh fish or seafood, unsalted savoury mince, unsalted cooked chicken, grated carrot, thinly sliced zucchini, unsalted sweet corn kernels, sliced tomato, herbs, nuts.

Wholemeal scone dough pizza base (Serves 4)

 1 cup wholemeal flour
 1 cup plain white flour
 2 tsp Salt Skip Baking Powder
 1 tbs unsalted margarine
 1/2 cup skim milk
 1/2–1/3 cup water
 Mix flours and baking powder in mixing bowl. Rub in margarine until mixture resembles breadcrumbs. Mix in milk and enough water to form a soft dough. Roll or pat out to form pizza shape (individual or larger ones). Spread with tomato paste or sauce and other ingredients (as above). Bake in hot oven at 200°C for 15 minutes or until golden.

Stir-fries

Wok cooking (stir-frying) tosses the food continuously on a very hot steel surface. In the few minutes that it takes to cook vegetables, they remain deliciously crisp and crunchy, with no loss of flavour or mineral content, and hardly any loss of vitamins. If meat is used, it is often only a small quantity of lean meat, more for flavour than for substance.

Few people realise when they stir-fry with soy sauce that the sodium content of soy sauce can range from 6000 to 9000 mg/100 g — six to nine times more salty than seawater. Low salt or low sodium soy sauces (up to 120 mg/100 g) and reduced salt or reduced sodium ones (up to 600 mg/100 g) don't exist, but people who love stir-fries can make a very satisfactory stir-fry sauce at home. Don Gazzaniga's cookbook (see Chapter 5) has a no-salt stir-fry sauce recipe sent to him by a friend in Thailand.[3] Salt skipper Jack Kane translated the American brands into Australian equivalents as follows:

Don Gazzaniga's low salt stir-fry sauce
3/4 cup garlic vinegar (vinegar with 2 garlic cloves soaked in it for about 20 hours)
3 tbs molasses (bought in bulk from a health food shop)
3 tsp MasterFoods onion powder seasoning
Mixed, this will store for several weeks in the fridge. Contrary perhaps to expectations this mixture is nothing like a sweet-and-sour sauce — the balance of flavours is savoury and very agreeable.

Pastry and pastry alternatives

The high fat content of ordinary pastry has made some people give up eating pastry altogether, but pastry can be made with far less fat than traditional recipes use. Unsaturated oils and margarines can replace butter and lard. At cooking temperatures high enough for pastry there is a preference now for using monounsaturated oils (olive oil, peanut oil, canola oil), because they are 'good fats' that will not raise your blood cholesterol.

You will soon find it easy and quick to make pastry with oil and wholemeal flour. Some people like to rest it up to half an hour in the fridge, but if left any longer it breaks up when you roll it.

It is not always necessary to use the same amount of pastry that a recipe might call for. For example, you can leave out the bottom layer of pastry in a pie dish, or you can use a light pastry case that has been baked blind. If the pastry is rolled thinly, less will be needed. Two tips for making better pastry are to start with cool ingredients and to avoid over-handling of the dough, which makes the pastry tougher.

Plain pastry

1/3 cup plain white flour
1/4 cup wholemeal flour
1 tsp Salt Skip Baking Powder
2 tbs evaporated skim milk
100 mL apple juice or extra skim milk
1/2 tsp mixed herbs may be added if desired

Mix all dry ingredients, add liquids and make into dough. Allow pastry to rest for 30 minutes, then place on a lightly floured board and roll out. Use as desired. For sweet pastry, use apple juice or sweetened skim milk. A little lemon rind and juice may also be added.

Crumb crust

1 1/4 cups wholemeal NAS breadcrumbs, or crumbed Lite-Bix
1 egg white, lightly beaten
(For a sweet flan) 1 tsp sugar or 3 tsp apple juice concentrate (from health food shops)
4 tsp lemon juice

Combine all ingredients thoroughly. Place in a pie or flan dish (23–24 cm, non-stick or lightly oiled), press down with lightly floured fingers. Bake at 180°C for 10 minutes.

Wholemeal potato pastry

250 g wholemeal plain flour
1 medium potato, peeled and finely grated
3 cups water
3 tbs lemon juice

Combine all the ingredients (this is best done in a food processor) until mixture becomes a smooth ball. Leave pastry to rest, then use as desired.

Wholemeal pastry

(Makes enough pastry for top and bottom crusts for a 22 cm pie plate.)

1/2 cup canola oil
1/2 cup water
2 cups wholemeal flour

Beat oil and water together until thick, add to the flour and mix gently. Divide in half and roll out each half. Cook at 225°C. A convenient way to handle this pastry is to roll it out inside a plastic bag. Cut away one side of the bag, arrange the pastry on a pie dish, then remove the plastic from the other side.

Variations

Instead of all wholemeal flour, use 1 cup wholemeal and 1 cup white flour. For a lighter crust add 3 tsp Salt Skip Baking Powder.

Crepes (Makes 12)

1¹/₂ cups water
¹/₄ cup cornflour
³/₄ cup wholemeal cake flour
2 tsp Salt Skip Baking Powder

Place water in blender and flours in a jug. Turn on blender and pour flours in gradually, blend for 30 seconds. Cook in a non-stick crepe pan or lightly oiled pan.

Salad dressing

Avocado dressing

This dressing can also supply both lubrication and flavour to sandwiches without adding any fat. It goes well with cucumber, tomato, lettuce and most other salads, and stores well for 3–6 months in the fridge, but once you taste it you are more likely to use it quickly than to keep it. Use dry peppercorns (bottled peppercorns are packed in heavily salted vinegar). Most people prefer the dressing sweetened, so aspartame (Equal or Nutrasweet) can replace some or all of the sugar.

500 g ripe tomatoes, scalded and skinned (or use canned tomatoes)
2 tsp dry green peppercorns, crushed
2 tsp dried mixed herbs
1 tsp dry mustard powder
200 g (1 cup) sugar or equivalent in aspartame (Equal or Nutrasweet)
375 mL (1¹/₂ cups) white vinegar or cider vinegar

Mix all ingredients in a food processor until the mixture is a suitable consistency for bottling. Store in the fridge.

Sauces and pickles

Tomato sauce for pasta *(Makes 3 cups, serves 6)*

  1 clove garlic, crushed
  1 medium onion, diced
  125 g mushrooms, chopped
  1 green capsicum, finely diced
  2 tsp polyunsaturated oil
  $1/2$ tsp dried rosemary
  1 bay leaf
  1 tsp dried oregano
  1 cup red or white wine
  180 g NAS tomato paste
  400 g NAS canned peeled tomatoes

Cook the garlic, onion, mushrooms and green capsicum in oil until soft, about 4 minutes. Add rosemary, bay leaf and oregano, and mix well. Cover with a lid and simmer for 5 minutes. Add wine, tomato paste and peeled tomatoes. Cook slowly for 1 hour or until sauce is thick. Remove bay leaf before serving.

Worcestershire sauce *(Makes about 500 mL)*

There is no commercial no-added-salt Worcestershire sauce. Two tasty recipes from salt skipper Debbie Seen are provided here.

  500 mL malt vinegar
  1 tsp cayenne pepper
  4 tsp ground cloves
  $1/4$ tsp ground allspice
  $1/2$ tsp ground mace
  $1/2$ tsp ground ginger
  1 clove garlic, crushed
  $1^1/2$ tbs brown sugar
  $1^1/2$ tbs treacle
  $1/4$ cup cold water

While bringing the vinegar to the boil, mix the other ingredients and stir into the water. Add this to the boiling vinegar, and simmer for 1 hour. Strain into a bottle through an open fabric, so that some of the sediment is included in the bottle.

Worcestershire sauce with plums   *(Makes about 4¹/₂ L)*

2 kg sour dark red plums, stoned
200 g minced garlic
20 small red chillies
4 L malt vinegar
1 kg dark brown sugar
1¹/₂ tins treacle
1 tbs cayenne pepper
2 tbs white pepper
2 tbs ground ginger
20 g fresh minced ginger
1 tbs ground cloves

Blend plums, garlic and chillies with enough vinegar to purée them. Place with all the other ingredients in a large saucepan and boil for 2 hours. Strain through muslin and return to vinegar bottles to store. You can store the mixture from the muslin bag in jam jars in the fridge to use later as a base in hot dishes.

Date chutney

250 g stoned dates, chopped
1 tbs dry mustard
1 tbs ground ginger (or 4 cups crystallised ginger, chopped)
1 tsp cinnamon
1 cup boiling water
1 cup vinegar

Bring all the ingredients to the boil in a saucepan, simmer for 5 minutes, stirring occasionally. Place into warm jars and seal when cool. This recipe may be varied by adding 4 cups chopped peanuts. It is delicious with cold meat, and with low salt cheese and salad in a sandwich.

Apple pickle

1 kg apples
4 cups cider vinegar
400 g sugar
1 tsp whole cloves
1 cinnamon stick

This makes a spicy (but not hot) apple sauce for roast pork. Peel, core and quarter the apples, bring vinegar and spices to the boil and add sugar, stirring until dissolved. Simmer for 20 minutes, strain off the spices and return the liquid to the saucepan. Add the apples and simmer for another 5 minutes. Pack the pickle into jars, cover each with a layer of hot syrup, seal and store.

Pickled cherries

1 kg sour (Morello) cherries
3 cloves
1 tsp fresh ginger root, roughly chopped
2–3 cm cinnamon stick
1 1/2 cups white wine vinegar
400 g sugar

This makes another good accompaniment for pork. Wash cherries and remove stems. Put spices in a saucepan, tied in a muslin bag, and add vinegar and sugar. Boil and stir until the sugar dissolves. Add cherries, cover and cook until tender. Strain the cherries and pack into jars. Return vinegar to the saucepan and simmer uncovered until the liquid is reduced to a syrup. Pour over the cherries and seal when cool.

French or American mustard

1/4 cup mustard seeds
6 tbs dry mustard
1 tsp dried tarragon
1 1/4 cups boiling water
1/2 cup tarragon vinegar
1/2 cup dry white wine
1 tbs peanut or canola oil
1/4 cup sugar
1/2 cup onion, finely chopped
2 tsp garlic, finely minced
1/4 tsp ground allspice
1/4 tsp ground cinnamon
1/4 tsp ground cloves
For American mustard add:
1 tbs turmeric

Combine mustard seeds, mustard, turmeric (if used), tarragon and water in a small bowl and let stand for 1 hour. Combine vinegar, wine, oil, sugar, onion, garlic, allspice, cinnamon and cloves in a saucepan, bring to the boil and simmer for 5 minutes. Blend both mixtures in a blender for about 2 minutes. Spoon combined mixture into a double saucepan, cook over boiling water for 5 minutes, stirring often and scraping the sides with a rubber spatula to make sure it all cooks evenly. Scrape the mustard into a mixing bowl and set aside to cool. Store, sealed in jars, in the fridge.

Italian fruit mustard pickle

1 kg mixed stone fruit (such as apricots, plums, peaches, cherries)
1 cup water
$1/2$–1 cup white wine vinegar
2 cups sugar
$1/3$ cup mustard powder

Wash and stone the fruit and chop into quarters. Boil the water and dissolve 1 cup sugar, then add the fruit and simmer until cooked but not too soft. Leave to cool. Dissolve the other cup of sugar in the vinegar, cool, add the mustard and stir it into the fruit. Bottle and use after one week.

Soups

Soup is a food that often seems essential on a cold day and the problem of making soup without additional salt can be overcome. Of two approaches (labour-saving and labour-intensive), the second is better if you have the time.

Salt reduced canned soups

Low salt canned soups have been discontinued, but two salt reduced tomato soups (Rosella and Heinz) have a declared sodium content when served of 150 mg/100 g. This is only 25 per cent above the limit for a low salt food, so they can be used if you dilute them with an extra half can of liquid, or add vegetables, no-added-salt baked beans or a can of no-added-salt chopped tomatoes. Sweet potato and pumpkin are both ideal vegetables with which to dilute the canned tomato soups. A herb and garlic mixture from Spice World (see Appendix 5) adds a flavour that makes a tasty variation to this.

Salt reduced packet soups

Most packet soups that are labelled 'salt reduced' declare a sodium content of 250 mg/100 g or more when ready to drink — too high to compensate by adding no-added-salt ingredients. One so-called salt reduced packet soup has 328 mg/100 g (many restaurant soups have about 350 mg/100 g).

This so-called salt reduced packet soup contravenes the Food Standards Code, in which salt reduced foods must meet the following requirements:

• The sodium content must be compared with the 'reference' food (the same food with the usual sodium content)
• The salt reduced food must have at least 25 per cent less sodium than the reference food
• It must have at least 90 mg/100 g less sodium than the reference food
• It must not exceed a total sodium content of 600 mg/100 g.

Very few salt reduced foods are low enough in sodium to be converted to low salt foods by dilution with no-added-salt (NAS) ingredients to bring the sodium down to no more than 120 mg/100 g, but you will find exceptions.

Two exceptions are Continental Salt Reduced Chicken Noodle Soup and Continental Salt Reduced French Onion Soup, with a declared sodium content of 155 and 170 mg/100 g respectively at the time of going to press. The Chicken Noodle packet provides a recipe for making Chinese chicken and corn soup, using a can of creamed sweet corn — so salt skippers can use Coles no-added-salt creamed sweet corn. The Continental French Onion salt reduced packet soup can be diluted with vegetables in the same way as the canned soups.

Instant no-added-salt stock

Salt Skip no-added-stock stock powders can be bought in chicken, beef and vegetable flavours from health food shops or by mail order (see Chapter 11 and Appendix 5). Used as directed (1 level metric tsp to 1 cup, 250 mL), they all have a sodium content below 60 mg/100 g, so 2 tsp still make a low salt stock. Homemade soup has a lot more flavour if you start with this instead of water.

The serious business of making proper soup

A good low salt soup can be made just as quickly as a good high salt soup if you have previously made a good stock, as directed in all good cookbooks. Follow the recipe — except for adding salt when 'season to taste' is advised at the end.

This small collection of recipes only scratches the surface of the myriad gastronomic opportunities that are waiting to be exploited by the adventurous salt skipper. Salt skippers are often keen to share their own newly discovered hints, tips and recipes with other salt skippers. I would be pleased to hear from any readers with contributions to make to our collection in the Salt Skip newsletter.

8
Eating out

This chapter deals with some of the practical problems of skipping salt when eating away from home — at restaurants or friends' homes, while on holiday or travelling overseas. It also suggests some recipes for special occasions such as Christmas or other celebrations.

Restaurant meals

Good restaurants are always happy to meet customers' requirements. If eating out, book a table by phone at least a day ahead. When you are going to the restaurant for the first time, ask whether they can provide a salt-free and low fat meal. Unlike supermarkets, restaurants have no precise definition of 'low' and 'salt free' is the only safe description. If they can't do it, don't argue — chefs persuaded against their better judgement can hardly be expected to do very well. Since the start of the Salt Skip Program in 1983 we have heard of only three Australian restaurants that have been unwilling to provide a salt-free, low fat meal. Success is naturally variable, but almost every restaurant is willing to try. It is worth becoming a regular customer of a few local chefs who seem to be getting better at catering for salt skippers.

Try to book a table soon after the restaurant's opening time. Special requests are difficult when a restaurant is busy, and salt skippers may need to get into the habit of eating early, and early in the week, when it is easier for staff to give you their full attention. Letting the restaurant know in advance of your no salt requirement also allows them the chance to come up with a tasty and attractive alternative, instead of being forced to take items out of a dish already on the menu.

Some chefs are tempted to use more pepper when they omit salt, so if you don't want this, remember to let them know. Many soups, salads, marinades, batters and sauces may have already been made with salt or soy sauce, so check the menu for dishes that can be made to order from fresh ingredients. Resourceful chefs can often adapt the menu, and may be interested in doing something different when they are not too busy. Discuss this with the staff when they take your order, and let them see if there are dishes on the menu that might be adapted fairly easily.

Soups may be possible with advance notice, especially at restaurants that make their own well-flavoured stocks by classic methods — starting without salt and withholding it until the very end, when the time comes to 'season to taste'. They simply omit this last step for customers who want soup without salt. Salt skippers with their keener palates often enjoy the superb and subtle flavours of these soups unmasked by salt. A melon purée in summer served as a cold soup or a hot sweet potato soup spiced with ginger are examples of salt-free soups.

Some entrées and main courses are acceptable if served without the salty gravy or sauces that have been prepared ahead, using salt. Alternatively, ask for a fruit sauce, as some chefs can work wonders with apples or plums, apricots, vinegar or lemon juice and spices — making a sort of instant chutney that is salt free and milder than a bottled chutney.

Many restaurants steam their vegetables without salt, but should be reminded not to butter the vegetables (as well as saturated fat, butter usually has 2 per cent salt, and sodium 800 mg/100 g). They may have salad vegetables that can be put together without a dressing, or with a plain oil and vinegar, lemon juice, or yoghurt dressing, with perhaps a sprinkling of chopped herbs.

Sugar and saturated fat are very common in desserts, which makes this area difficult, but fresh fruit salad without cream or ice-cream can be very nice, particularly if served with a liqueur, or perhaps mint leaves. The low fat yoghurt used in home cooking (0.2 per cent fat) is not common in Australian restaurants, but natural yoghurt is only about 4 per cent fat — far better than ordinary cream at 36 per cent fat, or reduced fat cream at 27 per cent fat — and makes a nice accompaniment.

Pastry is not only very fatty, but is usually made with salted butter or margarine, so it becomes a high salt item. Choose an apple baked with dried fruit rather than apple pie. If all the desserts seem unsuitable, ask for a fruit platter.

If you want salt-free bread with a restaurant meal you usually have to take your own.

Some ethnic cuisines contain higher levels of salt than others. Lebanese restaurants find it difficult to cater for just two salt skippers, because Lebanese food is labour-intensive, prepared ahead of time and therefore will normally be pre-salted. Otherwise the spices of the Middle East make Lebanese cuisine ideal for low salt meals, and memorable Lebanese meals can be prepared for large groups. Asian foods are often marinated with soy sauce, oyster sauce, black bean sauce or fish sauce, all high in salt, so avoid dishes containing these ingredients. However, it is customary for chefs from mainland China to steam rice without salt, and Nathan Pritikin pointed out that Chinese restaurants cook many dishes from fresh ingredients, so it may be quite practical to ask for vegetables and chicken to be cooked without salt, soy sauce or MSG. For example, a local Chinese restaurant in Hobart makes excellent low salt lemon chicken, orange chicken and sweet-and-sour dishes.

People who need to monitor their *sodium* intake, for example to combat fluid retention, can check it accurately on food labels, but sometimes become worried in restaurants. They have no need to get technical however about 'sodium', as distinct from 'salt'. About 90 per cent of all the sodium added to processed foods is sodium chloride or common salt, and this would apply to restaurant meals. People in this situation can just ask for meals without salt or salted ingredients, such as cheese, olives, and so on.

Holidays

The advice on restaurant meals also applies to holiday meals. It should be possible to book hotels that agree to provide low salt meals. Coach tours with overnight stops at good hotels can usually supply suitable meals. You will probably need to take your own salt-free bread, biscuits or rice cakes, and buy bananas or other fruit and a cup of tea or coffee to make a snack.

If you have access to a kitchenette in a caravan or campervan, you can bake fresh bread every day, because bread machines are so small and compact.

Meals with friends

Salt skippers certainly discover who their real friends are. The urge to convert others to a better diet must be postponed — some of your best friends 'know' they wouldn't enjoy their meals without salt (watch their eyes glaze over as you speak). A painless approach is to entertain them without salt, surprising them with some of your best recipes. If necessary lend them some of your recipes when they invite you back.

When friends invite you to a dinner party at which you may be the only salt skipper, it requires thoughtful discussion with your hosts, but salt skippers find with experience that almost every menu can be adapted fairly simply and painlessly. Be accommodating, and go for the company, not for a fussy meal.

Special occasions, such as Christmas or family celebrations

Nibbles

For a delicious start to the meal that will cleanse the palate and not be too filling, arrange a large platter with a variety of raw, bite-sized vegetables and fruits. Use a variety of colours and a variety of shapes such as slices, cubes, whole cherry tomatoes, celery sticks, and so on.

If you wish to use potato chips, corn chips or nuts be careful to select low salt varieties (but note the high fat content). No-added-salt varieties of sun-dried tomatoes, corn chips and nuts, and dried olives are also available.

Starters

Try something light and unusual like gazpacho or chilled cucumber soup.

Gazpacho (Serves 6–8)
    425 g can NAS chopped tomatoes
    825 mL can NAS tomato juice (Coles)
    1 onion, chopped
    1 cucumber, peeled and chopped
    1 green capsicum, seeded and chopped

2 garlic cloves, chopped
$1/4$ tsp Tabasco sauce
freshly ground black pepper to taste

Blend all the ingredients except the chopped tomatoes, then add the chopped tomatoes and mix well. Chill thoroughly. Garnish each serving with chopped chives and lemon quarters.

Cucumber soup (Serves 3–4)

2 cucumbers, peeled, seeded and diced
2 cups NAS chicken or vegetable stock
$1/2$ cup skim milk
1 tbs cornflour mixed with skim milk to 'dissolve' it
$1/2$ cup low fat yoghurt
2 cm piece of ginger root, peeled

Sauté the cucumber gently in 1 tbs of stock until soft (15 minutes). Add remaining stock, milk and ginger and simmer gently for 30 minutes. Remove ginger. Purée and sieve the soup. Thicken by adding dissolved cornflour, and stir while reheating gently. Cool. Stir in yoghurt. Chill and serve.

Main course

Roast turkey

Remove as much fat as possible from under the skin of the turkey before cooking, and remove the skin after cooking.

Veal, pork and celery stuffing

2 tsp NAS margarine
3 sticks celery, finely diced
1 medium onion, finely diced
1 tsp mixed dried herbs
pepper to taste
400 g lean pork and veal mince

Heat margarine in a non-stick frypan. Add celery and onion and sauté until transparent. Add herbs and pepper. Remove from heat and cool slightly. Combine with mince. Stuff mixture loosely into the turkey. (Add no-added-salt breadcrumbs if it's a very large turkey.)

Jacket potatoes can be served with a yoghurt and chive topping, accompanied by spicy vegetables. The next recipe for spicy vegetables makes an excellent accompaniment to hot meat.

Spicy vegetables (Serves 6)

2 tsp NAS margarine
1/2 tsp cumin
1/2 tsp black mustard seeds
1/2 tsp turmeric
1/2–1 tsp chilli powder
1 capsicum, seeded, cut into strips
6 zucchini, sliced
2 bananas, thinly sliced
freshly ground black pepper
1 tbs chopped parsley

Heat margarine in a non-stick frying pan, add the spices and chilli powder and fry for 3 minutes. Add the capsicum, zucchini and bananas. Cover the saucepan with a lid and cook over medium heat for 5 minutes. Season with black pepper, and serve on a bed of rice with salad accompaniment. Garnish with chopped parsley.

Cold leftovers

Serve with salads of raw fresh vegetables and fruit, with a simple lemon juice or vinegar dressing with herbs or garlic.

Festive salad (per person)

4 small asparagus spears
1/2 medium beetroot
1/2 cup tarragon vinegar
4 segments cantaloupe melon
small bunch green seedless grapes
3 snow peas

Steam asparagus (not too long — it should still be crisp) and cut off the ends. Peel beetroot. Simmer in just enough water to cover and add 1/2 cup tarragon vinegar. Cook until tender, then drain. Cool and refrigerate. Slice cantaloupe into small segments. Wash the grapes. Cook snow peas for 2–3 minutes and plunge into cold water, and drain. Arrange salad on individual plates.

Dessert

Microwave Christmas pudding   (Serves 6–8)

100 g fresh NAS bread, crumbed
4 tbs brandy
1/2 cup orange juice
400 g mixed fruit, including dates
50 g chopped blanched almonds
1/4 tsp each of nutmeg and mixed spice
1/2 tsp ground ginger
60 g plain wholemeal flour
3 egg whites, beaten
2 tbs black treacle, warmed
2 tsp Parisian essence

Soak bread in brandy and orange juice. Stir in dry ingredients until well mixed, then fold in egg whites, treacle and Parisian essence. Spoon into a plastic 18 cm pudding basin, and cover with Gladwrap. Microwave on medium (80 per cent) for 7 minutes, then low (40 per cent) for 8 minutes. Take out and cover the Gladwrap with foil until cold. To reheat, turn pudding on to a serving plate. Cover with Gladwrap, microwave at 100 per cent for 3 minutes. Serve with low joule custard or low joule brandy sauce.

Low joule brandy sauce

6 tbs cornflour
1 L skim milk
150 ml brandy
sugar (Equal/Nutrasweet)

Blend cornflour with skim milk and bring the liquid to the boil, stirring until thick. Flavour with brandy and sweeten to taste with sugar or aspartame (Equal or Nutrasweet).

Brandy 'butter'

1 ripe banana
1/4 cup stewed apple
1/4 cup apple juice
1/2 cup low fat ricotta cheese
brandy to taste

Purée banana with stewed apple and apple juice, plus low fat ricotta and brandy. Serve instead of brandy butter.

Airline meals

Book a low salt, low fat meal when you make your seat reservation. Airline snacks currently offered in economy class allow limited scope for observing the dietary guidelines. Salt skippers will need to take with them slices of salt-free bread.

Because salt skippers are not eating salt, they should be able to fly a long trip such as the one to Europe without suffering swollen ankles. Although some of this travel oedema is due to the posture, inactivity and sluggish circulation involved in the airline flight, skipping salt greatly reduces the swelling seen after 'normal' meals.

Eating in overseas countries

Countries vary a great deal in the ease with which low salt meals can be obtained. One of the best countries for salt-free meals is Holland and one of the worst is Britain. Keep requests for low salt meals simple, for example ask for potatoes baked in their jackets. Craig Claiborne, an American food writer who became a salt skipper, wrote 'If I dine in a restaurant, I ask that I be served a simple grilled dish — fish, chicken or veal — and that the chef not use salt'. In America you can also ask for a 'Pritikin meal'. Requesting low salt food may also bring some unexpected surprises. For example, the best salt-free bread my wife and I have ever tasted was a rye and wholemeal bread supplied fresh each day to a hotel in Limassol, Cyprus, by a local bakery.

Bushwalking

Because they have to carry their food, bushwalkers need to consider very carefully the sorts of foods they take. Most foods are about 80 per cent water, so carry mainly dried and dehydrated foods to which you can add water at each destination. Most dehydrated foods are very salty, but low salt versions are ideal and often low in fat and sugar as well.

For breakfast use a low salt, ready-to-eat breakfast cereal or oatmeal porridge with dried fruit or cinnamon. Instant oats can be cooked by just adding boiling water. Take skim milk powder with you, and dried fruit.

Lunch can be sandwiches of low salt bread or pita bread, rice crackers, rice cakes or crisps (several brands), bean sprouts, no-added-salt margarine and peanut butter, other nut butters and tahini paste, jam and honey. There is also Salt Skip Low Salt Cheddar and Lactos Fruit Cheese.

Ideas for the evening meal include making a quick soup from tomato paste or Tomato Magic granules with dried herbs. Soup can be thickened with pearl barley. For the main course filling meals can be made from a base of pasta, rice, lentils, beans, rolled oats, couscous or bourghul. Pre-cooked cereals are convenient for short bushwalks.

Couscous is pre-cooked. Simply add 3 parts boiling water to 2 parts couscous, leave for 10 minutes, and then fluff it with a fork. Sunbrown Quick Rice is steam-cooked brown rice which cooks in half the time of ordinary brown rice, or you can just add boiling water 2 hours before you need it, during which time it will cook and become ready to eat, cold or reheated. Bourghul is cracked wheat pre-cooked by steaming. Cover it with cold water, drain and leave it for 20 minutes to swell and soften. It is the cereal component of the Lebanese salad *tabbouli*.

Take dried herbs and spices for flavour, for example mustard, pepper, garlic cloves or powder, onion flakes, curry powder, caraway seeds, celery seeds, mixed herbs, tomato paste, no-added-salt sun-dried tomatoes, Salt Skip No-Added-Salt Stock Powder. Health food shops carry several brands of freeze-dried tofu (soy bean curd) that can be reconstituted by soaking for 10 minutes in hot or cold water. Supermarkets now have several brands of low salt dried vegetables. Edgell Chunky Roma Tomatoes are preserved by UHT without salt in a small square carton that is easy to pack. Chinese and Asian food shops stock no-added-salt dried mushrooms. Small tins of no-added-salt tuna, salmon or sardines are useful for a main meal or lunch. Alliance makes a dehydrated steak without added salt.

For snacks between meals take a mix of nuts and dried fruit, or homemade 'scroggin' made with dried fruits such as apricots, sultanas, raisins, peaches, apples, bananas, pears, plus any of the low salt cereals in the supermarkets, and nuts and seeds such as sunflower seeds, pepitas, no-added-salt peanuts, or almonds. Dark chocolate may be acceptable if you have no weight problem. The no-added-salt margarines have acceptable fats, and so do peanut butter, olive oil and canola oil (all mainly monounsaturated). Damper can be made with plain flour and Salt Skip Baking Powder. Lite-Bix and Mini-Wheats make good 'biscuits' on bushwalks, and Sustagen Gold (now available in a Light version with less saturated fat) can be used as an occasional meal replacement.

Pain tablets

Disprin Direct tablets are sodium free and can be taken without water (suitable for sucking), which is ideal for bushwalkers.

Salt skippers in hospital

Low salt hospital diets

A big problem for hospitals is that sick people lose their appetite, especially when sick enough to be in hospital. Educators couldn't choose a worse moment to teach a captive audience how to choose a healthier diet — it's hard enough to get sick people to eat the foods they are familiar with. This often makes it difficult for hospitals to observe the dietary guidelines.

Nevertheless, low salt diets in modern hospitals need to use cooking methods that conserve flavour and make fuller use of the wide range of herbs and spices that can be used for flavouring instead of salt. Meanwhile a portable kit for salt skippers in hospital might contain some of the following, modified to suit the individual's palate: a small shaker bottle of balsamic vinegar, Red Kelly Salad Dressing or a favourite homemade recipe, Red Label horseradish sauce, garlic powder, Jane's Krazy Mixed-Up Pepper, a low salt breakfast cereal, salt-free bread, Salt Skip Stock Powder, a packet of dried fruit and nuts.

Intravenous saline

A member of the New South Wales Meniere's Support Group had two attacks of vertigo while in hospital for orthopaedic surgery. She vomited in both attacks. Skipping salt at home had been highly effective in preventing vertigo, but in hospital the vertigo occurred following intravenous injections of antibiotics with a fairly large infusion of saline.

It is probably safer for Meniere's patients to avoid sodium loads from intravenous saline as a vehicle for intravenous drugs. Alternatives to normal saline would include fifth-normal saline with 4 per cent dextrose (except for patients with diabetes), or distilled water.

Take-away foods

You may have noticed that fish shops these days ask if you want salt on your chips (they no longer shake it on automatically). Potato chips are not salted before frying, and salt will not dissolve in oil, so chips are a take-away food you can buy with no added salt. The fat content is high after deep-frying, but one Hobart fish shop (Mures) advertises that it uses peanut oil (a 'good' fat). Some fish shops offer steamed rice as an alternative. Potatoes baked in their jackets are a good choice at many take-aways if you ask for them to be served with no sour cream or butter. Fish can be grilled, providing a low fat and no-added-salt alternative to crumbed fish, which also tends to have a little salt in the crumbs. I should admit, however, that it is possible to have a very good 24-hour urine result the day after an evening meal that included crumbed fish.

Sandwich bars that sell filled rolls at lunchtime can usually supply a very suitable low salt meal to salt skippers who take their own bread when visiting another city. Occasionally a sandwich bar may have nothing but salted meats such as ham, corned beef and 'luncheon meat', and you may have to confine yourself to salad without dressing, but most sandwich bars have cooked chicken and/or plain roast beef. Plan ahead and take some Red Kelly Salad Dressing (see Chapter 11), which is sold in narrow bottles that fit most pockets and handbags. At Myers Food Hall in Little Bourke Street, Melbourne, you can buy a sliced wholemeal salt-free loaf at the bakery and buy your own filling(s) from the wide choice available at numerous other counters in the food hall.

Perhaps the most popular take-away food is a pizza. Picking up a pizza on the way home doesn't have to be a fading memory if salt skippers who shop around can find a pizza outlet that uses a low salt dough. The rule of thumb for bread with a sodium content of 120 mg/100 g is that salt must not be added at more than 0.5 per cent of the flour weight, and the slightly higher moisture content of pizza dough brings the sodium down a little, providing a small but welcome safety margin. In Hobart one pizza outlet makes its dough with a level dessertspoonful of salt (10 g) to 6 kilograms of flour (0.17 per cent of the flour weight), which predicts a sodium content of only about 40 mg/100 g in the finished dough. This shop will use the customer's shredded Salt Skip Low Salt Reduced Fat Cheddar (a very good melting cheese) with the customer's no-added-salt tomato paste, sliced fresh mushrooms and dried basil to make a very palatable low salt pizza. Low salt variations on the topping are limited only by your imagination. Finding a shop with low salt pizza dough is the first and only hurdle.

Another Italian restaurant in Hobart serves gnocchi made with no added salt, with an excellent dressing of tomatoes, no-added-salt tomato paste and sliced fresh mushrooms. They will supply gnocchi as a take-away or for eating on the BYO premises. Thus, finding helpful restaurants is possible.

Skipping salt while eating out is still difficult at first, but becomes easier with experience, and is a lot easier for new salt skippers today than it was in 1980. The salt skipping message is in line with the international consensus of scientific medical opinion, and is already reaching the market for take-away foods, as well as the rest of the food market. I predict in Chapter 17 that the great breakthrough will come when salt skipping districts begin to appear, where the local salt skippers have reached what is called a 'critical mass'. Such districts would become a place of pilgrimage and/or residence for other salt skippers who want to live near shops that are well stocked with suitable foods, and near restaurants that are accustomed to catering for salt skippers.

9
Getting enough iodine

Some salt skippers ask how they can get enough iodine when they stop using iodised salt. The thyroid gland needs iodine to make thyroxine, a hormone essential for good health, growth, physical development and life itself. This requires only a trace of iodine (measured in micrograms — millionths of a gram), but we depend on a steady supply.

A curious difference between salt and iodine is that all human habitats have enough salt, yet iodine is scarce in some geographical districts, especially where melting ice sheets removed topsoil after the last Ice Age, exposing rock that lacked iodine. Most of the available iodine is in the ocean, in marine plants and animals. Living seaweed and sea creatures compete for this iodine and constantly remove it, making seawater itself — and sea salt — poor sources of iodine. Thus no human society has ever been offered salt as a public health measure — except as a convenient vehicle for iodine in societies that add salt to their food.

The most obvious sign of iodine deficiency is a goitre, a swelling in the neck due to enlargement of the thyroid gland. Although extremely visible, this condition is easy to treat, as the swelling goes down with adequate iodine intake. Other conditions caused by iodine deficiency, however, are not as easy to treat. Serious iodine deficiency during pregnancy can lead to the birth of a child with severe and incurable mental retardation, a condition known as cretinism.

Mild iodine deficiency can affect brain development and intelligence in the growing child, even without causing goitre. Whole districts may be intellectually and economically backward — a major international health problem. The United Nations Declaration for the Survival, Protection and Development of Children states that

'Every child has the right to an adequate supply of iodine to ensure its normal development'.

Goitre has occurred in most Australian states except Western Australia. Cases of goitre have revealed iodine deficiency in regions such as the Atherton Tablelands, the mountains behind Mackay, and the granite belt in the south-west of Queensland; the valleys of the Great Dividing Range, and the Hunter Valley in New South Wales; the high plains of the Southern Alps around the Canberra district and the Wyalong Plains in New South Wales and the Australian Capital Territory; the Southern Alps and Eastern Gippsland in Victoria; the hills east of Adelaide in South Australia; and the whole of Tasmania.

During the mid-20th century goitre gradually disappeared in many developed countries, often without government action. National and international distribution of fresh and processed foods masked regional differences in soil iodine. The salt added to food at the table was iodised, alginates (from seaweed) were used as thickeners in foods like ice cream, custards and sauces, and dairies used iodine compounds to sterilise equipment, leaving residues of iodine in the milk. Some bakers also used potassium iodate as a dough improver. By the 1980s the United States and New Zealand considered that iodised salt was no longer necessary[1,2], but the World Health Organization (WHO) has now set stricter standards to ensure an adequate intake.

The return of mild iodine deficiency

Full-blown goitre remains rare today, but recent studies of urinary iodine excretion have shown levels below the new WHO standard in Sydney, Melbourne and Tasmania.[3–5] Other developed nations report similar results. Risk is higher in former goitre districts, especially where access to seafood is limited and people depend on home-grown produce and milk their own cows, fed only on local pasture. Iodine intake may have declined in cities as a result of dairies sterilising equipment by methods other than using iodine compounds.

Table salt is the only form of salt that is iodised. People who heed the 'eat less salt' health message and give up using iodised table salt have had no help from the overload of salt in processed foods because none of it is iodised. In the 1995 Hobart Salt Study, for example, more than half the people interviewed 'never or rarely' cooked with salt or added salt at the table.[6] Sea salt and rock salt, although now popular, contain only minute traces of iodine of no value for rectifying iodine deficiency. In 2002 shoppers could see for themselves that less than half the salt on sale in Hobart and Sydney supermarkets was iodised salt, a situation that may change as a result of publicity.

Individual medical treatment

Doctors usually treat serious iodine deficiency with potassium iodide and, after correcting the deficiency, recommend iodised salt as a regular iodine supplement. Fortunately salt skippers have access to several good alternatives to iodised salt.

Personal protection by self-medication

The RDI for iodine is 150 micrograms (mcg)/day for men and 120 mcg/day for women, increasing to 175 mcg/day in pregnancy and 200 mcg/day when breastfeeding. If you are getting at least two-thirds of the RDI daily from other sources (such as seafood, milk, meat, fruit and vegetables produced in non–iodine–deficient areas of Australia and delivered to your supermarket in semi–trailer loads), a supplement of 150 mcg is enough for three days, so you don't need the whole of the RDI as a supplement every day.

People whose thyroid gland is underactive due to autoimmune thyroid disease need great care with the dose of iodine they take. Luckily this condition is rare, but an iodine supplement more than about three times the RDI (450 mcg/day for men and 360 mcg for women, may make the disease paradoxically worse. When symptoms point to the thyroid, a correct medical diagnosis is important.

Eating seafood

Before white settlement, there was no goitre in Tasmania.[7] Seafood gave Aboriginal Tasmanians all the iodine they needed. Eating seafood once or twice a week should provide enough iodine for most people. Canned seafood can also be eaten as it has the same iodine content as fresh fish, as well as being cheaper. Nutritionists recommend two to three fish meals a week also, because marine fish oils help to prevent heart disease.

Kelp tablets

Kelp is an edible seaweed and is available in tablet form. The salt content in one kelp tablet (made from about 1 gram of kelp) is small enough to be ignored, but buy a brand of tablet that gives the iodine content. For example, Blackmores claim their tablets contain 150 mcg of iodine per tablet, so one tablet is equivalent to a supplement of 50 mcg/day for three days.

Multivitamins

People who eat a healthy diet shouldn't need a vitamin supplement. The lower risk of colon cancer reported in women who take multivitamin supplements may be due solely to folic acid.[8] The leafy vegetables and salad greens that are recommended in the dietary guidelines should supply enough folic acid (Latin *folium*, a leaf).

Some patients do need multivitamins to treat conditions like macular degeneration of the retina, or to compensate for restricted diets (for example, a diet for irritable bowel syndrome), and many brands of multivitamins provide minerals and trace elements including iodine. Check the label to find the iodine in micrograms (mcg) per tablet or capsule.

Protecting the whole population

The bugbear of medication is remembering to take it, and relying upon self-medication is not a practical way to protect the whole population from iodine deficiency. The standard way to give everybody a supplement has been to sell iodised salt.

Iodised salt

The problem with promoting iodised salt as a remedy for iodine deficiency is that the general population has taken on board the message to 'eat less salt'. So many people skip salt in cooking and at the table that iodising salt would only reach about half of the population.[6]

An interim measure might be to iodise *all food grade salt*, so that *all processed foods* are iodised. In the next ten years the salt content of processed foods may be reduced by 50 per cent if manufacturers comply with the official health policy already being promoted in the United States, but the iodine content of salt could be increased in step with it.

Iodised bread

As an alternative to using iodised salt, the best vehicle for iodine would be a staple food that is not threatened with declining use. Such an iodised staple food would automatically give children a pro-portional dose. Bread is a more universal food than milk, and iodine could be included in the dough improver. Potassium iodate is a good dough improver. As the sole ingredient in a dough improver it sup-plies too much iodine, but the food regulations could standardise the iodine content of iodised dough improvers (which are usually mix-tures of several substances). The iodine content of bread would then be independent of the salt content, allowing salt to be reduced or omitted for customers who want low salt or salt-free bread.

Tasmanian bread was iodised in the 1960s with potassium iodate in the dough improver, to combat the epidemic of goitre in school-children at that time and was iodised again in 2002 by a regulation to use iodised salt (as an interim measure). This was enough to supply about 15 mcg of iodine per 30 g slice of bread. As a result, iodine levels in the population have gone up.

While we are waiting for iodised dough improvers, salt skippers can make iodised bread with kelp tablets or potassium iodide drops.

Kelp tablets in bread

By adding a Blackmore's kelp tablet (150 mcg iodine per tablet) to bread, you could get 15 mcg per slice by adding one kelp tablet for every ten slices of bread or two to three tablets per mix, depending on the size of the loaf and the number of slices it makes. The tablets would have to be crushed to ensure even distribution. It may be more convenient to add potassium iodide drops to the water in the recipe.

Potassium iodide drops

A pharmacist can make up potassium iodide solution in a concen-tration (4 g per litre) to give about 150 mcg of iodine per drop when using a dropper that averages 20 drops per millilitre. One drop is then equivalent to one kelp tablet, and can be used at the rate shown above for kelp tablets. The pharmacist uses water with 20 per cent alcohol as a preservative. For greater precision an insulin syringe with a weaker solution (1 g per litre) will deliver 153 micrograms in 0.2 mL. Keep the potassium iodide with the other accessories you use with your breadmaker.

Other issues

Sea salt

It is worth repeating — and stressing — that most of the iodine in the ocean is in marine plants and animals. Seawater and sea salt are not only poor sources of iodine, but they also happen to be more harmful than pure salt (see Chapter 4).

Iodine overdose

A form of goitre due to too much iodine occurs in Japan in people who are too fond of edible seaweed. It was also seen at a time when large doses of potassium iodide were taken in cough mixtures for long periods for chronic lung conditions such as bronchiectasis.

Getting the level of iodine right is very important. Too much iodine can be harmful. Various authors put the short-term safe upper limit at 1000–2000 mcg/day, except when reduced by autoimmune thyroid disease (as mentioned earlier). For long-term protection there is no point in having a total intake that exceeds the RDI of iodine.

Iodine sensitivity

The air we breathe contains traces of pure iodine, and no adverse reaction has been attributed to the extra traces that are essential to life and good health. True allergy with an antibody reaction to iodine has not been reported, but some people are sensitive to large doses of iodine if it is applied to the skin or given by injection. Possible adverse reactions are contact dermatitis when applied to the skin or dose-related intolerance when iodine compounds are injected into a vein to provide the contrast needed to show up blood vessels or parts of the urinary tract in an X-ray. These reactions are caused by complex organic compounds of iodine suitable for injection into a vein. Most people, but not everybody, can tolerate the temporary high dose of iodine in these compounds.

In summary, the inhabitants of iodine-deficient geographic regions need an iodine supplement to ensure healthy growth and development. Seafood and kelp are natural sources of iodine. Many people, guided by recent public health advice on the links between salt intake and high blood pressure, no longer use table salt, which is the only salt being iodised at present.

As a possible interim public health measure, one option is that the salt in processed foods could be iodised. Another possible solution, already in use in Tasmania, is to use iodised bread as a more permanent vehicle for iodine. Iodised dough improvers would be ideal for making iodised bread (both for the trade and for home bakers). Meanwhile salt skippers can make their own iodised bread by adding kelp or potassium iodide drops to the recipe.

III   Shopping for health

10
Shopping within the dietary guidelines

It is one thing to read the Dietary Guidelines for Australian Adults, and another to implement them with the nutrition information presented on food labels. This chapter helps you to reconcile the general dietary advice with the numbers printed in the nutrition information panel on food labels.

The Dietary Guidelines for Australian Adults (2003)

The dietary guidelines consist of five main headings, with dot points under each of the first two:

Enjoy a wide variety of nutritious foods

- Eat plenty of vegetables, legumes and fruits
- Eat plenty of cereals (including breads, rice, pasta and noodles), preferably wholegrain
- Include lean meat, fish, poultry and/or alternatives
- Include milks, yoghurts, cheeses and/or alternatives. Reduced-fat varieties should be chosen, where possible
- Drink plenty of water

Take care to

- Limit saturated fat and moderate total fat intake
- Choose foods low in salt
- Limit your alcohol intake if you choose to drink
- Consume only moderate amounts of sugars and foods containing added sugars.

Prevent weight gain: be physically active and eat according to your energy needs

Care for your food: prepare and store it safely

Encourage and support breastfeeding

Source: National Health and Medical Research Council, 2003

Fresh foods such as fruit, vegetables and fish comply with the dietary guidelines for Australians.[1] They provide enough energy, protein, fat, carbohydrate and sodium for health and longevity.

The invention of agriculture about 10 000 years ago increased our supplies of fresh meat and poultry, but today's fat livestock supply too much fat to comply with the dietary guidelines. This is why health recommendations now suggest that visible fat should be removed from meat. The bigger grains of cultivated grasses produce edible cereals that have greatly increased our carbohydrate intake and further reduced our dependence on fat for energy.

Today's **processed foods** provide convenience, food hygiene and long shelf life, but their salt, fat and sugar content increase the risk of about a dozen 'Western' diseases including overweight, adult-onset diabetes, heart disease and high blood pressure.[2]

Australian food labels

In Australia, all processed foods must carry a food label, with a nutrition information panel that gives consumers information about five aspects of the food — the energy it provides and the quantities of protein, fat, carbohydrates and sodium it contains. It must also include information about any other nutrient (such as calcium) about which it makes a claim (see the figure below). This chapter gives a short overview of four labelling requirements — **energy, protein, fat** and **carbohydrate**. Chapter 11 will look at **sodium** labelling and the salt guideline.

The dietary guideline for energy

Energy is measured in joules (J) (named after James Joule, an English physicist). The dietary guideline for energy is: *Prevent weight gain: be physically active and eat according to your needs.* A normal weight is much more important for good health than for appearance, and the more kilojoules the food provides (kJ/100 g), the more walking (running, aerobics, cycling, swimming or other exercise) you need to impose on yourself.

Exercise is good of course — indeed essential — for other reasons

```
                    NUTRITION INFORMATION
Servings per package: 3
Serving size: 150 g

                            Quantity           Quantity
                           per serving        per 100 g
Energy                       608 kJ             405 kJ
Protein                       4.2 g              2.8 g
Fat, total                    7.4 g              4.9 g
   – saturated                4.5 g              3.0 g
Carbohydrate, total          18.6 g             12.4 g
   – sugars                  18.6 g             12.4 g
Sodium                        90 mg              60 mg
Calcium                  300 mg (38%)*          200 mg
* Percentage of recommended dietary intake

Ingredients: Whole milk, concentrated skim milk
             sugar, strawberries (9%), gelatine,
             culture, thickener (1442).
```

Figure 10.1 A nutrition information panel for a yoghurt that claims a high calcium content

as well as controlling your weight. Every day we need at least half an hour of brisk walking (or the equivalent in other exercise) for general fitness and longevity. Fresh foods can provide all the fuel we need for exercise, as they did for our ancestors who were far more physically active than we are today, and had only fresh foods.

The Food Standards Code defines low energy or low joule foods as solids up to 70 kJ/100 g, and liquids up to 70 kJ/100 mL. As a result, most fresh foods are high energy foods; there are only a few fresh foods that are low in energy.

The following table shows the energy provided by a range of fresh foods.

Fresh foods	Energy (kJ/100 g)
Lettuce, tomato, cucumber, radish, celery, cabbage, lychee, mango, melon, passionfruit, pear	Up to 70
Asparagus, broccoli, broad bean, beetroot, carrot, mushroom, onion, turnip, pumpkin, pineapple, grapefruit, apricot	71–200
Green peas, kidney bean, potato, sweet corn, olives, apple, cherry, whole milk	201–500
Avocado, *lean* meat trimmed of fat (beef, lamb, pork, chicken, game)	501–1000
Wheat, rye, barley, oats, rice	1001–2000

The problem of energy-density

Our ancestors had to eat a big meal in order to get a little energy. The capacity of the human stomach was appropriate for the foods that were available — the stomach could hold as much as was needed before feeling full.

Today we are in trouble if we fill our stomachs, because they are still as large as ever. An apple has 230 kJ/100 g but an apple pie has 1300 kJ/100 g — just one of countless examples — so a full stomach today often contains too much energy. Our ancestors found it easy to work off the energy in the food they ate. With no other means of transport they walked or ran everywhere; today it is very easy to take the car to drive two blocks to buy a packet of biscuits. Many children watch television indoors rather than playing physical games outdoors. The result has been an alarming and growing epidemic of overweight and obesity, even in childhood.

The remedy is to balance lower energy foods against a higher energy lifestyle. Although this is not a book on weight loss, Chapter 12 on high blood pressure makes a few further comments on how to manage this balance.

The dietary guideline for protein foods

The dietary guidelines recommend meals that *include* lean meat, fish, poultry and/or alternatives such as legumes and nuts. A daily protein intake of 55 g for men and 45 g for women is suggested.[1] If we average that at 50 g/day and estimate the average daily intake of solid food at 1.6 kg, the average protein content would be 3 g/100 g. Compare this with the protein content of a few common foods shown in this table.

Fresh foods	Protein content (g/100 g)
Lemon 0.6, tomato 1.0, lettuce 1.2, strawberry 1.7, leek 2.1, green bean 2.2, butter bean 2.3	Up to 3
Milk 3.3, green pea 5.8, broad bean 6.9, tofu 6.9	3.1–10
Wholemeal flour 12.1, oyster 12.2, egg 12.7, kidney bean 12.8, mullet 19.3, whiting 19.8	10.1–20
Lean shoulder of lamb 20.5, lean chicken breast 22.6, lean beef steak 31.3, dried soy bean 31.3	20.1–40

Vegetarians need more advice on protein intake because plant and animal proteins are not of equal value. Most plant proteins are less digestible and of lower quality than animal protein. This is well explained in other books. Nevertheless, well-planned vegetarian meals are compatible with perfect health.

While our most distant ancestors probably lived on fruit and vegetables, like modern gorillas (chimpanzees are only occasional meat eaters), some of our more recent hunter-gatherer ancestors are thought to have consumed a lot of animal protein, like the modern Inuit (Eskimo) peoples. However, the meat intake of modern industrialised societies is greater than we need, and unsustainable on this small planet if every human society tried to consume at the same high rate as the affluent societies. Furthermore, protein, like salt, increases the excretion of calcium in the urine (see Chapter 13), so it is a good idea for people who want an active old age, without osteoporosis, to control their protein intake. Don't cover the plate with meat and add a few vegetables. Reverse that ratio — have vegetables with a little meat.

The dietary guidelines for fat

The dietary guidelines mention fat in two places:
- *Reduced fat varieties* [of dairy foods] *should be chosen, where possible*
- *Limit saturated fat and moderate total fat intake.*

Saturated fat

When agriculture began about 10 000 years ago it made saturated fat abundant. Animals grew fat when caught alive and bred in captivity because they had more food and less exercise. We ate *fat* animals for the first time in history. New fat deposited artificially in overweight animals as 'depot' fat is chemically different from the fat that occurs naturally in the tissues of wild animals, and is called 'saturated' fat. Diets that contain large quantities of saturated fat usually increase the risk of heart disease by raising blood cholesterol.

Drinking milk is unnatural for any adult — even the cow itself — but after inventing the bucket, human adults were able to drink cow's milk. Full-cream milk is 3.8 per cent fat, with a high proportion of saturated fat. Although harmless to the calf, saturated fat raises adult human blood cholesterol, especially when concentrated in foods like cheese (cheddar is 34 per cent fat), cream (36 per cent fat) and butter (81 per cent fat).

Total fat intake

Even 'good fats', such as olive oil and the fats in nuts and avocadoes, are fattening, hence the limit on total fat in the dietary guidelines.

Reduced fat dairy foods

The Australian Food Standards Code requires reduced fat foods to contain not more than 75 per cent of the usual fat content, and a reduction of at least 3 g/100 g in a solid food, so *reduced* fat foods are not *low* fat foods by any means.

Low fat foods

A low fat food must contain no more than 3 grams of fat per 100 grams of solid food (3 g/100 g) and no more than 1.5 grams of fat per 100 grams of liquid food (1.5 g/100 g) — because drinking is quick and easy, and most people who drink a glass of milk (200 g) would be equally satisfied with only 100 g of solid food.

The National Heart Foundation 'Tick' Program

The Heart Foundation invites food manufacturers to apply for permission to print its official 'Tick' (indicating its approval) on the labels of foods that meet required nutritional criteria. The National Heart Foundation 'Tick' Program has different criteria for fat content for different foods. It allows **total fat** up to 2 g/100 g for liquid milk, and up to 5 g/100 g for breakfast cereals. For hard yellow cheese such as cheddar it allows up to 25 g/100 g. All oils are 100 per cent fat, but some can carry the 'Tick' so long as the saturated fat content is no more than 20 per cent of total fats.

Limitations of the 'Tick' program

The 'Tick' program is often misunderstood. When salt skippers see the 'Tick' on a few processed foods with a high sodium content, they are confused. However, the 'Tick' was never meant to be a guide to the *best* diet — it would be unrealistic to expect the whole population to adopt the best diet in a single step, making all the radical changes that sick people need (and are prepared to make). The 'Tick' program is a means by which the Heart Foundation is trying to *improve the national food supply in the right direction*. This has to be a gradual process, as discussed more fully in Chapter 17.

The dietary guideline for carbohydrates

Cereals form the largest single component of the modern diet of industrialised countries. The carbohydrates in cereals are starches. Germinating grains such as sprouting barley (malt) form sugars from the starches. Human digestion must convert all starches into the simplest sugar (glucose) before the carbohydrate can be absorbed into the bloodstream.

The other food carbohydrates are the sugars, such as sucrose (cane sugar and beet sugar), fructose (honey) and glucose (manufactured from starches). Fruit and honey are the most abundant natural sources of sugars. Complex sugars are digested and absorbed as glucose.

The **carbohydrate** dietary guidelines ignore the cakes, pastries and biscuits restricted by the **fat** guideline, and promote other carbohydrates:

- *Eat plenty of cereals (including breads, rice, pasta and noodles), preferably wholegrain*
- *Consume only moderate amounts of sugars and foods containing added sugars.*

The simple classification into starches and sugars has progressed into a distinction between refined starches (such as white flour) and unrefined starches (such as wholemeal or wholegrain flour), with discussion of fibre, glycaemic index and 'resistant starch'. These are well covered in other books.

Carbohydrates also come in many foods covered by another guideline:

- *Eat plenty of vegetables (including legumes) and fruits.*

Fruits have a large natural sugar content, hence the need to limit added sugars. Sugars provide only energy (kJ) — they do not provide any fibre, minerals, vitamins or protein — and are criticised as 'empty kilojoules'.

The Food Standards Code regulates claims about sugar and fibre (the less sugar the better, and the more fibre the better):

- *Reduced sugar* means at least 75 per cent less than the usual amount
- *Low sugar* means no more than 5 g/100 g
- *High or increased fibre* means at least 3 g/serving
- *Very high fibre* means at least 6 g/serving.

It is not clear why the Food Standards Code should suddenly introduce 'serving' sizes in relation to dietary fibre. The strong objection to quantifying by serving sizes is that this prevents comparison — different foods have different serving sizes. This is a problem with American food labels, as you will see in the next chapter.

The Heart Foundation 'Tick' is not allowed for any cereal food with a fibre content less than 3 g/100 g, and flour must have at least 5 g/100 g, which rules out white flour.

While salt-related illness provides a good reason for following the salt guideline, *everybody* has an excellent reason for following *every one of the dietary guidelines* — it's a recipe for a healthy and long life. Nutrition information panels on food labels show quantitative data on the five main areas that can maintain or restore your health (or wreck it if you ignore them). This chapter has discussed four of them and the next chapter concentrates on the fifth area — salt.

11
Low salt shopping

You can find low salt foods by checking food labels, but you will soon discover that you might need this chapter — low salt processed foods sometimes seem like needles in a haystack. This chapter starts with special notes on reading food labels for sodium content, and then follows with a list of low salt products, presented in alphabetical order. The situation is better than it looks at first sight. For example, few people have heard of Lite-Bix, a low salt Weet-Bix, yet Australian supermarkets have stocked it since 1993 (usually next to the Weet-Bix, on the same shelf). You should find it there when you look (ask the store to order it if you can't find it, or shop around, using the phone book if necessary). Salt skippers find Coles supermarkets especially helpful with their no–added–salt range of canned and frozen foods, such as baked beans and oven-ready crumbed fish fillets.

Fresh foods listed in the Australian Tables of Food Composition are low in salt, with rare exceptions (listed in Chapter 15) that you can ignore if you eat a large variety of fresh fruit and vegetables. Fruit and vegetables without added salt will guarantee that your sodium intake stays well below a daily average of 120 mg/100 g.

Processed foods are the battleground for skipping salt, and success in identifying low salt foods depends on how well you read the food labels.

Australian food labels

Salt skippers should check the sodium line on the nutrition information panel (see the figure below) to see if the food is safe to eat (sodium up to 120 mg/100 g). When the label indicates that the food has a safe level of sodium, and is preferably within the other dietary guidelines (see Chapter 10), salt skippers can feel free to eat as much or as little of that item as they wish. If the sodium level of the food item is above 120 mg/100 g, look for another food item that is safe.

```
NUTRITION INFORMATION
Servings per package: 3
Serving size: 150 g

                      Quantity        Quantity
                     per serving      per 100 g
Energy                608 kJ           405 kJ
Protein               4.2 g            2.8 g
Fat, total            7.4 g            4.9 g
  – saturated         4.5 g            3.0 g
Carbohydrate, total   18.6 g           12.4 g
  – sugars            18.6 g           12.4 g
Sodium                90 mg            60 mg
Calcium               300 mg (38%)*    200 mg
* Percentage of recommended dietary intake

Ingredients: Whole milk, concentrated skim milk
             sugar, strawberries (9%), gelatine,
             culture, thickener (1442).
```

Figure 11.1 The standard layout of the Australian and New Zealand nutrition information panel

Imported food labels

Australia imports processed foods from around the world, especially from Europe and the United States. Foreign labels that don't conform to Australian and New Zealand food standards are illegal, but inadequate inspection by understaffed and underfunded agencies often allows importers to break the law with impunity. This means that consumers need to take more care in reading labels on imported foods.

European food labels

European labels report sodium in grams per 100 g, with a choice of 0.1 g/100 g or 0.2 g/100 g and nothing in between. Just as 1 metre equals 1000 millimetres, 1gram equals 1000 milligrams, so 120 mg/100 g equals 0.12 g/100 g. European food labels would normally print 0.12 g as 0.1 g.

The figure below shows a food label for a European brand of rye crispbread. On Australian food labels, the 100 g column is usually on the right, so at first glance this rye crispbread has only a trace of sodium. Checking the column headings, however, reveals that *one slice, not 100 g*, has a trace of sodium. The 100 g column has been printed on the left, and it shows a sodium content of 0.7 g/100 g. As 1 gram is 1000 milligrams, the sodium content of this crispbread is 700 mg/100 g — almost six times saltier than the recommendation of the salt guideline.

INGREDIENTS
Wheat Flour, Rye Flour, Water, Wheat Bran, Vegetable Fat, Sugar (Sucrose), Salt, Bakers Yeast. pH-controlling agents: Vinegar, Sour Dough.
STORAGE INSTRUCTIONS
Store in a dry, dark place. For 'Best Before End' see side of pack.

NUTRITION INFORMATION

Typical Analysis	Per 100g	Per slice (8.4g)
Energy	1527kJ (365kcal)	128kJ (30kcal)
Protein	11.4g	1.0g
Carbohydrate	65.0g	5.4g
(of which sugars)	2.6g	0.2g
Fat	6.0g	0.6g
(of which saturates)	1.0g	trace
Dietary Fibre	7.5g	0.6g
Sodium	0.7g	trace

18 slices per box.

Figure 11.2 Nutrition information panel from an imported European food label

American food labels

American labels give the sodium analysis in milligrams per serving. Look at the food labels on the next page. The one on the left tells us that one serving is '3 cookies'. Each cookie weighs 34 g and contains 80 mg of sodium. But servings vary from one food to another, and you need a pocket calculator to compare them. The American food label on the right from a packet of rye crispbread says that one serving is one piece weighing 11 g, which has only 30 mg of sodium — much less than the cookie. But wait! A pocket calculator shows that the cookies have 235 mg/100 g, but the rye crispbread has 273 mg/100 g. A crispbread with 30 mg per serving is saltier than the cookies with 80 mg.

Nutrition Facts
Serving Size 3 cookies (34g/1.2 oz)
Servings Per Container About 5

Amount Per Serving
Calories 180   Calories from Fat 90

% Daily Value*
Total Fat 10g — 15%
  Saturated Fat 3.5g — 18%
  Polyunsaturated Fat 1g
  Monounsaturated Fat 5g
Cholesterol 10mg — 3%
Sodium 80mg — 3%
Total Carbohydrate 21g — 7%
  Dietary Fiber 1g — 4%
  Sugars 11g
Protein 2g

Nutrition Facts
Serving Size: 1 piece (11g)
Servings Per Container: about 20

Amount Per Serving
Calories 40   Calories from Fat 0

% Daily Value*
Total Fat 0g — 0%
  Saturated Fat 0g — 0%
Cholesterol 0mg — 0%
Sodium 30mg — 1%
Total Carbohydrate 9g — 3%
  Dietary Fiber 2g — 8%
  Sugars 0g
Protein 1g

Figures 11.3 and 11.4 Nutrition facts panels from two American food labels

Food serving sizes

American food labels highlight the difficulty in standardising food 'serving' sizes across a variety of food items. There may also be significant differences in serving sizes of two similar foods because in Australia the decision about what is a standard food serving is left to each manufacturer. What individuals may eat is yet another factor — unless they are on a diet. On another day they may eat a different amount.

With most diseases people need to know what to eat — and how much — and serving sizes can be written down and memorised. Salt-related diseases are different because *everybody* needs to choose low salt foods, and their more natural salt content makes low salt foods safe at any serving size, small or large.

Identifying safe levels of sodium in food items

1   **Australian food labels** — Look at the 100 g column and check that sodium is no more than 120 mg/100 g.

2   **European food labels** — Don't buy the food if you find it too confusing to convert grams into milligrams.

3   **American food labels** — Avoid foods with American labels unless you shop with a pocket calculator to do sums to compare different serving sizes.

Low salt shopping overseas

Supermarkets in Europe will be dominated by European food labels, so it may be necessary to live as far as possible on fresh foods. If you buy any processed foods, take 0.2 g/100 g as the upper limit and buy only salt-free bread. (Many small bakeries are happy to take an order for it.) In North America one option is to check sodium contents with a pocket calculator, but a simpler alternative is to select foods by comparing sodium and energy — the sodium in milligrams should not be more than half the energy in calories. This is foolproof for most but not quite all foods (for example, with the American labels shown in the figure above, it would protect you from the rye crispbread but not the cookies).

★★★★★

The shopping list

The rest of this chapter provides a shopping list of commonly used processed foods that you can buy in Australia in a low salt version at the time of going to press, with notes about availability, possible alternatives, and things to watch for when buying them. Appendix 5 gives contact details for suppliers mentioned here.

Abbreviations
LS = low salt
NAS = no added salt

Baby foods   Added salt is illegal in foods for *infants* under twelve months old. Baby foods are sold everywhere, here and overseas, and some make convenient sandwich fillings. Avoid foods for *toddlers*, as these contain added salt, with sodium often well over 120 mg/100 g.

Baking powder   Supermarket baking powders all have a very high sodium content. Buy Salt Skip Baking Powder (see Appendix 4) or make your own by mixing 3 parts cream of tartar from the supermarket with 2 parts potassium bicarbonate, available from the local pharmacy. However, most pharmacists have to order it in, and sell only the relatively expensive pharmaceutical grade of potassium bicarbonate. Salt Skip Potassium Bicarbonate of food grade is stocked by health food shops or available by mail order.

Salt Skip Baking Powder is a modern product with better performance than cream of tartar. It is a mixture of calcium phosphate with potassium bicarbonate and calcium carbonate, as described in Appendix 4. You can buy it retail from health food shops or by mail order from the address in Appendix 5. To make brown baked goods like Anzac biscuits, add a teaspoonful of Salt Skip Potassium Bicarbonate.

Barbecue sauce   Low salt brands include Abundant Earth and Maleny Clean Cuisine BBQ Mango Sauce.

Beer   Despite a common rumour, there is no salt in Australian or imported beers; nor do home brewing kits and recipes use salt. Liquorice is popular in home-brewed stout, but the usual objections to liquorice (that it causes fluid retention and high blood pressure) can be ignored because recipes seldom use more than about 2 rounded teaspoonfuls of liquorice powder to 25 litres of water.

Beverages   *See* separate entries for Beer, Cereal beverages, Chocolate, Cocoa, Coffee, Cordials, Fruit juices, Mineral water, Soda water, Soft drinks, Soy milk, Sustagen, Tomato juice, Water, Wines and spirits.

Biscuits   Check the label very carefully because very few sweet or savoury biscuits, crispbreads or crackers have a low sodium content. Choose biscuits with fat up to 5 g/100 g and added sugar up to 15 g/100 g. (These are the eligibility criteria for the Heart Foundation 'Tick'.)

Black salt   Imported from India, this variety of rock salt is 98 per cent sodium chloride (common salt). It is just as harmful as any other form of common salt, contrary to the impression given in some books about spices.

Bottled water   *See* Drinking water.

Bread   Low salt bread is not currently available, but many small local bakeries will take orders for what everybody calls 'salt-free' bread. You can also use bread machines to make salt-free bread (see Chapter 6), but remember to use *plain flour* — there are no salt-free premixes on the market. Occasionally Pritikin bread is salt free (but more often reduced salt bread with sodium over 200 mg/100 g).

Supermarkets have salt-free *chapati* (unleavened Indian flat bread) from the Indian Bread Company, which is similar to pita bread and suitable to use as a pizza base.

Bread dough improvers   Salt acts as a dough improver by strengthening the gluten present in wheat flour. The baking trade uses up to a dozen other dough improvers, all of which work without salt and can replace salt. Extra gluten flour can be added as a mild dough improver, and ascorbic acid can be used. Supermarkets and health food shops carry Lowan Bread Improver. Carol Bates's Bread Improver can be bought from health food shops and by mail order. Basic Ingredients also sell a dough improver at their Queensland outlets and by mail order.

Breadcrumbs   Actual breadcrumbs must be homemade from salt-free bread. An alternative is Freedom Foods NAS All-Purpose Crumbs made from rice. These are available in health food shops, the health food sections of supermarkets and by mail order.

Burghul (bulgur wheat)   This is cracked wheat that has been steam-cooked. After soaking in water for an hour and draining in a muslin bag, it is ready for making Lebanese tabbouli. Alternatively, add an equal volume of boiling water and use when all the water is absorbed. It has the sodium content of wheat (3 mg/100 g) and is sold in health food shops.

Butter   The saturated fat in butter contravenes the fat guideline. Some unsalted brands available in Australia include Coles, Devondale, Falcon, King Island, Lactos, Norco, UMT and Home Brand Continental. In continental Europe unsalted butter is more common than salted butter. The unique flavour of continental butter comes from the special culture used, which won't work if salt is added.

Cakes   For low sodium content, cakes must be homemade using Salt Skip Baking Powder (see Baking powder and Appendix 5), or with FG Roberts gluten-free self-raising flour.

Celery salt   This is ordinary table salt with added celery flavour, so should be avoided.

Cereal bars   Check the label. Low salt brands include Kellogg's Sustain cereal bar and Just Right cereal bar, several Uncle Tobys muesli bars and Woolworths muesli bars.

Cereal beverages   Low salt brands include Bambu, Caro, Ecco, Fini, Nature's Cuppa and Sipp.

Cereals   In their natural unsalted state cereals have only a very low sodium content. A few processed cereals such as rolled oats, semolina, polenta, wheat germ, partially processed bran and couscous have no added salt.

Ready-to-eat breakfast cereals   You will see from the labels that about 30 per cent of the breakfast cereals are low in salt, especially the mueslis. There are no low salt cornflakes (in a health food shop 'NAS cornflakes' means 'no added sugar'), but people who miss cornflakes will find Kellogg's have two cereal mixtures of dried fruit and flakes called 'Just Right' that are low in salt. Note, however, that a third one with the same name has a sodium content over 200 mg/100 g. Sanitarium make a NAS version of Weet-Bix called Lite-Bix.

Choose breakfast cereals with fat up to 5 g/100 g, added sugar up to 15 g/100 g and dietary fibre not less than 3 g/100 g. Check the label carefully for the sodium content of 'instant' or 'quick' cereals (some have salt added).

Cheese   The only *hard cheese* low in salt as well as reduced in fat (under 25 g/100 g) is Salt Skip Low Salt Cheddar, sold retail in Hobart and by mail order. Hard cheese can have **fat** up to 25 g/100 g, and Salt Skip Low Salt Cheddar is eligible for the Heart Foundation 'Tick'.

Soft cheeses like cream cheese, cottage cheese and ricotta may be low in salt — read the labels carefully. Look for **fat** not more than 8 g/100 g. Several brands of *bocconcini* (small round white Italian cheeses) are low salt. Fromage Frais ('fresh cheese') is available in one low salt brand, Fruche Fromage Frais Dairy Dessert.

Fruit cheeses often contain enough salt to raise the sodium content to about 400 mg/100 g, but Lactos Cradle Valley Neufchatel with apricot, sultanas and ginger is made with no added salt. It is a reduced fat cheese with a sodium content of 31 mg/100 g. This cheese won a silver medal at the Royal Melbourne Dairy Show in 1997. Although sold in a large 2 kg pack, it keeps well and is highly recommended.

Chips or crisps   Several brands of oven-baked potato chips are available with about 3 per cent fat (3 g/100 g) and sodium under 120 mg/100 g, and Birdseye make four varieties. Freedom Foods, Freers and Lips make packets of NAS potato chips. Freedom Foods also make LS corn chips. Avoid all the snack foods of thin chips or potato wafers (crisps) as they are high in fat.

Chocolate and drinking chocolate   Check the food label carefully. Some brands of chocolate and drinking chocolate are LS.

Cocoa   Some brands of cocoa with a high sodium content are made by a process that uses sodium bicarbonate, but some brands use potassium bicarbonate. Nestlé Baking Cocoa has a sodium level of 10 mg/100 g.

Coconut milk   Canned coconut milk is sometimes heavily salted. Imported brands with no added salt appear and disappear from time to time. Coles Farmland Coconut Cream has a sodium level of 12 mg/100 g.

Coffee   Ground coffee and decaffeinated ground coffee are unsalted; so are caffeinated and decaffeinated instant coffees.

Confectionery   Nearly always low in sodium except for some chocolates, especially those with fillings such as mint. Dutch liquorice is sold with *salt* and *double salt* but other liquorice is usually low in salt. Eat liquorice in moderation as it contains a plant steroid that causes sodium retention.[1]

Cordials   The label usually shows a very low sodium content.

Corn chips   *See* Chips or crisps.

Couscous   Two common brands are Gault and Le Caid. Couscous is made from semolina, a coarse flour made from durum (hard) wheat and is pre-cooked. It's an ideal food for bushwalkers (just add boiling water). It has the sodium content of other wheat flours (3 mg/100 g) and is sold in supermarkets and health food shops.

Curry powders and pastes   Many curry powders and pastes are heavily salted. Small bottles may be exempt from the legal requirement to show the sodium content, but an ingredient list is mandatory. Brands of NAS curry powder are Bolst, Crosse & Blackwell, Keen's Thai Green Curry Powder, Parrot Brand and Yeo's Malaysian Curry Powder. Spice World can supply thirteen different NAS curry powders by mail order. Garnisha's excellent curry pastes are all NAS except two containing fish sauce and two containing prawn paste.

Custard powders   Some brands are too salty, but LS brands include White Wings, Bird's, Bird's Low Fat, Four Roses, Savings and Uncle Tobys.

Custard, liquid   Look for Dairy Farmers Dairy Custard, Devondale Handy Custard, Devondale Light Custard (1 per cent fat), Norco Nimbin Country Low Fat Custard (0.2 per cent fat) and Pura Light Start (1 per cent fat).

Dips   Very few commercial dips would have a good shelf life without a high salt content. Golden Circle Salsa Dips are nearly all too salty (as would be expected), but one of them (Golden Circle Sweet & Spicy Salsa Dip) has no salt in the ingredient list and has a declared sodium content of 21 mg/100 g.

Dressings   *See* Mayonnaise and salad dressings.

Drinking water   Tap water in parts of Adelaide and Perth may be above 100 mg/L in summer. For bottled water, check the label for sodium content. The acceptable sodium limit for low salt water in the Salt Skip Program is 100 mg/L (10 mg/100 mL). Chapter 15 supplies further information on Australian drinking water.

Eggs   Buy whole eggs, frozen egg whites, Country Harvest Egg-Like (sodium 10 mg/100 g, fat 1.4 per cent), Scramblers Yolk-free Egg Mix. The natural sodium content of a whole fresh egg is about 133 mg/100 g, but the Salt Skip Program treats it as a low salt food.

Essences (Parisienne or Parisian, vanilla)   Parisian essence (gravy browning) contains salt, but in normal use (1–2 drops) the amount of sodium can be ignored.

Fish   All freshwater and sea fish with backbones are normally low salt when bought fresh or frozen (if unprocessed), but prawns, shrimps, oysters and scallops are too salty even when freshly caught (see also Appendix 6).

Frozen low salt brands include Birdseye Cape Hake fish steak, Coles Oven Fry NAS fish fingers and Oven Fry NAS crumbed fish fillets and Catch of the Day frozen fish.

Canned low salt brands include Ally NAS pink salmon, Coles NAS pink salmon, red salmon and Australian salmon, Greenseas Albacore Tuna, John West NAS tuna, Seakist NAS tuna and pink salmon, King Oscar, Brunswick and Paramount NAS sardines.

Notes about canned fish:

1 Coles have tuna *canned without salt* showing a sodium content of 300 mg/100 g and labelled 'reduced salt'. The tuna boats are out for several weeks and fish caught on the first day spend several weeks stored in refrigerated seawater. All tuna canned without salt may be affected.

2 The phrase 'in Spring Water' is often misleading, as some products have salt added (usually enough to raise the sodium content above 120 mg/100 g).

Flour Any brand of plain flour, white, unbleached white and wholemeal flour, gluten flour and strong bread flour is unsalted and very low in sodium. So too is any brand of maize cornflour, wheat cornflour, semolina, soy flour, gluten-free plain flour, rye flour, potato flour, triticale flour, rice flour, buckwheat flour, polenta or oatmeal. Strong bread flour has a high natural gluten content, and is sold in health food shops and some supermarkets, also by mail order from Carol Bates and Basic Ingredients.

Self-raising flour Only FG Roberts gluten-free self-raising (SR) flour is low in sodium. Sodium content of other brands is about 700 mg/100 g, except McAlpin cream of tartar SR flour which is 209 mg/100 g.

Fruit All brands of fresh, frozen or dried fruit, fruit canned in syrup or fruit juice concentrates are low salt. Dried fruit such as apricots, raisins and sultanas treated with sodium metabisulphite (preservative 223) are still low, because food regulations only permit a very small amount. If you prefer, you can also buy 'unsulphured' sultanas and other dried fruits with a darker colour and more flavour.

Fruit juices The label usually shows a very low sodium content.

Garlic salt Avoid garlic salt as it consists mainly of salt.

Gelatine Gelatine powder, agar, sweetened jelly and jelly crystals are all low in salt. Although the sodium content of Davis Gelatine

Powder is shown as 330 mg/100 g, so much water is added to the powder that the final sodium content of the jelly is only 7 mg/100 g.

Gluten-free flour   *See* Flour.

Gravy browning (Parisian essence)   This contains salt, but cooks who use only 1–2 drops can ignore the salt content, as with Tabasco sauce.

Herbs   Fresh herbs, dried or processed, are NAS, but avoid them if they are labelled 'seasoned'. Freshly chopped ginger, chilli, horse-radish and crushed garlic may be sold stored in vinegar and heavily salted, but Variety Dash and Newman Red Label are two brands that use vinegar without any added salt. MasterFoods herbs are one of the brands that have no added salt. NAS herbs and spices are available from Spice World.

Horseradish   *See* Sauces and pickles.

Ice cream   Both ice cream and low fat ice cream are usually low salt. Brands include the Pauls, Peters and Streets plain and flavoured tubs, 1–4 litres; Peters Light, Vanilla and Strawberry; Streets Blue Ribbon Light, Vanilla and Strawberry; Oak Reduced-Fat Oak Classic; Vitari frozen fruit soft whipped ice cream.

Iodine   *See* Kelp, also Chapter 9.

Iodised salt   Avoid iodised salt as it consists of salt with a small iodine supplement. Chapter 9 contains information on iodine.

Jams and spreads   All brands of fruit jam, marmalade, honey and fruit spreads are low in salt. When sodium bisulphite or sodium benzoate is added as a preservative the total sodium content remains below 120 mg/100 g.

Kelp   Blackmore's kelp tablets (iodine 150 mcg) is the only brand that declares the iodine content. The RDI for iodine from all sources is 150 mcg/day for men and 120 mcg for women (175 mcg/day in pregnancy and 200 mcg/day when breastfeeding). Assuming an intake of at least two-thirds of the RDI from other sources, men and women at normal times need less than one tablet per day as a supplement unless medically prescribed. The sodium in one tablet is low enough to ignore.

Liquorice   *See* Confectionery.

Margarine   There are no low salt margarines, but three unsalted brands are Becel Light polyunsaturated, salt-free reduced fat

(40 per cent fat); Coles Sunspread canola, salt-free, milk-free; Meadowlea canola, salt-free, milk-free.

Mayonnaise and salad dressings, other dressings Most dressings are excessively salty, particularly mayonnaise. One brand of low salt salad dressings (Red Kelly) with a sodium content of 55 mg/100 mL or less is found in Coles supermarkets, also Woolworths in some states, where its flavour enables it to compete successfully against competitors with a sodium content between 600 mg/100 g and 2200 mg/100 g. The Red Kelly range includes Traditional Salad Dressing, Spicy Cajun Dressing, Italian Basil & Garlic Dressing and two Tasmanian flavours (Pepperberry Dressing and Lemon & Myrtle Dressing). The Red Kelly Sweet Hot Chilli Dressing may be found either among the mayonnaises and salad dressings or in the specialty foods section. At the moment, it is the only low salt sweet chilli sauce on the market.

Other low salt brands are confined to health food shops, the health food sections of some supermarkets, and mail order suppliers. They include Abundant Earth Dressings (Herb & Spice, French, Italian); Australian Sunshine Rosemary & Mint Dressing; Basco Mayonnaise unsalted; Freedom Foods low fat (0.7 per cent) low salt mayonnaise, Freedom Foods Caesar Salad (serve without the parmesan cheese and anchovies!); Hains Real Mayonnaise and Imitation Eggless Mayonnaise; Healtheries Soy Mayonnaise, French Dressing, Thousand Island Dressing; Maleny Clean Cuisine salad dressings (Queensland and New South Wales); Mayvers Healthtime Mayonnaise (canola, highly recommended flavour); Nature's Cuisine NAS Salad and Pasta Dressing; and Norganic Tofu Mayonnaise.

Meat and meat products Fresh meat and mincemeat have no added salt or salted ingredients. When butchers add the permitted small amount of sodium metabisulphite to fresh mincemeat to keep the bright pink colour, the sodium content remains below 20 mg/100 g. At present there is no low salt processed meat.

Milk Milk is a low salt food whether from cows, goats or sheep, and whether whole or skimmed, fresh, powdered, UHT, evaporated or condensed, or sweetened condensed. Also low salt are soy milks such as Sanitarium So Good and Becel non-dairy soy drink, and Weight Watchers milk drink mixes.

Mineral water   *See* Drinking water.

Monosodium glutamate (MSG)   MSG is sold in Asian food stores as a flavour enhancer. True allergy to MSG has never been demonstrated although some people report symptoms of food intolerance (see Chapter 13). MSG is not suitable for salt skippers as it has 40 per cent of the sodium content of salt.

Mustard   *See* Sauces and pickles.

Natex   This is a reduced salt version of Marmite, and an alternative to Marmite, Promite and Vegemite (see Vegemite).

Nuts   All brands of unsalted nuts, seeds, pine nuts and coconut are low salt, including freshly made unsalted nut butters. Some pistachios and occasionally peanuts may be salted even when sold in their shells (the pistachio shell is partly open, and peanuts can be salted if the intact but porous shells are soaked in brine). Peanut butter machines in health food shops usually use unsalted peanuts. Brands of ready-made unsalted peanut butter include Basco, Coles Farmland, Crown, Hains, Kraft and Sanitarium.

Oils   Oils contain no sodium at all (sodium compounds are insoluble in oil and need water to dissolve them).

Olives   Dried olives with NAS are available from Osborne Olives. These are a delicacy worth pursuing.

Onion salt   Avoid onion salt as it consists of salt with onion flavour.

Parisian essence   Gravy browning contains salt, but cooks who use only 1–2 drops can ignore the salt content, as with Tabasco sauce.

Pasta   Most brands and varieties are low salt. Try wholemeal or added fibre varieties. Check the label on egg pasta and noodles. Coles have NAS canned spaghetti.

Pasta sauces   *See* Sauces and pickles.

Peanut butter   *See* Nuts.

Pies   Meat pies and other savoury pies and pasties are unobtainable in low salt versions, and even frozen fruit pies and tarts may go above 120 mg/100 g. One exception is Nanna's *Light* Apple Pie (sodium 60 mg/100 g).

Potato crisps   *See* Chips or crisps.

Rock salt   Avoid rock salt as it consists mainly of salt.

Salad dressings   *See* Mayonnaise and salad dressings.

Salt substitutes   Two brands of potassium chloride called No Salt (Cenovis and Wallace) carry a warning notice (explained in

Chapter 4) that potassium chloride is not suitable for diets requiring low or restricted sodium or potassium intake, without medical advice, and it is not suitable for use with certain diuretics.

Salt Skip Flavour Booster and a herb blend (with or without cayenne) are suitable for all salt skippers. Both are available by mail order or retail from Spice World.

Beware some bogus 'salt substitutes' listed in Chapter 4.

Salt varieties   Avoid black salt, celery salt, garlic salt, iodised salt, onion salt, rock salt and sea salt. All consist mainly of salt.

Sardines   *See* Fish.

Sauces and pickles   Red Kelly's Sweet Hot Chilli Dressing is the only low salt sweet chilli sauce currently on the supermarket shelves. You will find it in Coles (also in Woolworths in some states) among the salad dressings. On the health food shelves and in health food shops the low salt brands include Abundant Earth Pasta Sauce, Salsa Tangy Sauce and Ketchup; Aristocrat Sweet Chilli Sauce; Farmland, Fountain and Rosella NAS tomato sauces; Fountain fruit sauces, apple sauce and cranberry sauce; Freedom Foods range (see Appendix 5); Gardener Peach and Date Chutney; Hain Natural Stone Ground Mustard; Hill Farm Herbs (Tas.) Green Peppercorn Mustard, Dijon Mustard, Sir John's Mustard, Honey Mustard, Tarragon Mustard, Ploughman's Mustard, Mustard with Horseradish; Hill Farm chutneys (apple and mint, apple and Brazil nut, apricot), Hill Farm relishes (Ratatouille, Rosemary Jelly, Redcurrant Jelly, Gamekeeper's Jelly, Mint Jelly); Healtheries Tomato Sauce and Tartare Sauce; Home Made Fare (NSW) NAS Horseradish Sauce and Apricot Mustard; House of Winston low salt pasta sauces: Amatriciana, Arrabbiata, Bolognese and Carbonara; Keen's Dry Mustard Powder; Leggo's 'Salt to Taste' Italian Napolitana Cooking Sauce with Mushrooms and Herbs; Nature's Garden NAS Lemon and Garlic Chutney and Mango Chutney; Newman Red Label NAS Horseradish Sauce (*highly recommended*) made by BJ Meakins; Prue Sobers Classic, Chunky, Spinach and Serendipity pasta sauces; Prue Sobers Barbeque Marinade and Fruit Chutney; Socomin NAS Sweet Chilli Sauce and NAS Hot Chilli Sauce; Weight Watchers NAS Pasta Sauce; Wild's Ezi-Sauce (for home pickling). Maleny Clean Cuisine produces for the Queensland and New South Wales markets seven NAS sauces, including a sweet chilli sauce, and four NAS chutneys.

Seasonings and spices   *See* separate entries for Curry powders and pastes, and Sauces and pickles. Most natural herbs and spices (fresh and dried) are unsalted except for some brands of curry powders and pastes, and nearly all brands of lemon pepper. Brands that are NAS include most peppers and Jane's Krazy Mixed-up Pepper (*highly recommended*), MasterFoods Cuisine Essentials (Indian, Mexican, Thai), McCormick Citrus Pepper (other brands of citrus pepper are too salty). See Appendix 5 for mail order addresses for seasonings.

Snack foods   *See* Beverages, Cereal bars, Chips or crisps and Nuts.

Soda water   Bottled soda water often contains added sodium bicarbonate (but not always). Check the label for the sodium content. The Schweppes brand of soda water uses potassium bicarbonate. The Sparklet bulbs of compressed carbon dioxide for making your own soda water come with instructions to add 'bicarbonate of soda', but plain water can be used instead.

Soft drinks   The low sodium content on the labels show that sodium bicarbonate is seldom added, even though the industry adds it to soda water.

Soups   Australia has no canned or packet soups that are low salt, but some reduced salt brands can be used with modification (for example by diluting with plenty of mixed vegetables, or pumpkin or sweet potato, as well as by the measured addition of water).

Canned soups   Rosella and Heinz both have a reduced salt Tomato Soup containing 150 mg/100 g after dilution for serving. This is only 25 per cent over the sodium limit, and can be used to make low salt soup by adding vegetables, or a tin of NAS baked beans or sweet corn.

Packet soups   Most packet soups are far too salty. Continental Reduced Salt French Onion and Chicken Noodle Soups have a declared sodium content of 159 and 155 mg/100 g respectively (as served, making 1 litre), which if made with 1.5 litres of water brings the sodium level down to below 120 mg/100 g. They make a labour-saving stock, suitable as a base for homemade soups.

There are many good recipes for excellent low salt homemade soups.

Soy and linseed for bread-making   These grains are both free from added salt, and are sold separately in bulk in health food shops. Weston Milling also sells them as a salt-free mixture with kibbled wheat for adding to bread machine recipes. The 360 g packet is enough for three loaves, and the packet carries instructions for four different brands of breadmaker. It is available in all major supermarkets in the baking section, or you can write to Weston Milling Customer Service Department, PO Box 227, Enfield, NSW 2136.

Soy milk   Sometimes soy milk has sodium below 10 mg/100 g, but in some cases salt has been added to raise it to the natural sodium content of cow's milk. *See also* Milk.

Soy sauce   Soy sauce has a sodium content of about 6000–9000 mg/100 g (six to nine times saltier than seawater). The sodium content of what used to be called 'reduced salt' soy sauces is always over 3000 mg/100 g, and the words 'reduced salt' can no longer be used for foods with a sodium content greater than 600 mg/100 g. *Low salt* soy, tamari or teryaki sauce is not available either here or overseas. The so-called 'low salt soy sauce' in American recipes is what used to be called 'reduced salt' soy sauce in Australia. US food laws are based on serving size.

Spreads   *See* Margarine and Nuts for various brands of NAS peanut and other nut butters. Tahini paste (ground sesame seeds) is usually NAS or low salt. It is rather oily and runny, but mixing with lemon juice gives it a thicker spreading consistency. Margarines are 80 per cent fat, except Becel Diet Margarine (40 per cent); alternatives such as low salt mayonnaises (varying from 0.7 to 30 per cent fat) and low fat yoghurt (1 per cent fat) are lower in fat.

Stock cubes and stock powder   There are no low salt stock cubes, and only one low salt stock powder, on the Australian market. Avoid Massel 'reduced salt' stock powder as salt comes second in a list of ten ingredients.

Salt Skip NAS Stock Powder (sodium under 60 mg/100 g) is made in beef, chicken and vegetable flavours, and is highly recommended. It is made in bulk for hospitals by Massel and distributed by Eumarrah Wholefoods in 200 g plastic bags. It retails in health food shops and by mail order.

Sugar All forms of sugar — white, brown, raw, golden syrup, treacle, glucose, honey, molasses light and dark, cinnamon sugar — are
low in salt.

Sustagen The pharmaceutical company Mead Johnson makes this
as a liquid meal replacement for patients who are unable to eat
solid food, and the hospital pack is sold in pharmacies as a dry
powder for mixing with water. You can also buy a 250 mL ready-
mixed retail pack flavoured with Dutch Chocolate (and sold with
a drinking straw) from the cold soft-drink cabinets of some supermarkets and retail shops. Sustagen is less than 2 per cent fat, has a
low glycaemic index of only 31, and sodium 110 mg/100 mL.

Sustagen Sport Powder provides a liquid meal for athletes and
sportspeople. Don't be misled by the declared sodium content of
250 mg/100g (it refers to the dry powder). When you mix 3
scoops in 165 mL water as directed, the liquid when ready to drink
has 91 mg/100g.

Tabasco sauce The chilli used in this sauce is so powerful that
recipes often call for one-eighth of a teaspoonful, or measure the
dose in drops. As with gravy browning (Parisian essence), the salt
content of using just a few drops can be ignored for most purposes.

Taco shells Some are made without salt for use with sweet fillings. Brands include Casa Fiesta Taco Shells and Old El Paso Taco
trays.

Tofu Fresh tofu (soy bean curd) is available from Asian food stores
and some supermarkets. Kikkoman and several other companies
also produce long-life UHT tofu (ultra heat-treated) which will
keep without refrigeration until the packet is opened.

Tomato juice Coles sell NAS tomato juice with a sodium level
of 4 mg/100 g.

Tomato paste, purée and flakes The days have gone when
tomato paste was usually salted (although caterers still use it salted).
Brands of NAS tomato paste include Ardmona Tomato Magic
(plain and Italian style) and Tomato Purée; Campbell's Tomato
Paste; Farmland Tomato Paste; IXL No Waste Tomato Paste
Sachets; Leggo NAS Tomato Paste (avoid Leggo 'salted'), Tomato
Paste and 'Salt to Taste' Napolitana Italian Cooking Sauce with
Mushrooms and Herbs; Rosella NAS Tomato Paste; Woolworths
Home Brand NAS Tomato Paste.

Vegemite   The sodium content of 3060 mg/100 g makes Vegemite unusable for those seeking low salt foods. Vegemite, Promite and Aussie Mite are copies of Marmite (the first yeast spread); a reduced salt version of Marmite (Natex) is available. Although its sodium content of 400 mg/100 g is still too high, a Natex sandwich with two slices of salt-free bread will make a low salt food (sodium under 120 mg/100 g). The flavour is more reminiscent of Marmite and Promite than Vegemite. It is essential to use Natex (not Vegemite), and salt-free bread (not ordinary bread). Natex is sold in health food shops and the health food sections of supermarkets.

Vegetables   All fresh and most frozen vegetables are low salt (check the labels). So are soy bean curd (tofu) and most dried vegetables, including dried beans, peas and lentils. Avoid 'instant' mashed potato.

Canned vegetables   Low salt and NAS brands of tomatoes, chopped tomatoes and chopped tomatoes with herbs include Ardmona, Coles, Edgells, Gardenland, Goulburn Valley, Lagina and Letona. Brands of canned NAS baked beans include Coles and Heinz. Other canned vegetables in the Coles and Coles Farmland NAS range include beetroot, green asparagus spears, corn kernels, creamed sweet corn, green peas, sliced mushrooms in butter sauce, and red kidney beans. Other vegetables in Edgells NAS/LS range include corn kernels, green peas, tomatoes, and chunky Roma tomatoes.

Dried vegetables   Brands of low salt and NAS dried vegetables include Chilsea dried mushrooms (from Asian food shops), Dewcrisp Dried Vegetables and Noodles, Dry Ideas Tasmanian Dried Mushrooms, and Dried Chopped Onions, and Riverina dried tomatoes, loose and in 125 g packets.

Deep-frozen vegetables   Except when there has been additional processing, for example minted peas, frozen vegetables are nearly all NAS. They are too numerous to list individually, except to mention Logan Farm deep-frozen soy beans (quite a delicacy), and Quickpulse chickpeas and lentils (pre-cooked).

Water   *See* Drinking water.

Wines and spirits   All wines and spirits are low in salt and sodium.

Yeast   The Australian Tables of Food Composition show a sodium content of 50 mg/100 g for fresh (compressed) yeast and 170 mg/100 g for dried yeast. Most brands of dried yeast claim a sodium content close to 170 mg/100 g, but Tandaco declares 440 mg/100 g, and the company believes this is correct. The first step in drying is to immerse fresh yeast in strong brine to dehydrate it. Salt cannot be rinsed off without reversing the dehydration, so it is carried over as a contaminant (and should probably be declared in the ingredient list).

The sodium content of the active yeast cells would be much lower when reconstituted with water and allowed to swell again, and brands with 170 mg/100 g probably come close to 120 mg/100 g. Even bread made with Tandaco yeast (sodium 440 mg/100 g) would be a low salt food and fit to eat, because one teaspoonful of yeast is such a small proportion of the finished loaf.

Yeast extracts   *See* Vegemite.

Yoghurt   All brands are low salt, and skim milk yoghurts are low fat as well. Some are sweetened. All make an excellent alternative to cream with fresh or stewed fruit.

IV Health problems linked with salt

12
Salt and high blood pressure

This chapter explains why there is a massive international consensus linking salt with high blood pressure, and why it is so important. While other aspects of diet and lifestyle (such as overweight, sedentary lifestyles, excess alcohol and stress) can affect blood pressure, none of these factors are essential (high blood pressure can occur in their absence). Excess salt seems to be the one essential factor, as blood pressure rises with age — without exception — in every society that uses salt, yet there is little if any rise of blood pressure with age in societies that add no salt to their food. This chapter outlines the current scientific position.

High blood pressure is common enough to be called an epidemic, affecting about 50 per cent of urban Australians before their seventieth birthday, and 60 per cent of Americans aged sixty-five to seventy-four.[1,2] A fifty-year follow-up of a sample of the population of Framingham, Massachusetts, has found that the middle-aged and elderly have in what remains of their lifetime a risk of high blood pressure of no less than 90 per cent.[3] In industrialised societies high blood pressure is all but universal in those who live long enough.

Increased blood pressure causes escalating damage to the heart and blood vessels, especially those of the brain, heart and kidney, ending in deaths from stroke, heart attack, heart failure or kidney failure. The higher the blood pressure, the more common such complications are. The long-running Framingham study (quoted above) found that the risk of stroke and heart attack increased gradually with every increase in blood pressure above 110/70.[4]

Until recently we only knew that blood pressure rose with age and was 'high' when permanently above 140/90. Blood pressure is now considered 'normal' up to 120/80 millimetres of mercury, and borderline ('prehypertension') between 120/80 and 140/90.[5]

For some patients high blood pressure can be dramatically 'cured' by treating a specific cause, such as a tumour of the suprarenal gland or a disease of the kidney, or the artery to one or both kidneys. However, cure by surgery or drugs for a specific cause doesn't prevent the steady increase of blood pressure with age, and it is important for everyone to adopt a diet and lifestyle that can limit this age-related increase.

European settlers brought high blood pressure to Australia in 1788, along with other preventable diseases of diet and lifestyle such as obesity, coronary heart disease and type 2 diabetes.[6] Even today (as in 1788), the blood pressure of tribal Aboriginal Australians is about 100/60 and remains the same at age seventy as it is at age eighteen. This is not due to racial immunity. If Aboriginal people choose to live in an Australian city they have the same risk of high blood pressure as their neighbours.

When a specific cause for high blood pressure cannot be found, the diagnosis is *'essential' hypertension*, indicating that no abnormality has been found except high blood pressure. The WHO and the International Society of Hypertension attribute essential hypertension to an interaction between *genetic predisposition* and six errors of diet and lifestyle:[7]

- overweight and obesity
- lack of exercise
- excess alcohol
- inadequate potassium intake
- psychological factors
- excess salt.

Genetic predisposition

As several genes are suspected, the question 'Am I susceptible to high blood pressure?' cannot be answered 'yes' or 'no'. Science can only estimate relative risk, which will nearly always be above zero. A strong family history of high blood pressure and stroke increases the risk, and borderline blood pressure above 120/80 (prehypertension) doubles the risk of developing high blood pressure.[5]

Genetic predisposition affects all ethnic groups, with evidence of greater sensitivity in African Americans, and greater resistance in the Kuna Indians of Panama.[8] Although there are about twenty tribal populations around the world who show little if any increase in blood pressure with age, the genetic predisposition of these groups *is* revealed in members who migrate. In places with unhealthy diets and lifestyles the migrants have the same risk as the host population.[9]

Although natural (Darwinian) selection has had 5000 years to weed out salt-sensitive people, the 'survival of the fittest' has not affected blood pressure because most people have children to whom they pass on their genetic predisposition before their blood pressure is high enough to impair their capacity to reproduce.

Genetic engineering can already protect a crop of soybeans from Monsanto's weed-killer Roundup, and in principle gene technology could one day transfer 'salt resistance', enabling humans to reach old age with a normal blood pressure at high salt intakes (provided they were also lean, active, and moderate in their use of alcohol). However, there is a cheaper and simpler remedy — tribal Aboriginal Australians are one of about twenty societies with good lifestyles who reach old age with a normal blood pressure if they skip salt.[9]

Overweight and obesity

The increasing epidemic of obesity in industrialised societies increases the risk of heart disease and type 2 diabetes, as well as the risk of high blood pressure. Obesity makes the heart beat with greater force to circulate blood around a larger and heavier body, so a higher blood pressure is not surprising. The overweight may also be more sensitive to sodium as their blood pressure usually shows a greater response to skipping salt.[10] Overweight people should do everything they can to lose weight, and certainly to avoid further weight gain.

Unfortunately deliberate weight loss triggers the body's response to famine, and it struggles to use energy more economically. You suddenly need about 15 per cent less food than others of similar build with no history of weight loss.[11–13] You need a permanent change to a healthy diet and lifestyle with a lot of exercise — permitting weight loss with satisfying meals that will not leave you hungry. Don't worry about losing only half a kilo in a month. Dietitian and food writer Rosemary Stanton keeps 500 g of margarine on a plate in her office fridge, to show people what half a kilo of fat looks like.

One glance at 500 g of margarine convinces them they are making real progress.

Weight loss without a lot of exercise would mean starvation — a diet psychologically unbearable, and lacking vitamins and trace elements. Regular exercise to build and maintain muscle gives you fat loss without muscle loss. More exercise gives still more weight loss, limited only by your stamina and spare time. Exercise just before the main meal of the day tends to help by suppressing the appetite.

Lack of exercise

Even a small amount of exercise has a direct effect on blood pressure that is independent of the effect of weight loss. A landmark study at the Baker Institute in Melbourne in the mid-1980s confirmed that exercise lowered high blood pressure, and half an hour on an exercise bicycle three times a week had the full effect, while the same exercise five days a week had no further effect on blood pressure.[14] Exercise relaxes blood vessels just as effectively as a drug for high blood pressure called clonidine, which helps to explain why people who exercise daily usually have lower blood pressure than people with relatively stagnant circulation.[14] As other factors are at work, however, blood pressure can still rise with age in athletes. Like dogs and horses of normal weight, people of normal weight still need exercise; sedentary lifestyles are unnatural. However, frail people, especially heart patients and chronic invalids, may be wise to get medical advice about taking active exercise.

Excess alcohol

Alcohol raises blood pressure in ways that are not yet fully explained, but there may be very high stress levels during recovery from a bout of heavy drinking. Heavy drinkers in hospital for 'drying out' can enter with a blood pressure of 200/120 and leave a few days later with levels about 140/90 or less. Individual susceptibility is very variable. Some heavy drinkers have normal blood pressure, but many drinkers are moderately sensitive (some to as little as one or two drinks a day). A group of regular beer drinkers showed a significant fall in blood pressure when they changed from Swan Beer to Swan Extra Light (0.9 per cent alcohol), and a rise when they crossed back to the other beer.[15]

Inadequate potassium intake

Fresh unprocessed foods supply more potassium than sodium. With a few exceptions such as eggs, kidneys, and invertebrate seafood such as oysters and prawns, fresh foods gave our ancestors more potassium than sodium, but food processing now reverses that ratio, increasing the sodium content from ten to thirty times and reducing potassium by 20–70 per cent.[16] You can get more potassium by choosing more fresh unprocessed foods, and by cooking in ways that conserve potassium — and incidentally conserve flavour too (see Chapter 5).

Potassium resembles sodium in chemical and physical properties, and works in partnership with sodium in the electrical control of nerve conduction and muscle contraction. The natural, unsalted, foods on which the human body evolved provide up to ten times more potassium than sodium.[16] However, a multinational blood pressure study has shown that some populations excreted up to seven times more sodium than potassium in 24-hour urine collections.[17] Potassium supplements lower blood pressure at high salt intakes, and presumably work through the partial return to the natural sodium/potassium balance.[18]

Psychological factors

The word 'hypertension' has no reference to the individual's mental state. It refers only to physical pressure that can be measured with a pressure gauge, like the air pressure in a car tyre. A very relaxed and placid person can still have dangerously high blood pressure. Many people like to blame stress (and nothing else) for high blood pressure. However, constant tribal warfare didn't prevent the members of two salt-free societies from having normal blood pressure throughout life. The Asaro of Papua New Guinea and the Yanomama of the rainforests near the upper reaches of the Amazon had an average (mean) blood pressure of 108/63, and 96/61, respectively — not a bad advertisement for constant tribal warfare.[17]

An experiment with mice showed that permanent high blood pressure can be induced by the social stress of overcrowding and competition for space, but the diet of laboratory animals contains an excess of added salt, so this experiment really tested the effects of stress combined with added salt.[19,20]

A detailed Australian study of work stress found no direct effect of stress itself on blood pressure, although some people had unhealthy ways of coping with stress such as alcohol and drug abuse, smoking, binge eating, or withdrawal from social contact. Poor stress management did have a link with blood pressure.[21]

Excess salt

Sceptics could argue that the normal blood pressure of the salt-free societies might really be due to the fact that they are not overweight or sedentary, that they abstain from alcohol, that they eat more potassium than sodium, and that many (although not all) avoid severe stress. In other words there is no *proof* that being salt free has a great deal to do with their normal blood pressure.

Nevertheless, their normal body weight is not a complete protection — every doctor has a few thin patients with high blood pressure. Being physically active and abstemious with alcohol helps them, but athletes sometimes develop high blood pressure and so do total abstainers. By no means all of these societies are free from stress. They all eat food with its full potassium content, but a lot of people with high blood pressure have a high potassium intake. The diet of the salt-free societies is very varied, with some subsisting entirely on fruit and vegetables while tribal Aboriginal Australians eat little else but meat and seafood. So what do they all have in common, apart from a normal blood pressure? They all skip salt, giving them among other things a diet containing more potassium than sodium (the natural ratio).[9]

Societies where blood pressure increases with age all add large amounts of salt to their food, so that it supplies ten to thirty times more than their biological need for either sodium or chloride. High salt intake causes fluid retention and a larger blood volume. Stress of rapid mental arithmetic gives people a greater (temporary) rise of blood pressure when their blood volume is swollen by salt than when it is contracted by prescribing a diuretic — a drug that makes the kidneys work faster.[22] Salt excretion must keep up with salt intake (accumulation would be fatal) and the kidney's role is crucial.

In one experiment a rat's kidney continued working for several hours on a laboratory bench, producing urine and removing salt from its artificial blood supply. The rate of removal was very sensitive to the pressure in the blood supply, with a stepwise increase in rate at every rise of pressure, limited only by the bursting point of the whole system.[23] Kidney transplants cured rats with high blood pressure when they received kidneys from normal rats. When the normal rats got the other kidneys in exchange it was their turn to develop high blood pressure.[24] Thus the kidney's ability to raise blood pressure gives it a powerful and life-saving weapon against accumulating a dangerous backlog, if it happens to be a slow kidney confronted with an overload of salt to excrete.[25]

Proof that salt causes high blood pressure in animals

It has been shown that added salt causes high blood pressure in rats, dogs, chimpanzees and chickens. Because our closest animal relative, the chimpanzee, has 98.4 per cent of human DNA sequences, defenders of animal rights already question the ethics of experiments on primates. When high blood pressure was discovered in zoo chimpanzees in the United States the only identifiable factor, apart from the stress of captivity, was the salt in the 'Monkey Chow' biscuits that replaced their natural diet of fruit and vegetables.[26] The Monkey Chow — special food for primates — had more potassium than sodium (the natural ratio), and its sodium content of 240 mg/100 g was less than that of any of Australia's top ten best-selling ready-to-eat breakfast cereals at the time of the study.[26,27]

This disconcerting discovery prompted a controlled trial in French Equatorial Africa with a colony of captive chimpanzees that were fed on the fruit and vegetables eaten by wild chimpanzees.[26] The animals were divided into two groups of thirteen. One group received added salt, in a dose of 250 mmol/day, except for a young animal that received half the amount and two that refused the full amount. The control group showed no change in blood pressure but the diet group had an average increase within two years of 33 mm systolic (the upper figure) and 10 mm diastolic (the lower figure). All had a normal blood pressure within six months of returning to their natural diet.

With every other factor held constant, including the social and emotional stability of the group, this study provides unequivocal proof that a salt intake within the range of many human diets — and salt alone — caused the majority of chimpanzees to develop high blood pressure within two years.[26] It has been suggested that the dose of salt (250 mmol) was high for the chimpanzees' average body weight of 51 kg[28], but the People's Republic of China bases its nutrition policy on an average body weight of 60 kg for men and 50 kg for women[29], and the average (mean) 24-hour sodium excretion in Tianjin in the Intersalt study was 246 mmol.[17] These figures are so similar that the chimpanzee study must be of more than passing interest in China, where by 1990 stroke was the leading cause of death.[30] Note that a single Chinese take-away meal in London in 1982 supplied 238 mmol on analysis (admittedly the saltiest dishes were deliberately chosen, but this was a single meal).[31]

Proof that salt causes high blood pressure in humans

The evidence from the salt-free societies is very persuasive, but it doesn't match the standard of proof set by the chimpanzee experiment. We must look elsewhere for proof that salt (when acting alone) would be as harmful to humans as it is to chimpanzees.

In the 1980s it was still considered ethical to offer salt to a salt-free society at Kalugaluvi in the highlands of Papua New Guinea. Those who agreed to participate were divided into two groups, one of which had salt added in 'normal' amounts to their vegetable and cereal diet with no other change in their natural diet and lifestyle, while the other (the control group) maintained their usual salt-free diet. Within ten days the blood pressure in the experimental group began to rise above that of the control group.[32]

In a US study, fourteen urban volunteers received between 1200 and 1600 mmol of sodium per day, partly in food and partly by intravenous drip. All showed an increase in blood pressure within three days.[33] Again it was unethical to continue. Tests for salt sensitivity in industrialised societies provide irrefutable evidence that extra salt can cause a short-term rise of blood pressure in some individuals and a lower salt intake can significantly reduce it in some individuals.

Practical as well as ethical reasons prevent human trials from going any further — volunteers don't join trials that might give them high blood pressure and no doctor would ask them to. Thus, vested interests can claim there is 'no proof' that salt causes high blood pressure, repeating the parrot-cry of the tobacco companies about smoking and lung cancer.

Additional factors in high blood pressure

Additional factors that may add to the problem of increased blood pressure include high caffeine intake and smoking (an independent risk factor for stroke and heart disease). Liquorice contains a plant steroid that can cause sodium retention and raise blood pressure when consumed in excess.[34] Occupational exposure to heavy metals in some industries can raise blood pressure through kidney damage.

Drugs called NSAIDS (non-steroidal anti-inflammatory drugs) can cause sodium retention and increased blood pressure, and may reduce the effectiveness of other drugs prescribed for high blood pressure. Women who take the pill sometimes need an alternative contraceptive. Remedies for coughs and colds containing a few drugs such as ephedrine can raise blood pressure temporarily. Even snoring can contribute to high blood pressure, especially if breathing is severely obstructed through sleep apnoea. This is apparently the effect of prolonged arousal, and deprivation of proper sleep by the breathing problem. Diabetes also predisposes people to an increase in blood pressure, and 70 per cent of Australians with type 2 diabetes (the common form) have high blood pressure.

Reversing high blood pressure

Many smokers will quit smoking when they develop lung cancer or emphysema. No one expects either cancer or emphysema to improve by this action, although cigarettes can cause both problems. Smokers with cancer quit in order to make themselves fitter for major surgery and smokers with emphysema quit to preserve what lung function is left and to stop it getting worse.

A few academic sceptics (see Chapter 16) assist the salt industry with the spurious argument that salt can't be very important, as high blood pressure is not fully reversible in a few weeks by adopting a low salt intake. It is fortunate it is reversible at all; in fact, a few cases are irreversible. These people have self-sustaining hypertension.

Self-sustaining hypertension

It has been known since the 1940s that blood pressure may remain permanently elevated even after the cause is removed. A plausible explanation is that a rise in blood pressure may cause permanent damage, both to the blood vessels and the kidney, in ways that maintain the higher pressure. When the blood pressure is completely normal at 100/60 the body has many life-saving mechanisms to keep it from falling. The body sometimes accepts a high blood pressure as 'normal' and tries to uphold it with the usual defence mechanisms. Defences probably include the stress hormones, and hormones that control sodium.[35] Drugs work in many of these areas. Beta-blockers counteract stress hormones and ACE inhibitors and angiotensin antagonists interfere with the sodium–handling hormones.

In one of Dahl's classic experiments, 40 per cent of rats with high blood pressure due to a high salt intake had permanent high blood pressure (it stayed up when salt was removed), even though their diet contained nothing else to keep the pressure raised. Salt had given them self-sustaining hypertension.[36] People with self-sustaining hypertension often abandon their new diet and lifestyle believing that the new diet and lifestyle made no difference to the condition. Although medication is very good nowadays, it is by no means infallible, and drugs will usually work better at lower doses and with fewer side-effects when assisted by an appropriate diet and lifestyle.[37]

Chimpanzees all recovered fully in six months after exposure to salt for two years, but Dahl's rats received relatively long exposure (two years is about the natural lifespan of a rat), indicating that prolonged exposure to salt seems to increase the risk of self-sustaining hypertension.[36] In humans an operation that removes the cause may be too late to 'cure' secondary hypertension due to a tumour.

Paradoxically, older people usually do better than the young when they skip salt as a treatment for high blood pressure. The body's defences against a fall in blood pressure are apparently stronger in youth and weaker with advancing age. The older you are, and the higher your blood pressure, the greater the likely fall in blood pressure after skipping salt.[38]

Salt sensitivity

It is often assumed that people with self-sustaining hypertension are 'not salt-sensitive'. In fact, however, some or all of them may be people who didn't recover when the cause was removed, and the cause may have been salt. It makes no sense to say that Dahl's rats with self-sustaining hypertension were 'not salt-sensitive' — the rats in that particular experiment would not have developed high blood pressure in the first place unless they had been salt-sensitive.[36]

Nevertheless, some salt-resistant rats can maintain a normal blood pressure at a high salt intake. Tests for salt sensitivity are being developed in an effort to identify salt-resistant humans. In theory salt-resistant people could have developed high blood pressure as a result of other factors such as being overweight, lack of exercise or excess alcohol, while at the same time salt-resistance would save them from having to pay much attention to their salt intake.

Salt sensitivity, however, is apparently very common. Of the 10 079 participants in the Intersalt study of salt intake and high blood pressure in fifty-two centres in thirty-six countries, 8344 had a 'normal' blood pressure (the increase with age was not yet high enough for a diagnosis of high blood pressure). The strong link between sodium excretion and blood pressure was just as strong among those with 'normal' blood pressure, indicating that salt sensitivity of varying degrees is as widespread in the rest of the population as in those with high blood pressure.[39]

A typical test for salt sensitivity measures blood pressure in people exposed alternately to a higher salt intake and a lower salt intake (sometimes as low as 10 mmol/day), and divides the group into 'salt-sensitive' and 'salt-resistant' according to their short-term responses. A typical interval for the test is two weeks at each salt intake

Unfortunately, a short-term test cannot predict with confidence the effect of *lifelong* exposure, because some people respond differently when tested again and salt sensitivity measured in this way increases with age.[40,41] It would take more than fifty years to validate a test predicting the final outcome of lifelong exposure — a young diet group has to reach old age.

Genetic research may be more promising. If we can identify all the genes for salt sensitivity it may one day be possible to treat people with those genes to reduce their salt sensitivity before their blood pressure rises. Salt resistance through genetic engineering may or may not be practical eventually, but an earlier spin-off of genetic research may be to develop new drugs with more highly specific action and negligible side-effects. If anyone wants to take drugs to *prevent* high blood pressure in spite of eating salty foods the option may be available one day. Meanwhile we do have the other and simpler option: to skip salty foods.

The DASH-Sodium Study, 2001

DASH stands for Dietary Approaches to Stop Hypertension. The DASH–Sodium Study set a new standard of dietary compliance in research on salt — it supplied the food, and participants only had to take it away and eat it.

The first DASH trial compared the standard American diet with a diet that followed all the dietary guidelines, except the salt guideline. It held sodium intake constant at 130 mmol/day (about average for American women but a 30 per cent drop from the male average). It had better blood pressure results compared with many past trials of low salt diets.[42]

The second DASH trial (DASH-Sodium) compared the standard American diet again with the DASH diet, but at three levels of salt intake — 143 mmol/day, 104 mmol/day and 65 mmol/day.[43] Thus DASH-Sodium tested a lower salt intake on its own. The only difference between DASH and DASH-Sodium was the salt intake.

When salt was controlled to 104 mmol/day, it was better than the previous DASH diet, and at 65 mmol/day the effect on high blood pressure was even better. DASH–Sodium also made 'normal' blood pressure more normal. It reversed some of the usual increase in blood pressure with age. The rise in blood pressure with age is the basic problem — reversing it would prevent the modern epidemic of high blood pressure.

The study findings were released at a conference (in advance of full publication in 2001) and the American National Institutes of Health reported some details on the official US government website in May 2000, urging all Americans to reduce their sodium intake to an upper limit of 65 mmol/day (1500 mg), in addition to following all the other dietary guidelines, with special emphasis on eating fruit and vegetables.[44] As in all trials, these impressive results from DASH-Sodium are group results. They are the average, made up of responders and good responders — including some excellent responders — and a few non-responders.

salt and high blood pressure

In industrialised societies high blood pressure is almost universal among those who live long enough. The common form ('essential hypertension') is incurable, and all that can be offered for the foreseeable future is lifelong treatment. There is good evidence, however, that it is preventable, and far more attention should be given to prevention.

You may be one of those rare people whose genetic predisposition to high blood pressure is so small that your own blood pressure and that of all your relatives is below 110/70, regardless of age, and you may therefore assume that you too can tolerate a high salt intake indefinitely and have no need to skip salt. Otherwise, your risk of high blood pressure is probably proportional to your genetic predisposition, your age and your errors of diet and lifestyle, which include your salt intake.[7] Moreover, if your blood pressure is already 120/80 or above, you have prehypertension, which needs prompt and permanent treatment with an ideal diet and lifestyle.[5]

Future geneticists who measure individual genetic predisposition to salt sensitivity are unlikely to report zero sensitivity very often. To retire with a normal blood pressure, most people are likely to find the cheapest and safest option is a healthy lifestyle that includes skipping salt.[5,7]

13
Salt and other health problems

A high salt intake increases thirst and fluid retention, with one whole group of health problems resulting from this artificial accumulation of fluid. It also causes loss of calcium in the urine, increasing the risk of stones of the kidney and bladder that contain calcium (the common kind) and the risk of osteoporosis ('chalky bones'). Acute salt poisoning can be fatal if the patient who is given salt as an emetic fails to vomit it, and the danger of salt causing acute illness is greater in early infancy. There is evidence that the high salt content of some Chinese foods may be more important than MSG in causing symptoms of 'Chinese restaurant syndrome'. Other problems linked with a high salt intake include stomach cancer, enlargement of the heart (independently of the blood pressure), and asthma.

Fluid retention

As the kidneys excrete all the salt we eat, many people wonder how salt can be harmful. One effect is thirst, when we swallow surplus water to balance our surplus salt intake. People with very high salt intakes drink about twice as much (in the form of water, tea or other beverages) as people who eat completely unsalted foods.[1] The kidneys are forced to work against a permanent backlog that makes most Australians about 1–2 kilograms heavier than they would be if they followed the national dietary guideline on salt.[2,3] This degree of fluid retention is seldom noticed, although some (especially women) can see it in their ankles, particularly in hot weather, and just before menstruation.

Swollen ankles (idiopathic oedema)

Swollen ankles are often attributed to poor nutrition, circulation and hormones. However, it has been shown that the condition improves with a lower salt intake and often disappears completely on the Salt Skip Program, with no other treatment.

Many people try avoiding salt, see no reduction in their swollen ankles, and tell their doctors that skipping salt didn't work. However, doctors who order a 24-hour urine collection (see Appendix 2) find these people are excreting a lot of sodium. Some people who cook without salt and add no salt at the table have a sodium excretion rate of over 200 mmol/day. They fail to realise that 75 per cent of the salt they eat is coming from processed foods (see Chapter 2). Swollen ankles can occur when salt intake is less than 100 mmol/day. A woman who entered the Salt Skip Program with swollen ankles at 65 mmol/day had complete relief at 20–30 mmol/day, and remained symptom-free throughout eighteen months of follow-up.

Dependence on diuretics (fluid tablets)

Modern diuretics (powerful prescription drugs) were hailed as a breakthrough when they replaced herbal diuretics. Doctors prescribed them to get rid of swollen ankles without putting patients on the unpalatable low salt diets of the 1950s. Many patients prefer a tablet to a radical change of diet, and doctors find it quicker and easier to prescribe a drug than a diet. Diuretics are still very popular but, as Appendix 1 points out, they have some significant drawbacks.

Some women become 'hooked' on diuretics to control swollen ankles. When they stop taking the diuretics the swelling comes back, often worse than before. Ankles may also swell for the first time when stopping a diuretic that has been prescribed for other reasons. This is really a form of drug dependence dating from the introduction of modern diuretics.[4] Patients with this form of drug dependence can stop taking the tablets if they follow the salt guideline closely and adopt the other dietary guidelines (especially the guideline to eat more fruit and vegetables). The natural answer — a lower salt intake — is both effective and permanent. People who start the Salt Skip Program stop taking the diuretic and drink plenty of water.[5] Salt — not plain water — causes fluid retention. The worst cases may need elastic stockings for a few weeks, but that is unusual, and all cases can expect a natural recovery.[5]

Travel oedema

Passengers on long-distance flights often find that, having taken off their shoes during the flight, they are unable to get them on again at the end of the journey, due to swollen feet and ankles. This swelling ('travel oedema') — due to stagnant circulation in artificial conditions that restrict movement and make it difficult to raise the legs — is much less at a low salt intake.

The swelling can be greatly reduced by skipping salt thoroughly for at least a week before the journey and requesting low salt meals when booking the ticket. Most international airlines serve good salt-free meals, although not all meals are controlled for fat at the same time. Travellers can choose from more than a dozen special diets (although no single meal currently available complies with all of the international dietary guidelines). Some airlines offer a Pritikin diet, very low in fat and theoretically low in salt. If you are unsure about the compromises you are being asked to make, a fruit platter is a flavoursome option.

Carpal tunnel syndrome

The carpal tunnel is a bony channel at the wrist containing tendons and a large nerve. Occupational injury or arthritis may encroach on the limited space, causing pressure on the nerve. You can make more room in the tunnel by removing fluid retention. Symptoms include numbness and/or pain and tingling in the thumb, index and middle fingers, which is usually worse at night.

Diuretics can help mild cases. The Salt Skip Program can also give complete relief in mild cases and replace the use of diuretics. When bony enlargement of the wrist joints from osteoarthritis reduces the space in the carpal tunnel too severely, surgery to the ligament that covers the carpal tunnel may be the only way to relieve the constriction and the symptoms.

Meniere's syndrome

Meniere's syndrome causes deafness, ringing in the ears (tinnitus) and giddy attacks (vertigo). In severe cases vertigo can strike suddenly without warning, making sufferers feel that the room is spinning violently, and leaving them incapable of doing anything except lying still. The severe nausea and vomiting that accompany severe vertigo can make these attacks extremely distressing. Vertigo responds well to a lower salt intake and is rare with good 24-hour sodium excretion results (under 50 mmol for men and under 40 mmol for women, with potassium higher than sodium excretion).

Medical professionals, being naturally sceptical, sometimes ask if there is 'good evidence' that low salt diets help Meniere's disease. They know that placebos (inert pills) are very effective for subjective symptoms like pain, headache or vertigo, especially when used by an enthusiast. It has been known since 1934 that salt is a very important trigger for vertigo and that 24-hour urinary sodium excretion rates below 50 mmol give dramatic relief. It became the standard medical treatment in Michigan, and similar results were obtained in London.[6-8]

In the 1960s the National Hospital for Nervous Diseases at Queen Square, London, had no problem with a remission of vertigo when sodium excretion was below 50 mmol/day but the hospital's ethics committee stopped the research after complaints about the severe vertigo attacks from patients who regretted that they had agreed to take the risk.[8,9] The result is that a randomised controlled trial has never been carried out, as it would expose participants to the risk of another vertigo attack, and informed consent is unobtainable. How could a food additive that is completely harmless invariably cause this insurmountable ethical problem?

Unfortunately for Meniere sufferers, the price for complete relief from vertigo seems to be an increased sensitivity to salt, as a single dietary mistake may now provoke an attack of vertigo within eight hours. Vertigo patients must avoid over-the-counter remedies for urinary infection (Ural is the most popular) which add over 200 mmol to the daily sodium intake (see Chapter 15). They should also avoid liquorice, which contains a plant steroid that causes sodium retention and fluid retention — significant for people who love liquorice and eat a lot of it.

When the vertigo persists

If all patients with Meniere's syndrome had 100 per cent recovery when skipping salt strictly, it would mean that salt was the only trigger for the vertigo. Apparently it isn't. Some patients with persistent vertigo, in spite of good urine results, may have other triggers, such as food allergy or intolerance.[10] They are candidates for further investigation, and for all the other treatments in current use by ear specialists. Diuretics would be unsafe unless they go back on a higher salt intake (see Appendix 1). Diuretics are still the standard medical treatment of course — because a salt intake low enough to work as well as a diuretic is still widely considered too difficult for most people, in spite of published evidence to the contrary from both America and Britain. This is likely to change when the Salt Skip Program becomes better known.[6-8] Doctors who suggest diuretics to treat Meniere's syndrome may be interested to look at Appendix 1, which has references for professional readers.

Premenstrual syndrome (PMS)

Some authors claim that PMS affects up to 50 per cent of women to some degree, and about 5 per cent of women severely. Symptoms of PMS may include swollen ankles and a bloated feeling, evident about seven to ten days before each period. Other symptoms may include tender breasts, headaches, depression, insomnia, perverted appetite, mood swings, irritability, anger, impaired capacity for work, or lethargy. Child abuse, marital breakdown, suicide and even homicide are more common in this part of the menstrual cycle. French courts accept PMS as a defence for homicide.

Yet even the most severe symptoms vanish abruptly at the onset of the period. As PMS is confined to women and governed rigidly by the menstrual cycle, it is usual to blame the balance of hormones, and to search for effective drugs to treat the symptoms. But if half the women of child-bearing age are sick, it is reasonable to ask if their environment is sick.[11] Most women's current sodium intake is ten to thirty times higher than they need, and could be reduced. A diuretic is inappropriate when there is an effective drug-free alternative.

By doing what their grandmothers might have told them — taking regular exercise, getting enough rest, stopping smoking, limiting their intake of saturated fat, salt, sugar, alcohol, caffeine and liquorice (if applicable), and eating more fresh fruits and vegetables, many women can expect benefit from a more natural lifestyle.

About 5 per cent of women with PMS have such severe symptoms that they are seriously incapacitated for several days to a week in every month. Two women who joined the Salt Skip Program with severe Meniere's syndrome discovered that the salt intake low enough to abolish their vertigo had abolished the symptoms of PMS so completely that they failed to realise when they were in their pre-menstrual week. Although PMS is notorious for placebo effects (when remedies work because people *think they will*), a placebo effect seems unlikely for these two people, considering that the remission was totally unexpected. This is not an isolated observation — cookbooks for PMS sufferers generally purport to be low salt cookbooks (though some recipes may include bacon and other salty ingredients, and fall far short of the requirements for a salt skipper).[12]

Glaucoma

Glaucoma is another disease affected by salt intake. The clear fluid at the front of the eyeball is constantly being produced and removed, and the pressure is maintained by a delicate balance between the rate of production and the rate of removal. An increase in pressure causes glaucoma, which (despite many advances) is the second most common cause of blindness in industrialised societies.

Sudden onset of glaucoma and other acute symptoms can lead to early diagnosis, but pressure rising gradually without symptoms over ten to twenty-five years is treacherous. Loss of sight is hard to restore if it is the first symptom, and it is essential to detect glaucoma as early as possible. Early treatment should prevent blindness. Medical treatment with eye drops may be enough, but some cases require surgery as well.

Some patients who adopted the Salt Skip Program for Meniere's syndrome have also had glaucoma, and found that their eye pressure dropped further than usual at a low salt intake. While a low salt intake is not sufficient as sole treatment, it often makes glaucoma easier to manage. Presumably it may help to prevent glaucoma or at least postpone its onset.

Calcium loss

When your kidneys excrete salt they also lose calcium. The more salt you excrete the more calcium you lose. Both humans and experimental animals lose calcium at a rate that is directly proportional to their sodium excretion rate, with a progressive increase in calcium loss in humans at every step from 70 mmol/day to 220 mmol/day. High salt intakes waste calcium, while low salt intakes are equivalent to a dietary calcium supplement.

Osteoporosis ('chalky bones')

Osteoporosis makes many people stooped and frail in old age, with weak bones deformed by pressure and fractures. Women are at higher risk after the menopause. The hard material that strengthens a bone is calcium phosphate. Bone is a living structure, constantly reshaped by mechanical forces, like a coral reef yielding to ocean currents, except that external forces make bone stronger and denser. Bones reach their greatest density (peak bone mass) in early adult life.

Some bone loss may be inevitable with age, and osteoporosis is diagnosed when 30 per cent or more of the peak bone mass has been lost. An estimated 15–20 million Americans have osteoporosis, with 1.3 million fractures a year as a direct result. Australian estimates are similar in proportion to the population. Community survey data in New Zealand indicate that a low salt diet at an average sodium excretion rate of 70 mmol/day would reduce calcium loss by 32 per cent in men and 27 per cent in women, equivalent to a generous calcium supplement — at no cost. The RDI for calcium could be set lower at a lower salt intake.[13]

At current salt intakes the RDI for calcium is set so high to prevent osteoporosis that it is very difficult to obtain enough from natural sources without eating a lot of dairy products that provide too much saturated fat unless they are made from skim milk. Some dairy products like ordinary cheese contain enough salt to increase the urinary wastage of calcium.

Calcium carbonate (food quality chalk) was added to the flour used in Britain during the Second World War to prevent calcium deficiency when dairy foods were rationed. That was artificial, but so is an excess of sodium chloride. Instead of adding both it would be cheaper and healthier to add neither.

A high calcium intake will not guarantee absorption, and wasting calcium with a high salt intake becomes more harmful when absorption from the gut is impaired, as in coeliac disease and with advancing age. Foods containing oxalic acid, such as spinach, rhubarb and sorrel, form calcium oxalate, which (being insoluble) is not absorbed. Also the phytic acid found in cereals and bran forms calcium phytate, which is also insoluble and not absorbed.

Impaired calcium absorption may explain why calcium supplements and dairy products often fail to benefit older people. When less exercise and weaker muscles increase the risk of bone loss, older people can ill afford to increase urinary calcium loss with an unnecessarily high salt intake. Osteoporosis is a 'disease of affluence', preventable by changes of diet and lifestyle.[14] Reducing the risk of osteoporosis is another benefit of skipping salt.

Kidney and bladder stones

Kidney and bladder stones are common. One in eight Americans has a stone in the urinary tract at some time in their lives, and Australian rates are similar. Up to 85 per cent of urinary stones are calcium stones. Stones in the urinary tract may be excruciatingly painful, they may require major surgery, and there is about a 50 per cent chance that they will recur within seven years — three good reasons for preventing them. Yet prevention is often neglected.

The tendency to form calcium stones runs in families. Such families excrete more calcium than the average person on their usual ('normal') diet. This condition is called familial hypercalciuria. It is another Western disease that should disappear with a better diet and lifestyle, because calcium excretion usually drops to normal at sodium excretion rates below 80 mmol/day.[14,15]

To prevent kidney stones the old advice was to drink more water, reduce calcium intake, and sometimes to take a diuretic. Reducing calcium intake has surprisingly little effect on calcium excretion, because about 98 per cent of all the calcium in the body is in the bones, and an excessive salt intake is able to go on wasting calcium (even at low intakes) by increasing bone loss and hastening the onset of osteoporosis. Although thiazide diuretics can reduce calcium excretion they are not a healthy alternative to a lower salt intake, particularly as their long term side-effects include low blood potassium, low blood sodium, diabetes and gout. These side-effects are more common at the high dose rates often used for hypercalciuria. Patients with high blood pressure are given diuretics at low doses nowadays to reduce these long-term side-effects.

A controlled trial has now demonstrated that reducing animal protein and salt — even modestly — reduces the recurrence rate of urinary calcium stones substantially.[16] A low calcium diet to prevent urinary calcium stones is no longer justifiable.[17] Patients with kidney and bladder stones can avoid diuretics, decrease their sodium excretion to 50 mmol/day or less on the Salt Skip Program, and eat more fruit and vegetables and less meat. They need to produce alkaline urine, and should let their doctors check their 24-hour urinary sodium and calcium excretion rates to confirm they are on the right track (see Appendix 2 for an explanation).

High blood sodium (hypernatraemia)

Chinese restaurant syndrome

Some people feel unwell after a Chinese meal, and the term 'Chinese restaurant syndrome' dates from the first report in 1968 in the *New England Journal of Medicine*. The author of the report, Chinese American Dr Kwok, suggested a high blood sodium as the likely cause.[18]

Dr Kwok felt unwell almost every time he had a meal at a Chinese restaurant. At first he suspected the soy sauce, but it was the same brand he used at home. He wrote that very salty food 'may produce temporary hypernatraemia' (high blood sodium) and gave technical reasons why MSG could make high blood sodium worse.

The media and public worldwide have ignored the author's opinion about salt and demonised MSG as the possible cause of this reaction. True allergy to MSG has never been identified. 'Allergy' is the correct word when an antigen such as pollen reacts with an antibody in the human tissues or bloodstream. The reaction to MSG is not like that. It takes the form of *intolerance* to large doses (the same principle seen with drug intolerance). No harm has ever been linked with the small dose of MSG that occurs naturally in breast milk, tomatoes and mushrooms and every case of MSG sensitivity identified so far has been a standard example of food intolerance, with symptoms only at doses above the individual's threshold of tolerance. The threshold for an effect in a double-blind trial (an experimental technique to avoid bias where neither the subject nor the person giving the test is aware of the particulars of the items being tested) was an intake of 2.5 g of MSG, which is more than would be obtained from any natural source.[19]

In Kwok's original description of Chinese restaurant syndrome, his symptoms began within twenty minutes of eating and faded within two hours. Seven volunteers who ate identical take-away meals from a Chinese restaurant in London felt unwell within one to four hours.[20] They all complained of severe thirst, abdominal distension and bloating — symptoms of an overload of salt. The total sodium content of an identical meal on analysis was 238 mmol (5474 mg), a lot more than the average man would eat in a whole day. The volunteers all showed a steep rise in blood sodium, and two who made urine collections excreted only 27 per cent of the sodium load within four hours, and still had about 174 mmol waiting to be excreted.

Chinese restaurant syndrome strikes before its victims have had time to drink much water, or to absorb any water. Salt skippers can order a Chinese meal with impunity by ordering a meal without added salt, MSG or soy sauce, as discussed in earlier chapters. Low salt Chinese meals can be accompanied safely by wine.

The general public may be able to reduce the risk of Chinese restaurant syndrome by avoiding an overload of salt, especially a *sudden* overload. This rules out salt-preserved foods such as black bean sauce, soy sauce, oyster sauce and brine-pickled vegetables. Eat plenty of rice (normally cooked without added salt in China). As this is a reduced salt meal, not a low salt meal, it would help to avoid wine (alcohol is dehydrating and it is important to dilute the excess sodium, not to concentrate it). Drinking plenty of water or a big pot of China tea will dilute the excess sodium.

Intolerance to MSG — confirmed by 'blind' testing — is uncommon, but those with confirmed intolerance who read food labels in order to avoid MSG (additive 621) may find they need to avoid the other glutamates as well (620–625 inclusive).

Fatal salt poisoning

Animals that are unable to vomit, or vomit rarely, are easily killed by salt. Pig breeders who believe they can increase a pig's appetite with salt must be very careful not to overdo it, because fatal salt poisoning with high blood sodium levels is a hazard if the pigs fail to drink and absorb water fast enough.

Humans are normally protected from an overdose of salt by

vomiting. In fact, salt was formerly used as an emetic. This danger-ous practice has now been abandoned because the survival of patients who fail to vomit may depend on the emergency use of a stomach pump.

The immature kidney of the young infant is especially vulnerable, and foods considered normal for adults can kill young infants with salt poisoning. It can be rapidly fatal when infants fail to vomit.

Fatal salt poisoning with 'normal' food

British papers reported in July 1999 that a three-month-old infant had died of salt poisoning after his parents tried to save money by feeding him adult foods instead of specially prepared baby foods. The mother told the coroner that they knew that babies should not be given too much salt and didn't understand what had gone wrong.

The baby became ill after eating a standard breakfast cereal, instant mashed potatoes and gravy instead of Baby Rice, and was admitted to hospital. He had a fit, breathing problems, high blood pressure and a fast heart rate, and died from extensive brain damage. Two special-ist paediatricians from the Sheffield Children's Hospital told the coroner that death was due to an excessively high level of sodium in the bloodstream, due to an attempt to wean him with adult foods that had a salt content totally inappropriate for an infant.

Although some UK breakfast cereals in 1999 had excessively high levels of sodium up to 1100 mg/100 g, the parents chose one of the very few low salt ones — Ready Brek, with only 100 mg/100 g — and reduced it to a pulp with a liquidiser. Considering the exces-sively salty alternatives they might so easily have chosen, it is tragic that the parents made only one big mistake. The fatal overdose of salt came from the gravy, which was made with ordinary commercial gravy granules.

The only way anyone (young or old) can survive an overdose of salt is by excreting it as rapidly as possible through the kidneys. No matter how much water is available, the best chance for survival is to concentrate the urine and excrete very salty urine. The coroner was told that the urine did contain a lot of salt, but infants cannot con-centrate urine as well as adults. Incidentally, the ability to excrete salt declines once again in old age.

Mothers usually wean infants at five to six months, and most makers of canned unsalted baby foods offer them for use for babies from six months onwards. Mothers who mash home-cooked food instead of buying commercial baby foods must eliminate any food cooked with salt, and never check the taste in the mistaken belief that the baby will share their own preference for salted vegetables. It is well known in childcare circles that added salt actually makes it more difficult to persuade an infant to accept solid foods.

The young of mammals like mice, chimpanzees and humans have been successfully weaned since the dawn of history with the foods naturally available. Human infants can start with fruit, vegetables or a cereal. It is an advantage to soften the food by cooking, and to sieve it. The essential precaution is this — *don't add salt.*

At what age is it safe to introduce salt?

It is illegal for manufacturers to add salt to foods intended for infants under twelve months old. After that age it may be legal to add salt, but whether it is quite safe — for perfect health from every viewpoint — is another matter. Opinions differ — it depends on what you want.

Does your definition of perfect health include having the same blood pressure at age seventy as you had when you were eighteen? The only intact human societies with perfect health by that definition are the salt-free societies. They wean their babies without adding salt to their food, either at weaning or at any later time in their lives. A research project in Holland (described below) has demonstrated harm from even a small increase in the salt content of an infant's diet above that of breast milk.

Premature rise of blood pressure in infancy

The blood pressure of young infants is so sensitive to salt that a Dutch research team was able to show that bottle feeds and commercial baby foods with a salt content that was standard in Holland in 1980 had a significant effect on blood pressure.[21] Standard bottle feeds in Holland in 1980 were made from partly diluted cow's milk, which provided about three times more sodium than the amount in breast milk.

The trial randomly assigned several hundred newborn infants into a high salt group given standard bottle feeds and a low salt group given bottle feeds with the same sodium content as breast milk. When solids were introduced at thirteen weeks, the high salt group had the usual lightly salted baby foods commercially available at that time, and the second group had identical baby foods manufactured without added salt. The original article stated that the low salt solid foods were 'demineralised', but it has now been confirmed that the vegetables were simply prepared without added salt.[21,22]

At twenty-five weeks the high salt group had a higher average blood pressure, taken by nurses with automatic equipment and without knowing which group each infant belonged to. About one-third (35 per cent) of the children from the original study were available for follow-up at age fifteen. In spite of eating ordinary foods in the interval, the two groups still showed a significant difference in blood pressure that persisted after statistical adjustments were made for exercise and other lifestyle factors that could affect blood pressure.[23] A difference detectable fifteen years later, regardless of the diet in the interval, may seem surprising, but a growing body of evidence links adult health problems (including high blood pressure) with the environment in pregnancy and early infancy.

Stomach cancer

Leaflets produced by cancer societies around the world warn readers of the clear association between stomach cancer and the consumption of salt-preserved foods such as anchovies, olives, salt pork and so on. Any form of chronic irritation, whether mechanical or chemical, can increase the risk of cancer, and salt in preservative concentration is a powerful irritant to the sensitive lining of the stomach.

In one study the risk of stomach cancer increased more than three-fold among people who frequently ate foods containing salt in preservative concentration, and the risk was proportional to the consumption (a dose response).[24] The country with the world's highest death rate from stomach cancer is Japan, where meals of salt-preserved foods are eaten without water to drink, which would have diluted the salt.

Many salted foods are also smoked, adding to the cancer risk when combined with salt. Experiments with rats confirm that salt itself at concentrations above 2.5 per cent (sodium 1000 mg/100 g) increases the effect of other cancer-promoting agents.[25]

Enlargement of the heart

Physical exercise strengthens and enlarges the muscles, including the heart muscle, and the enlargement that accompanies physical fitness is regarded as beneficial — it corrects the relative atrophy of disuse. An increase in blood pressure also tends to enlarge the heart, as a response to the extra work of maintaining a higher pressure.

A high salt intake has the unexpected effect of enlarging the heart independently of any effect on blood pressure. It can enlarge the heart of an animal even when the blood pressure fails to rise, and the same thing happens in reverse — when high blood pressure due to a high salt intake enlarges the heart, it becomes smaller at a lower salt intake, even in animals whose blood pressure remains high.[26]

A CAT scan can measure the degree of enlargement accurately in humans, and patients with larger hearts have a poorer health outlook due to a greater risk of heart attack, heart failure, sudden death and stroke. It remains unclear how changes in salt intake can alter heart size independently of the blood pressure, but a direct effect on the heart has been fully confirmed in both humans and animals. It is another recognised hazard of a high salt intake.[26]

Rigidity of the large arteries

The walls of the large arteries become stiffer and more rigid with advancing age, and stiffness affects the speed with which a pulse wave passes down the arm at each heart beat. It is easy to show with electronic equipment that the wave travels more slowly down a soft young artery, and faster down a stiff old artery.

It was natural to attribute loss of elasticity to ageing, but in China two populations with different salt intakes had different arterial stiffness at all ages, and stiffness was shown to be independent of blood pressure.[27] A pilot study by the same research team found that a group on the Salt Skip Program had more flexible arteries than a control group on an ordinary Australian diet. Some older salt skippers had the arterial flexibility of others half their age.[28]

Asthma

Although salt is not regarded as a cause of asthma, tests of lung function in asthmatic men have shown that it was worse at higher sodium excretion rates.[29] A double-blind trial with sodium tablets and placebo confirmed that a high salt intake makes asthma symptoms and lung function worse.[30] Higher salt intakes have several direct effects on the bronchial airways.[31,32]

Kidney function

Like the rest of the body, kidneys gradually wear out with advancing age. Microalbuminuria (urine containing small traces of protein) provides important early warning of declining kidney function. It improves when high blood pressure is treated with certain drugs, such as ACE inhibitors or calcium channel blockers, but there is less improvement when salt intake is high, independent of their effect on blood pressure.[33,34]

When sodium is thought to be lacking

The problems discussed so far are a result of a high salt intake. A different set of problems may be attributed (rightly or wrongly) to a lack of sodium. Salt skippers who think they may be lacking sodium must be guided by professional medical advice. These notes may make it easier to understand the advice given.

Low blood sodium (hyponatraemia)

One Melbourne laboratory found low blood sodium in 4.8 per cent of 326 923 blood samples it received (about one sample in twenty), and most of the patients had no symptoms.[35] Low results are not uncommon in laboratory reports because of the way they are defined. They are 'low' if they fall below the 'reference range' for each test, and the reference range is a statement of the upper and lower limits of the values found in 95 per cent of the general healthy population.

When no cause can be found for hyponatraemia in a patient who is not taking a diuretic and has no symptoms, the patient is usually kept under observation without treatment. When a cause is found the most common diagnosis is dilutional hyponatraemia, which is due to a maldistribution of the body fluids. The low blood sodium is caused by excess fluid (not a lack of sodium), which may be due to fluid retention from heart failure, cirrhosis of the liver, or some forms of kidney failure. Another cause is a hormone problem called

SIADH (Syndrome of Inappropriate Antidiuretic Hormone), which tends to accompany certain forms of cancer and diseases of the lungs or central nervous system, or occurs as a side-effect of ACE inhibitor drugs prescribed for high blood pressure, or a number of other drugs prescribed for arthritis or depression.[36] The street drug 'ecstasy' can also have this effect.[37]

When there is an actual lack of sodium the reason is usually excessive salt loss, a common side-effect of synthetic diuretics (prescription drugs that make the kidneys excrete salt faster than normal). Appendix 1 provides a detailed description of excessive salt loss from diuretics and various other causes such as a few rare diseases. Chapter 14 discusses salt loss from heavy sweating, and explains why salt skippers don't have that problem. The natural salt content of a balanced diet is more than adequate to prevent hyponatraemia in the absence of diseases or drugs that cause excessive salt loss.

Hyponatraemia may occur with diuretics at any salt intake, but (as would be expected) the risk is greater the lower the salt intake. This is a special reason for salt skippers to avoid diuretics, and a reason for warning everybody who is currently under medical treatment and/or taking medication of any kind to skip salt *only* with their doctor's full knowledge and consent. See Appendix 1 for a full discussion.

Appendix 1 also describes the symptoms of hyponatraemia. Everyone with symptoms needs urgent medical attention — the outlook may be serious, depending on the diagnosis. The exact cause may be uncertain even after full investigation in hospital (all tests for possible causes may come back negative). Difficult cases are a worry to their doctors.

If salt skippers have low blood sodium, the first step is to check if possible whether they are taking a diuretic and to seek professional medical advice. Some doctors are unfamiliar with the Salt Skip Program, so ideally salt skippers should invite their doctors to look at this book and make a professional judgement on the issues raised in Appendix 1.

Hair analysis and sodium levels

Some people have sent hair to a commercial laboratory in response to advertising on the Internet and been told their sodium was low and that they were not getting enough salt. Hair analysis may provide good evidence of poisoning, especially by mercury and arsenic, but there is no scientific evidence of any correlation between sodium in the hair and salt in the diet.[38] Hair analysis for sodium is very unreliable, with different results from different laboratories on the same hair. Six commercial laboratories that advertised hair mineral analysis for nutritional assessment gave widely varying reports on the sodium content of hair samples collected carefully on the same day by the Californian Department of Health Services from a single healthy volunteer.[38]

Stomach acid and salt

Some alternative practitioners tell some of their clients they don't have enough stomach acid (hypochlorhydria) because they are not eating enough salt. It is impossible to make the medical diagnosis of hypochlorhydria without passing a stomach tube — painless, and easier than it sounds. An increase in salt intake has no effect on stomach acid and has no place in the medical treatment of hypochlorhydria.

The natural sodium content of a balanced diet is entirely adequate for producing stomach acid. Newborn infants are able to make stomach acid from the salt in breast milk (sodium 14 mg/100 g). Salt skippers who choose low salt foods (sodium up to 120 mg/100 g) get nearly ten times more than that. Salt-free societies have not needed additional salt to help them make enough stomach acid. Mice in Australian mouse plagues can make enough stomach acid on a diet of wheat grains with a sodium content of 3 mg/100 g.

We have seen that the high salt intake of industrialised societies causes chronic fluid retention in the whole population — no one escapes — and it may have multiple symptoms, from swollen ankles to premenstrual syndrome (PMS), the vertigo of Meniere's syndrome and carpal tunnel syndrome. It causes loss of calcium in the urine, a factor in osteoporosis and calcium stones of the kidney and bladder. A high salt intake can be fatal to young infants, and to adults who are given salt as an emetic but fail to vomit. The many other problems include evidence that salt rather than MSG is the critical factor in Chinese restaurant syndrome, and that salt-preserved foods are linked with stomach cancer.

A laboratory report that the blood is low in sodium (hyponatraemia) is not uncommon in apparently healthy people without symptoms, but the presence of symptoms makes it urgent to have a medical diagnosis and treatment. Hyponatraemia is usually due to dilution of the blood by fluid imbalance resulting from various diseases or drugs. Another cause is excessive loss of sodium, which is usually due to drugs (especially diuretics) or heavy sweating or a few rare diseases. Salt skippers, however, can sweat heavily without much salt loss. The natural sodium content of a balanced diet is entirely adequate to prevent hyponatraemia in the absence of the diseases and drugs that can cause it.

V   Frequently asked questions

14

Hot weather, sport and cramp

Some of the Australian continent lies in the tropics, and if skipping salt led to health problems in hot weather it would be a serious mistake for the government to recommend that the entire population choose foods low in salt (sodium no more than 120 mg/100 g). This chapter explains why that recommendation is perfectly safe. It describes the various forms of heat illness, the role of acclimatisation, how first aid can save life in heat illness, and discusses the jigsaw puzzle of cramp and salt.

The vicious circle of eating salt in hot weather

Salt-free societies such as the Yanomama in Brazil and the Asaro in Papua New Guinea live in the tropics and sweat freely all day in steamy jungles, yet remain vigorous and well, without access to salt, salty foods or sports drinks. That is because their sweat consists mainly of water. Adding salt to their food would deprive them of this benefit. Within a few days they would have a high salt sweat — an artificial result of high salt intakes. Most Australians eat enough salt to give them a salty sweat, which is why they may need to replace salt as well as water if they sweat heavily. Skipping salt has the reverse effect and is equally rapid.

The perfect safety of skipping salt very strictly in a hot Canberra summer was tested by a group of athletes called The Canberra Runners, who were habitually running 10–20 kilometres daily in all weathers. Some of them joined a large study promoting a sodium excretion rate of 35 mmol/day.[1] They all remained very fit and well, and were delighted when their sweat no longer stung their eyes or tasted like brine. They confirmed that this improvement rapidly followed the change of diet to low salt foods.

Preventing salt loss

To prevent salt loss it is important to adopt a low salt intake before sweating occurs. A high salt intake only makes matters worse — salt is not stored but excreted in the urine and sweat, increasing the salt content of the sweat, with greater salt loss when sweating does occur.

Advice from the National Health and Medical Research Council is: 'Paradoxically it may be preferable for athletes or people going to a tropical area to be on a *low sodium intake*' (author italics).[2] The Australian army, navy and air force no longer issue salt tablets to troops working in the tropics as they are unnecessary, they increase water requirements and often cause vomiting if taken on an empty stomach.

Heat illness

It is well known that hot weather can make people ill. The most common form of heat illness is heat exhaustion, where the patient at first feels weak and giddy and then often faints. Heat stroke is more abrupt and severe, with rapid loss of consciousness. Although rare, heat stroke is dangerous in the absence of prompt first aid (vigorous cooling). Both conditions are due to heat and should be completely preventable by keeping cool.

A third form of heat illness is heat cramp (miner's, stoker's or cane-cutter's cramp) which affects the muscles most used at work (the arms and trunk as often as the legs). In some parts of the world miners drink salted beer after work. Heat cramp is usually attributed to sweat losses being replaced by water without replacing the artificial salt losses they suffer as a result of their high salt diet. Cramp is rare in acclimatised workers, however, even without supplementary salt, because acclimatisation reduces the salt content of the sweat.

Preventing heat illness

To prevent heat illness (heat exhaustion and heat stroke) it is essential to prevent over-heating of the body. Frail elderly people who are not salt skippers may develop heat illness even when sitting still and trying to keep cool. General debility increases the risk, but plenty of cold non-alcoholic drinks reduce it. When we need food we are hungry, but thirst is less reliable when we need water, especially with advancing age, and dehydration may prevent sweating and precipitate heat illness. Scanty and dark urine provides an early warning sign, so older people should watch the colour of their urine and keep drinking enough non-alcoholic drinks to pass plenty of pale urine. Many older people take diuretics, which increase the risk of heat illness by disturbing body chemistry and fluid balance, but salt skippers normally avoid diuretics (see Appendix 1).

The main candidates for the more severe form of heat illness called heat stroke are people like elite athletes, soldiers subjected to misguided 'toughening-up' in full combat uniform, or footballers or marathon runners who get no time to cool down. Also at risk are the frail elderly who are unable to fend for themselves in a severe heatwave, especially if living alone, and if air conditioning suddenly fails during peak demand periods.

Acclimatisation

Acclimatisation makes heat more tolerable within a few days, especially for active people. Acclimatisation is usually well underway at two weeks, but may continue for two months, with more comfort and less risk of heat disorders. Sweating increases, yet salt loss is less (acclimatisation independently reduces the salt content of sweat).

A high salt intake can produce sweat with a sodium level of up to 70 mmol/L before acclimatisation. Constant sweating and acclimatisation can reduce it to 10–20 mmol/L.[3] Salt skippers who choose low salt foods have a low salt sweat from the outset, independently of the added effect of acclimatisation. This limits their salt loss from the outset without having to wait for their bodies to acclimatise.

Cooler weather and less exercise rapidly reduce the effects of acclimatisation, but a return to the heat and more exercise lead to increased sweat volume and better heat tolerance again.

First aid for heat exhaustion

Patients with heat exhaustion are usually elderly. They complain of feeling weak, giddy, nauseated and faint, and may have a headache. They are usually over-breathing, look ashen-grey, have cold, clammy skin, and may vomit or faint. They generally recover before the ambulance arrives if they can lie down in a cool place shaded from the sun, with all excess clothing removed. If they are conscious, they should also be given sports drinks or oral rehydration fluids if available, or water.[4]

First aid for heat stroke

Patients with heat stroke may briefly feel weak, giddy, nauseated and faint, but lose consciousness so abruptly that this may be the first symptom. Some athletes are still sweating, but the elderly are nearly always 'burning hot and dry'. Their survival may depend on what first aid they receive before the ambulance arrives.

Heat stroke victims who are still conscious must stop all exercise (the main heat source) immediately and be shaded from the sun (another heat source). All unnecessary clothing must be removed, and the body must be continually sprayed or splashed with water and fanned to promote maximum air circulation and evaporative cooling.

Sport: sweat loss, salt loss and sports drinks

Salt-eating sportspeople who drink only water to replace heavy sweat losses may be at risk of developing low blood sodium or 'water intoxication' (hyponatraemia). Although this is usually rare, it can occur in prolonged sports events like marathons and ultramarathons.

Sports drinks consist of a weak solution of salt, sugars and potassium (sometimes with other minerals such as magnesium). This mixture reduces the risk of water intoxication. Its main benefit is that water is absorbed faster from a weak solution of salt and sugar, as in oral rehydration therapy (ORT). It was thought to improve performance in events where heavy sweating sometimes removed water faster than it could be absorbed from drinks. In the opinion of some experts, the advent of sports drinks has led to overdrinking. The latest guideline for athletes who sweat heavily is to be guided by thirst, and not to drink more than 400 mL per hour, or in extreme cases 800 mL.[5]

Salt skippers with heavy sweat loss can also be guided by thirst, and water is considered a satisfactory way to replace the fluid lost. If they choose sports drinks in the hope of absorbing fluid faster, they can see from the labels that commercial sports drinks are low in salt (sodium below 120 mg/100 g), so one serving of a typical sports drink adds less sodium than they would get from a serving of cornflakes. They can work out from the labels that 400 mL of Gatorade would boost a 24-hour urine result with 7 mmol of sodium, and 400 mL of Powerade would boost the urine result by 2 mmol (sports drink labels show the sodium content in millimoles as well as in milligrams). Even salt skippers might lose up to 2 mmol of sodium every hour with copious sweating, and the fruit flavours of sports drinks make it easier to drink more fluid.

Sporting events and heat illness

Heat illness can occur with all vigorous exercise, but it is more common in fun runs, which often attract untrained, unfit and overweight competitors. When hot weather is forecast fun runs should begin before 8 am, when the air is cool and the sun is low.

Some people tolerate hot weather better than others, but everybody engaged in vigorous exercise needs to take more care when any of the factors listed below are present:

- a sudden hot spell in early spring, when people are not yet acclimatised
- a warm or hot day (above 25°C) with high humidity and still air
- being a beginner, less trained and less fit
- being overweight (wearing a 'subcutaneous overcoat'). Weight control is of special benefit before the hot weather begins.
- wearing too much clothing, or wearing impervious clothing that does not allow sweat to evaporate
- trying to compete when ill, from simple virus infections or other causes of fever, and/or diseases of the heart, circulation and skin. Sick people need rest, especially in the heat.
- suffering dehydration from not drinking enough beforehand and at regular intervals during the race. Even when the body is at rest, hot weather demands frequent cool drinks throughout the day, especially for older people.
- suffering dehydration from diarrhoea and vomiting
- taking diuretics or alcohol, or drugs such as tranquillisers and motion-sickness remedies that impair body temperature regulation
- competing in great heat when not yet acclimatised
- overcrowding in a fun run in a pack of other hot people.

Muscle cramp

There is a common belief that muscle cramp can also be caused by lack of salt. Muscle cramp can occur independently of hot weather.

The few serious diseases that can cause cramp are usually diagnosed from other symptoms before cramp becomes a problem. Cramp may occur with varicose veins, with relief when the veins are treated, and leg cramp may occur in pregnancy. It may follow vigorous exercise, especially in muscles given unfamiliar use (such as the arms, after the season's first game of tennis). Some people experience cramp after drinking alcohol, even in moderation. A cold bed may precipitate it; swimmers are thought to be to be in greater danger of cramp in cold water.

The common muscle cramp that most healthy people notice at some time in their lives usually comes in the feet or legs, and usually during the night while lying in bed. The pain can be distressing, and the muscles may be tender next day, but recovery is complete and this form of cramp is compatible with perfect health. The classic attack affects healthy people of any age but is more common after age thirty, affecting women slightly more often than men. It usually occurs after a few hours of sleep, but sometimes also occurs on first waking. Either the toes curl painfully or the calf muscle contracts into a painful knot. It usually starts suddenly with a leg movement.

Cramp in the calf in the middle of the night can be relieved at once by stretching the muscle, and to some extent by massage. The strong calf muscle is sometimes easier to stretch by getting out of bed and standing on the floor. For a short time the cramp tends to return.

There has been no good explanation for leg cramps at night. It may be a simple postural accident, an inappropriate attempt while asleep to bend the ankle downwards when it is already bent, resulting in over-shortening of the calf muscle.[6]

Swimmers often suffer cramp also. To save lives, first aid for cramp in the water should be a mandatory part of all swimming instruction. It may develop like the cramp that occurs in bed, as a result of accidental over-shortening of the calf muscles when the toes are pointed. Experienced swimmers can stretch the muscle, and change to a backstroke that lifts the feet.

Cramp and salt

The verifiable facts about cramp provide no support for the common belief that cramp is due to lack of salt, or that salt can cure it. A medical expedition to the Yanomama — the world's most salt-free society — did not find a single case of cramp.[7] In one blood pressure trial the control group reported having both mild and severe cramp at sodium excretion rates of 175 mmol/day — how much salt would they need to cure it?[8] When warned to expect more cramp with less salt, the diet group expecting more cramp reported a slight improvement in both mild and severe cramp at 37 mmol/day.[8] Blood pressure trials in London and Dunedin reported no change in the frequency of muscle cramp, although the groups receiving the low salt diet in both trials had been warned to expect it.[9,10]

A study that recruited medical students in the People's Republic of China, however, did report more cramp on a low salt diet. It may be significant that the students had a very low potassium intake, bordering on potassium deficiency, as a result of their dependence on white rice.[11]

Salt may be implicated when cramp occurs as a recognised side-effect of diuretics and renal dialysis (treatment with an artificial kidney machine), because both can induce a rapid change in sodium balance. Also, salt skippers in the Salt Skip Program have connected cramp with dietary salt in the reverse direction. Although they report no cramp at any other time, a salty evening meal (unavoidable for social or other reasons) has been followed by severe cramp during the night. Because cramp is so sporadic and unpredictable, it is hard to investigate, but this association with salt loading could probably be tested, with control for alcohol intake, dehydration and other possible confounders such as potassium, magnesium and calcium levels.

The association with salt is reported most convincingly when there is a rapid change in salt intake — whether downwards with diuretics and renal dialysis, or upwards with salt loading. Few people realise that ordinary diets can provide very rapid change in salt intake in a matter of hours, for example some processed foods have a hundredfold increase in their natural sodium content, and multiple 24-hour urine collections reveal a huge random variation in salt intake in the Western diet, with big swings over a wide range from one day to the next.[12] No other nutrient with the chemical and electrical activity of sodium suffers such swings. Sporadic episodes of cramp may be symptoms of this unsuspected fluctuation in the daily electrolyte balance.

Preventing cramp

One published antidote is to stretch the calf muscles thoroughly at bedtime.[6] In flat slippers or bare feet, stand facing a wall, about a metre away from it, and lean forward while keeping the heels on the floor. Stretch the calf muscles for at least 10–15 seconds, and repeat this several times. Another antidote recommended in pregnancy is to sleep with a pillow at the bottom of the bed. This prevents people from bending the ankle downwards and pointing the toes.[13]

There is no evidence that the Australian dietary guideline on salt intake increases the risk of dehydration, heat illness or cramp.[2] On the contrary, there is evidence — that readers can verify for themselves by skipping salt — that it reduces these problems, which is why the official advice to athletes and tourists visiting tropical Australia is to adopt a low salt intake.[2]

15

Sodium in water and in the pharmacy

Food is not the only source of sodium. It also occurs in tap water, bottled drinking water and other bottled drinks. You also have to look out for sodium in some of the items you may have been buying from a pharmacy.

Sodium in Australian drinking water

Rainwater is virtually sodium free, except when contaminated with sea spray (which can carry traces of added sodium as far as 25 kilometres inland in stormy weather). When city tap water consists of upland surface water it is low in sodium, but any addition of artesian well water may greatly increase the sodium content in some districts.

A salt skipper who found that Sydney drinking water had a sodium content of 11 milligrams per litre (11 mg/L) wanted to know if this was a high or low level of sodium. This is how to work it out:

Local authorities, most reference books and some bottled mineral water labels use milligrams per litre (mg/L):

Sodium levels in water	
Very low	20 mg/L
Upper limit for low	100 mg/L
Upper limit for taste	180 mg/L

The food labels that became mandatory on 31 December 2003 and some bottled water and mineral water labels now use milligrams per 100 millilitres (mg/100 mL), which is ten times smaller than a litre:

Sodium levels in water	
Very low	2 mg/100 mL
Upper limit for low	10 mg/100 mL
Upper limit for taste	18 mg/100 mL

With a sodium content of 11 mg/L, Sydney drinking water is very low by these criteria. The figures of 20 and 180 for 'Very low' and 'Limit for taste' respectively have been set by the National Health and Medical Research Council (NHMRC). There is no official upper limit for 'Low', so the Salt Skip Program puts it at 100 (halfway between the two NHMRC figures).

Tap water in some very dry areas of Australia is far too salty in summer. The worst area listed in the Report of the Working Party on Sodium in the Australian Diet (1984) was the Eyre Peninsula in South Australia, which had an average of over 600 mg/L.[1] The capital city with the highest levels of sodium in the water is Adelaide, and Perth is the next saltiest. In summer, water in some parts of Adelaide approaches a sodium level of 200 mg/L, which is perceptibly salty to taste.[1]

The average daily water requirement is 30 mL/kg body weight.[2] Fat doesn't need water, so this refers to ideal body weight. A person whose ideal body weight for height is 70 kg needs about 2 litres of water a day. Most vegetables and fresh foods are between 80 per cent and 90 per cent water, so the volume of separate fluid a 70 kg person needs in a day as water or cups of tea or coffee is about 1 litre.

One litre of low salt water will give you up to 100 mg of sodium. As 24-hour urine results give sodium in millimoles (mmol) and 1 mmol equals 23 mg, 1 litre of low salt water would increase a 24-hour urine result of say 36 mmol/day to 40 mmol/day. You can check your local water supply by phoning the supplier. If in doubt, consider buying bottled water with a low sodium analysis on the label.

In hard water districts the hardness of the water is due to calcium and magnesium salts, and water softeners usually work by absorbing calcium and magnesium and replacing them with sodium. If you use a water softener it is essential for the plumber to provide a tap for drinking (and cooking) water that has not been softened.

Health drinks

A number of so-called health drinks sold as powders or granules to make water more palatable to drink are high in sodium. Some of them fizz in water and may look like a refreshing drink, but will fill you up with large quantities of sodium. The chief offenders are Alka-Seltzer, Dexsal, Efferdex, Eno's Fruit Salt, Fruit Saline and Sal Vital.

Sports drinks such as Powerade, Repalyte and Staminade may be prescribed medically for an acute illness such as gastroenteritis (diarrhoea and vomiting). Take them when prescribed as they are intended to replace sodium, potassium and chloride that your body may have lost. True depletion of sodium does need replacement — the mistake is self-medication with extra sodium that you didn't lose and don't need. For reasons explained in Chapter 14, sportspeople use them to accelerate the absorption of fluid.

Sodium in the pharmacy

Many drugs sold 'over the counter' (without a prescription) in pharmacies contain large amounts of sodium, but you can always ask the pharmacist for a low sodium or sodium-free alternative that works equally well.[3] None of the drugs sold over the counter have an effect that depends on the sodium content. Most prescription drugs, including most antibiotics, are low in sodium, so should not be a problem. You may be unable to take a urinary alkaliser, however, as there isn't one that will suit everybody, but these are not essential drugs.

Cough and cold remedies

None of the cough and cold remedies have a very high sodium content. However, some may contain ingredients that cause a temporary rise in blood pressure, like the pseudoephedrine in products such as Actifed and Sudafed. Check with the pharmacist if you have high blood pressure.

Sodium-free products

Actifed CC, Brondecon, Cosanyl, Drixine, Drixine Cough Suppressant, Elixophylline, Elixophylline KI, Linctus Tussinol, Orthoxicol Expectorant Cough Syrup, Polaramine Expectorant,

Quiactin Children's Cough Linctus, Sudafed, Sudafed Elixir, Sudalix, Tusselix, Vicks Formula 44.

Products with some sodium (less than 23 mg (1 mmol) per dose)

Benadryl Expectorant, Benatuss, Benyphed, Orthoxicol Cough Syrup for Children, Polaramine Cough Suppressant.

High sodium products to avoid

These may contain up to 92 mg (4 mmol) per dose and are best for occasional use only. These are Orthoxicol Syrup, Quiactin Adult Cough Mixture, Vicks Viscoat.

Low sodium tonics

A few drug companies have been supplying mixtures for the old-timers who still turn up for a bottle of 'tonic'. They are all low in sodium. Examples are Accomin, BCM, Clements Tonic.

Artificial sweeteners

Although artificial sweeteners preserve your 'sweet tooth' and prevent you from re-educating your palate, there are times when most people will want a sweetener. Two of the artificial sweeteners are sodium salts — sodium saccharin and sodium cyclamate — but in ordinary use the amount of sodium can be ignored. Aspartame (Equal, Nutrasweet) contains no sodium, but remember that aspartame is destroyed by cooking, and must be added to food or drinks after cooking, or at the time of consumption.

Indigestion remedies

Sodium bicarbonate must be avoided as an indigestion remedy, either when used alone or when mixed with slower ingredients that last longer. On its own it is especially unsuitable, as rebound acidity forces the sufferer to keep taking more bicarbonate and sodium.

Sodium-free indigestion antacids

Almacarb, Aludrox, Alu-Tab, Amphogel, Amphotabs, Andrews tums, Asilone, De-Gas, DeWitts antacid tablets (*avoid the powder*), Digestif

Rennie, Dijene, Gastreze, Gastrobrom, Gastrogel, Maalox, Maalox Plus, Mucaine, Mylanta and Mylanta II liquid and tablets, Quick-Eze Tabs, Rennies, Sodexol, Zantac plain.

Medium sodium antacids

Duoquel supplies a small amount of sodium. Gaviscon supplies almost 100 mg (4 mmol) per dose, and should preferably be avoided.

High sodium antacids to avoid

Some are powders and some are liquids or tablets: Alka-Seltzer, Bradburys Saline, Dexsal Regular, Dexsal Lemon, DeWitts Antacid Powder (DeWitts tablets are okay — read the label), Eno's Fruit Salt, Fruit Saline, Hardys Indigestion Powder, Meracote, Mylanta Plus, Neutralon, Pep-Uls-Ade, Roter Tablets, Sal Vital, Sodibic, Zantac effervescent.

Painkillers

The main traps to look out for are *soluble painkillers*, most of which contain sodium bicarbonate to make them fizz in water. Buy one of the brands of plain aspirin, or soluble tablets based on calcium carbonate with a soluble acid to dissolve it.

Sodium-free and safe to take

Use *plain tablets* containing plain aspirin or aspirin with codeine such as Aspalgin, Aspro, Asprodeine (plain), Bayer Aspirin, Bex, Bufferin, Codiphen, Codis, Codox, Codral, Ecotrin, Solcode and SRA sustained release aspirin.

Alternatively look for *soluble aspirin tablets based on calcium carbonate* such as Aspro Soluble, Disprin, Disprin Direct, Solprin (hospital pack), Veganin.

Both Disprin Direct and Solvin (aspirin glycinate) dissolve in the mouth without water, which is handy for bushwalkers.

Also look for sodium-free paracetamol tablets, plain or with codeine, including Codalgin, Codral Pain Relief, Di-Gesic, Panadol, Tempra.

High sodium pain tablets to avoid

Aspro Clear, Asprodeine Soluble, Panadol Soluble, sodium salicylate.

Premedication for colonoscopy

If salt skippers with Meniere's syndrome need a colonoscopy they are shocked to discover the high sodium content of the premedication prescribed. After controlling their vertigo with a sodium intake below 50 mmol/day, an extra 125 mmol looks extremely risky; in practice the risk is negligible, because the sodium is not absorbed.

Although nothing in medicine can be totally guaranteed (biological phenomena are intrinsically variable), the chances of vertigo are remote. An attack of vertigo would not affect the safety of the procedure, because there is no need for a general anaesthetic. Colonoscopy is usually done for very important medical reasons, and should seldom be deferred.

The drug used in the premedication for colonoscopy is able to pass through the bowel without being absorbed. Several Meniere's patients who control their vertigo with the Salt Skip Program have reported taking the premedication for colonoscopy without incident.

Toothpaste

Toothpastes contain a mild abrasive to remove plaque without damaging the surface of the teeth, so it may be worth avoiding brands that use sodium bicarbonate ('baking soda'), although very little toothpaste would normally be swallowed. Sodium saccharine, sodium cyclamate and sodium fluoride can all be ignored in toothpaste, as the total dose of sodium is extremely small.

Urinary alkalisers

To treat 'waterworks' troubles such as scalding and frequency, drug companies now supply ready-made mixtures and powders containing high doses of sodium citrate. To avoid sodium, a pharmacy can supply the original remedy (potassium citrate mixture).

Sodium-free

Unfortunately potassium citrate is not very palatable. It is also incompatible in high dosage with potassium-sparing diuretics, ACE inhibitors and angiotensin antagonists, and is unsuitable in kidney failure. However, urinary alkalisers have no curative effect.[4] Urinary infections need other medical treatment (discuss this with your doctor).

High sodium drugs to avoid

These include Citralka, Citravescent, Dexcit, Protea, Urade and Ural. Salt skippers who normally live below 50 mmol/day from all sources should note that full doses of Citralka add 370 mmol of sodium to the daily intake and the others supply over 200 mmol. These include Ural, the most popular. Note the special importance of avoiding Ural if you have the vertigo of Meniere's syndrome.

Vitamins and minerals

Healthy people with a good diet shouldn't need vitamin supplements. Some people, however, have irritable bowel syndrome, or other reasons for believing they have a genuine need for vitamins, and should check the sodium content. Nearly all fizzy tablets contain a lot of sodium bicarbonate.

Sodium-free

Most vitamin preparations are sodium free, and too numerous to list here.

High sodium vitamins and minerals to avoid

Those with a high sodium content include Supradyn, Berocca and Redoxon. Vitamin C in megadoses of sodium ascorbate is another product to avoid. Buy plain ascorbic acid or potassium or calcium ascorbate. To avoid giving you a very acid stomach, plain ascorbic acid is seldom sold in tablets larger than 250 mg.

Sandocal-1000 calcium supplement has a very high sodium content of 18 mmol per tablet (except in the UK, where the sodium is zero). For technical reasons Sandoz cannot import the sodium-free version in Australia.

Supradyn comes in two formulations — fizzy tablets and sodium-free capsules. Buy the capsules.

Berocca is available only as the fizzy tablet from Roche, but an alternative with no sodium bicarbonate is Allbee with C, made by AH Robbins. The vitamin content is similar except that Allbee with C has 300 mg of vitamin C instead of Berocca's 1000 mg. The tissues are saturated with vitamin C at 130 mg/day, but if you insist on a mega-dose you can use calcium ascorbate (see below).

Redoxon is Vitamin C in mega-doses (1000 mg), and Roche supplies only the fizzy tablets. Most mega-dose preparations of Vitamin C — including the ones that don't fizz — contain sodium ascorbate, which should be avoided. An alternative is to take two Bioglan calcium ascorbate, 500 mg per tablet. Calcium ascorbate supplies the vitamin with a small calcium supplement.

Thus environmental sources of extra sodium should be fairly easy to avoid. You can check the label when buying drinking water in bottles, and you can check the sodium content of tap water with the local authority. Pharmacies provide the ultimate consumer protection by providing the services of a qualified pharmacist during trading hours, who can answer every question, either from personal knowledge or by consulting the appropriate source. Whenever you are in doubt, have a word with the pharmacist.

16
The problem of what to believe

This book frequently refers to a 'massive international consensus' that 'salt matters', and points out that skipping salt is the uniform official policy worldwide, from the WHO down to the level of national governments, including our own (whose national policies are based on the independent advice of their own expert committees). By now readers must therefore wonder how such a massive consensus could escape the notice of the media, many doctors (sometimes including their own doctor), their favourite naturopath and the TV cooks who add salt liberally to a dish that already contains soy sauce.

Another question is how members of the general public can be expected to distinguish truth from falsehood. This chapter discusses these issues and explains the development of scientific medicine and the new discipline of Evidence-Based Medicine (EBM).

Vested interests

The health benefits of fruit, vegetables and grains have been public knowledge for fifty years, yet an eminent American academic and nutritionist with extensive experience at the interface between government and industry finds the public more confused today about what they are supposed to eat to stay healthy than they were fifty years ago.[1]

It is true that new research may overturn old beliefs, but that is the least of the problems. A stream of contradiction about what foods to choose comes from vested interests that resist modern nutrition policy. During the Second World War the British government tried to secure a 'balanced and varied diet' to prevent malnutrition and deficiency diseases by providing enough kilojoules, protein, fat, carbohydrate, minerals and vitamins. Wartime food policy gave no thought to preventing disorders of middle age; in fact their connection with nutrition was poorly understood. Within a single generation after the war, coronary heart disease became the leading cause of premature death in the industrialised societies, and evidence was mounting that this was only one of many 'diseases of affluence' such as high blood pressure and type 2 diabetes that are now known to be associated with a diet *too rich* in total fat, saturated fat, sugar and salt.[3] Governments were slow to act on the advice of their expert committees, but the food industry was predictably swift, and the media became a battleground for protecting vested interests.

A former best-selling book in Britain (now out of print, but still in the libraries) exposed this 'food scandal'.[2] The latest best-seller on food politics in the US is equally alarming and leaves its readers in no doubt that commercial manipulation, motivated by profit, not health, governs much of what we eat.[1] Vested interests pour out their advertising, political lobbying and other propaganda with huge budgets that far exceed government spending on health promotion.[1]

Big business is keen to stay in business, and a democracy with a free market must accept industrial propaganda as a fact of life. Business fights any health advice that is a genuine threat to its profitability, and there could be no better illustration than the threat the salt industry in the US faced in 1977.

The US Senate Select Committee on Nutrition and Human Needs (the McGovern Committee) recommended that Americans reduce their salt intake to 3 g/day (50 mmol). Fierce lobbying from the US Salt Institute saw the level increased to 5 g/day (85 mmol), but this was still a 50 per cent reduction from the national average of 10 g/day (170 mmol). That little drop of 5 g/day (just under a level teaspoonful) by 280 million Americans would cut annual production of salt by *over half a million tonnes* (check it on your pocket calculator). With that at stake, it was not surprising when media releases regularly contradicted government health messages about reducing salt.

Advice from health professionals

Although health professionals are a more trusted source than the media, they too may contribute to the problem of what to believe. People often mistrust doctors in general, but trust their own doctor; many trust a dietitian or pharmacist. There has been a huge increase in the number of people who rely upon 'alternative practitioners' such as herbalists or naturopaths.

Unfortunately alternative practitioners often promote sea salt, saying the problem with ordinary salt is 'the chemicals that are added to it'. They claim that 'natural sea salt' is not only safe but also an important part of a healthy diet. Trade literature on sea salt and a book by Jacques de Langre, founder of the Grain and Salt Society that distributes Celtic Sea Salt, also make this assertion.[4] Media articles on sea salt tend to quote de Langre as an expert, without revealing his vested interest in Celtic Sea Salt.[5]

It has been known since 1961 that rats develop high blood pressure more easily with sea salt than with ordinary salt.[6] A 1974 study of six tribal societies in the Solomon Islands confirmed that humans also find sea salt at least as harmful as ordinary salt. The group with the highest blood pressure in this study also had the highest salt intake — from cooking their vegetables in seawater.[7]

The president of the Australian Register of Homeopaths claimed in a letter to *The Age* newspaper in 2003 that salt 'in its whole, natural state' contains all the trace elements needed for human health including 2% iodine'.[8] Two per cent would give sea salt an iodine content of 20 000 parts per million (*20 000 micrograms [mcg] per gram*), a very dangerous overdose, while 1.5 micrograms (the real figure)[6] is well below the recommended dietary intake of 150 mcg/day for men and 120 mcg/day for women.

Celtic Sea Salt makes no statement about the iodine content of its product.[9] It doesn't risk court action over a false declaration. Australian iodised salt supplies 25–65 micrograms per gram. Chapter 9 explains how other good sources of iodine can replace iodised salt.

Some people ask if hawthorn, prescribed by their naturopath, is good for blood pressure. A small number of randomised controlled trials of herbal remedies have been published. If there is a good one on hawthorn it may be in the Cochrane Library of randomised controlled trials (discussed later in this chapter), which can be accessed free of charge in Australia.

Many alternative practitioners are sincere professionals who get excellent results with a faithful clientele. Doctors today are trained to recognise the placebo effect of everything they do — a point discussed below — and to remain sceptical about its intrinsic value (if any). At the same time there has been a tradition in British clinical practice to recognise the legitimacy of faith healing, including the method known in the Anglican Church as 'the laying on of hands'. With the right patient some doctors say they have seen this give better results than anything in the British Pharmacopoeia. The right patient is a person with subjective symptoms, such as pain, chronic fatigue, insomnia, or any other disease with a subjective component such as asthma.

Medical scepticism about salt

It is disappointing if your own doctor — the doctor you trust — is not convinced that salt is important. It is understandable, however, for several reasons:

- salt is scarcely mentioned during medical training
- postgraduate medical education still has the same gap
- drug representatives promote new drugs, not healthy lifestyles
- many patients who 'avoid salt' derive no obvious benefit (since they are unaware that the salt in processed foods provides 75 per cent of their salt intake)
- when patients say they 'avoid salt', doctors take their word for it
- doctors seldom check patients' salt intake with 24-hour urine collections, so they fail to discover the high salt intakes of many who believe they 'avoid salt'
- with blood pressure, patients who *really* avoid salt occasionally derive no obvious benefit (see Chapter 12)
- it is quicker to write a prescription than to give dietary and lifestyle advice (in any case patients really need special help — and books like this one — for effective control of their salt intake)
- non-compliance with medication is common, and experience teaches doctors to be even more sceptical about adherence to a change of diet and lifestyle that is radical enough to be effective
- doctors, as well as the general public, are the target of vested interests that conduct a relentless campaign to trivialise, misrepresent and cast doubt on health messages about the dangers of high salt intake.

In addition, no occupation is immune from prejudice. Obstetrician

Ignaz Semmelweis of Vienna provides medicine's classic example. His colleagues ridiculed his simple hygiene in the delivery room (hand washing and a chlorine water rinse). Although this method dramatically reduced the high death rate in the 1840s from childbed fever, and went on saving hundreds of lives — in contrast to the very high death rate in other maternity wards — Semmelweis died without convincing any of his colleagues to try it.[10] More recently, evidence that peptic ulcers respond dramatically to antibiotics was ignored for decades and denied publication in peer-reviewed journals, from what is recognised with hindsight as prejudice.

Some scepticism is valid. Some alternative practitioners argue that their conclusions can be supported by thousands of case histories and that even though they are willing to supply case histories for statistical analysis, herbal clinics can never get research grants. Readers might think thousands of clients should know if they felt better (and law courts listen to reliable witnesses) but the problem here is the placebo effect.

The placebo effect

'Remedies' with no active ingredient (placebos) are often 'beneficial'. They can be compared with any other 'beneficial' treatment to test whether it is really any better than leaving the patient without treatment.

Patients who take a sugar-coated pill that may or may not contain an active drug show that pills containing starch can 'relieve' pain. The placebo reveals how often the pain would have disappeared anyway. It may even have a crop of 'side-effects', for example 48 per cent of 669 men who joined one drug trial complained of sleepiness on the placebo, compared with only 38 per cent of those who took the active drug.[11]

The development of modern drug trials owes a great debt to the late Dr Archie Cochrane, an early champion of Britain's National Health Service, who was reluctant to charge taxpayers for drugs that didn't work. He believed that the health budget should pay for drugs that *actually do something*. Cochrane's legacy is the Cochrane Library, a large repository of randomised controlled trials providing reliable medical evidence.

Controlled trials

In the 18th century fresh fruit seemed to cure scurvy, but in 1747 James Lind was able to prove it. He selected twelve equally ill sailors, being treated by the same doctor in the same sick bay with the same diet, water supply and ventilation, and divided them into six pairs. He gave orthodox treatments (cider, vitriol, vinegar, seawater, nutmeg) to five pairs and after fourteen days none recovered. He gave oranges and lemons to the sixth pair and both recovered in eight days.[12] Trials with control groups are called 'controlled trials'; this one had five control groups.

Single-blind and double-blind trials

A modern criticism of Lind's study is that the sailors knew if they were given fruit, and may have believed that fruit would work. The patient's beliefs can radically change the course of many diseases (but not scurvy, as it happens). Concealing the identity of a tablet, how-ever, can provide 'blind' conditions in which patients are unaware of which treatment they have been given.

The need for 'blind' conditions is obvious when judging a Scotch whisky against an Australian whisky. 'Blind' tastings should give the tasting panel no unintended clues. Single-blind tastings make the panel 'blind' and double-blind tastings make people who serve the whisky 'blind' as well. Double-blind conditions remove the body language that can inadvertently give clues about what is happening. Tablets are identified by code numbers, and the code is broken when all the results are in.

Randomised trials

Originally the first patient was given the active treatment and the second patient the placebo, and so on, alternately. But doctors who knew which treatment was coming next might select a 'suitable' patient. Even minor differences between patients might affect the outcome. The order in which placebos are given needs to occur ran-domly, by tossing dice or by random computer selection.

People on low salt diets can swallow coated tablets that may or may not contain salt. People who get the salt tablets are not on a low salt intake. Again code numbers identify the tablets afterwards. As a double check the best trials make 24–hour urine collections, with results reported only at the end of the trial.

Crossover trials

It is more convincing when treatment and control groups cross over, especially if they cross back again. One trial to determine the effect of alcohol consumption on blood pressure compared a light beer and a normal beer and showed a convincing result by crossing over. Each group changed to the other beer after a month, and returned to its original beer in the third month. Every group had a lower blood pressure when drinking light beer.[13]

The herbal clinic

Where alternative practitioners are willing to present case studies to support their argument for the success of particular treatments, there is no way to separate the real effect from the placebo effect retrospectively in thousands of case histories. Drug companies investigate herbs in the constant search for more effective remedies with fewer side-effects (digitalis and ephedrine are two prescription drugs with herbal origins). Drug companies always seek reliable data by adhering strictly to controlled trials that allow for the placebo effect.

Meanwhile, the placebo effect of a herbal remedy for high blood pressure, such as hawthorn, can lead thousands of people to believe sincerely that it does them good (particularly if it is well promoted). Their doctors may be impressed too — by a small reduction in blood pressure (the placebo effect seen in randomised controlled trials). Modern prescription drugs cannot be sold legally until the drug company supplies evidence to the government that the drugs have an independent effect on the body, by performing better than the placebo in randomised controlled trials.

The illusion of controversy

Threatened food manufacturing industries can defend themselves by attacking the consensus on sugar, meat or salt and preserving the illusion of 'controversy'. In this way media messages from nutritionists and public health authorities become 'controversial' because they are promptly contradicted or undermined by media releases from the threatened industry.

Academic medical sceptics

The US Salt Institute has active professional support from academic medical sceptics with good access to the medical press, some of whom serve as paid consultants on the Salt Institute's medical advisory board to advise it on tactics.

Scepticism is good science, and the academic sceptics may still have various reservations about salt after examining all the scientific evidence. As every major issue in science generates controversy, it would be surprising if salt were different. Now that the controversy is being replaced by a broad international scientific agreement that high sodium intakes are largely responsible for increased blood pressure, the handful of remaining salt sceptics play a valuable role as devil's advocates, for which they deserve due attention and respect.

The US Salt Institute was able to find sixteen academic sceptics who were prepared to sign its 'Citizen's Petition' to the US Federal Drug Administration (FDA) in 1996. The FDA allows labels on low salt foods to say that a low salt diet would reduce the risk of high blood pressure. The petition summarised the best arguments the academic sceptics could produce and asked the FDA to rescind the regulation.[14] Before the FDA could respond, the Salt Institute withdrew the petition without giving a reason.[15]

Controversial American journalist Gary Taubes was able to interview twenty-two sceptics. He set the opinions of those twenty-two against those of twenty other researchers in an article for the journal *Science* that described the salt debate as 'one of the longest running, most vitriolic, and surreal disputes in all of medicine'.[16] He commented that 'all a researcher needs to do is to randomise subjects into two groups, one reducing salt intake, one eating normally, and then see what happens. But the results were as ambiguous as anything else in the salt dispute'.[16]

Taubes missed the central problem — *the variability of dietary compliance*. Epidemiology distinguishes between studies of *effectiveness* (the effectiveness of giving dietary advice) and *efficacy* (the efficacy of full compliance).[17] Effectiveness trials illustrate the difficulty of change in a food market that doesn't cater for change. The salt debate is all about efficacy — whether it is *worth* changing. It is easy to guess what happens to people who fail to change very much.

The cost of supplying the food makes *efficacy* trials rare. The last big one was the DASH–Sodium study which compared the standard American diet at three levels of salt intake with a healthier diet (the DASH diet) that was also delivered at the same three levels of salt intake (see Chapter 12). DASH–Sodium was about to begin when Taubes wrote his article. Its results were so convincing, both with high blood pressure and 'normal' blood pressure above 120/80 (pre-hypertension), that a US government web page recommended regulatory agencies to consider a dietary intake of 65 mmol/day as the upper limit for the general population for both treatment and *prevention* of high blood pressure.[18,19]

Conflict of interest

The devil's advocates associated with the Salt Institute nowadays face some discrimination. A letter to a medical journal may appear with an editor's note that the author has 'attended consulting meetings with the Salt Institute'.[20] This warns readers of the possibility of conflict of interest.

Conflict of interest became an issue when tobacco companies demanded 'proof' that cigarettes were harmful, and tried to disarm their critics by providing funds for scientific research. Research grants are very hard to get and the grant is usually smaller than the amount requested, but tobacco money was readily available and generous. Leading scientific journals responded by requiring authors to declare any 'conflict of interest', and the financial link with the tobacco industry suddenly made articles on smoking less convincing. Ultimately leading journals refused even to publish them.

Conflict of interest is a matter of judgement. A large amount of good research on nutrition in Australia depends on food industry sponsorship, and would be impossible without it. The Australian Meat & Livestock Corporation, for example, is one of several bodies that have gained wide respect for their support of worthwhile nutrition research.

In theory, conflict of interest shouldn't matter — a work should be judged 'on its merits, rather than on the inferred state of mind of the author'.[21] In practice the real world uses a test the Romans gave us

— *cui bono*? (who benefits?) — and takes less notice of a paper on the health benefits of butter if the dairy industry supports the study. Devil's advocates are helpful when they are independent, but less convincing when they are consultants to a threatened industry with a vested interest in what the consultants say.

Controlled trials are not always possible

When the tobacco industry made parrot-cries for 'further research' to prove the dangers of smoking, it knew perfectly well that randomised, double-blind, controlled trials were impossible. It could claim there was 'no proof' because no doctor or ethics committee would allow trials to give people lung cancer.

Cigarettes came under strong suspicion when it was found that lung cancer patients were nearly all smokers, while patients with other diseases had the normal ratio of smokers to non-smokers. Case comparisons like this ('case-control studies') led to a search for supporting evidence, and epidemiology provided that too.

A large number of British doctors supplied an annual report of their smoking habits and state of health. After twenty years the data showed that smoking doctors were twenty times more likely to get lung cancer than non-smokers. The risk tapered off in doctors who quit smoking, and fell to the same risk as non-smokers within ten years. No one could doubt any longer that smoking is the main cause of lung cancer.[22]

The power of evidence-based medicine

Nevertheless, when randomised controlled trials are feasible they provide the strong foundation for Evidence-Based Medicine (EBM), which treats long-held medical beliefs with suspicion until they are properly validated. In theory EBM gives medicine an open mind.

EBM might have saved us from spending several decades clinging to the traditional beliefs about peptic ulcers, ignoring the benefit of antibiotics and overlooking the infective origin of ulcers. But EBM arrived recently and is only a remedy (not a certain cure) for blind scepticism. When randomised controlled trials became the 'gold standard' of medical evidence, there was a further refinement. Analysis of data pooled from several trials (a 'meta-analysis') was thought to provide even greater certainty and meta-analysis became 'the ultimate gold standard'.

An international group of obstetricians collaborated in organising meta-analyses of randomised controlled trials on every aspect of pregnancy and delivery. They published a compendium of meta-analyses that has shaken obstetrics all over the world.[23,24] This dramatic step forward gave us the International Cochrane Collaboration. Interested groups (Cochrane Centres) are now developing meta-analyses of all the randomised trials so far published in all branches of medicine, in the expectation that similar advances in other fields would match the outstanding contribution of this method to obstetrics.

A misleading media release

Everybody expects a media release that quotes the Cochrane Collaboration to contain reliable evidence, yet the salt debate seems to be ill-fated. In January 2003 the Cochrane Collaboration's Hypertension Review Group issued a globally quoted media release claiming that two research teams studied 'over 100 trials', and *'available evidence does not suggest people with normal blood pressure should reduce the amount of salt in their food and drink'*.

Members of the Australian Medical Association saw this statement in their newsletter, quoting the Cochrane Collaboration, their most trusted source of EBM.[25] The general public learnt in the mainstream media that 'a review of the medical literature demonstrates that the benefits of a low salt diet are marginal' [26] and 'next time you're asked whether you'd like salt with your fish and chips you may accept guilt free'.[27]

This happened because the result of a meta-analysis depends on how the authors select the trials for inclusion. The selection criteria can convert 'the ultimate gold standard' into a disastrous blunder.

Two meta-analyses provided the total of 'over 100 trials'. In the first the average duration of trials with normal blood pressure was only eight days.[28] Even drugs need four to six weeks to show the full effect. Low salt diets need about five weeks and don't get far in eight days.[29] The study should have excluded short trials that were unable — and never intended — to measure the full effect (they measure other effects, such as short-term hormonal or metabolic changes). This is a rather basic mistake and one that the authors of the second meta-analysis said they were avoiding.[30–33] Yet peer review either failed to notice it, or was ignored after noticing it (as may happen).

However, both meta-analyses made another critical mistake. Both reported old *effectiveness* studies, with limited results due to limited dietary compliance. The salt debate is about *the efficacy of a low sodium excretion rate* (not the effectiveness of partial dietary compliance). This globally quoted media release turned a contentious conclusion into a potentially major setback to public health and good clinical practice. Global setbacks on this scale could be worth millions of dollars to the salt industry and some sections of the food industry.[34,35]

Fortunately Cochrane Reviews are ongoing. They are updated regularly every quarter when a Cochrane Collaboration receives comments from readers. Comments and criticisms are published and flagged along with the complete review, and the original authors of the review are invited to respond.[36] Future updates will point out the authenticity of efficacy studies like the DASH–Sodium study, and the critical error of diluting the results of an efficacy study in a meta-analysis that combines them with data from effectiveness studies. It is ironic that Cochrane himself gave modern epidemiology this fundamental distinction between studies of efficacy and studies of effectiveness.[37,38]

Some salt sceptics accuse public health advocates of using data of dubious quality contained in 'the totality of the evidence'. They stress the value of randomised controlled trials and EBM almost to the point of excluding other evidence.[39] EBM is a radical advance, but public health needs *all the available evidence, including extensive data based on observation and inference.* There are whole branches of modern science such as astronomy that depend almost exclusively on observation and inference. Observation and inference provided nearly everything we know about the cosmos — including a wealth of data used in the moon landing, without which the landing could never have happened. Public health is like that too.

For the wrong reasons, as we have seen, anecdotal evidence ('it worked for me') will remain the most powerful evidence for most people. Thus the readers with the least problem in deciding what to believe will be those who can abolish the severe vertigo of Meniere's syndrome by skipping salt. They will know very well that it's not a placebo effect if they return to a higher salt intake.

Women with the symptoms of severe PMS will know within a month if skipping salt helps them. They should not be satisfied with partial relief — they should ask their doctors in that case to let them check their progress with a 24-hour urine test to make quite sure their sodium excretion is below 40 mmol/day (the level that confirms they are following the Australian dietary guideline and choosing low salt foods exclusively).

To believe that skipping salt will also prevent high blood pressure, readers would need to spend a decade or two in a salt skipping community in which everybody's blood pressure behaved like that of the salt skipping tribal societies, and showed little if any rise with age. This incidentally would be much more convincing than anecdotal evidence — the devil's advocates would be hard-pressed to explain it away. The strong argument for setting up such communities is discussed in the next chapter.

17
Can we abolish high blood pressure?

Evidence that high blood pressure is preventable dates from 1904, but the 20th century has passed without a practical test of the mounting evidence.[1] Will the 21st century find a way to test this proposition? I believe it will. A test is long overdue, and this chapter is an outline of the main grounds for optimism.

It may be impossible to abolish high blood pressure in a society that eats only what the multinational food companies find most profitable to sell, but this chapter points out that salt skippers already have friends — food companies that sell low salt foods. A better-informed public needs to find these products and increase their turnover. At present decisive government action is obstructed by public ignorance and apathy — a stalemate that has to be broken, not just by community awareness but also by *community action*. A lot of people must start testing for themselves the long-term benefits of the healthy diet and lifestyle that works so well in the salt-free societies. With the right leadership coming in the first instance from outside government I believe anything is possible.

This chapter discusses a few of the practical and ethical difficulties of attempting to abolish high blood pressure and describes some small but promising advances that have already been made — advances that in my opinion point clearly to the ultimate feasibility of this dream that high blood pressure can one day be abolished. The dream has a very solid foundation — the unequivocal fact that a salt-skipping lifestyle, along with a normal body weight, regular exercise and moderation with alcohol, has been simple enough to allow about twenty salt-free tribal societies to prevent high blood pressure automatically for millennia.[2] Such a lifestyle gives these ordinary people virtually no high blood pressure and little if any increase in blood pressure with age.[3] If they can do it, surely we can do it.

Who controls what we eat?

A big problem in industrialised societies is that multinational firms manufacture and distribute most of our food and drink; *they* decide its fat, sugar and salt content, as well as manipulate through advertising and promotion the great majority of media messages about food.

Multinational food manufacturers infiltrate the bureaucracy and the legislature in many countries, manipulating administrative decisions to their own commercial advantage. The *Guardian* newspaper in London reported on 9 January 2003 that the food industry had even infiltrated the WHO, just as the tobacco industry did.[4] The first responsibility of these companies is to their shareholders, so that commercial profit will always come before the public health. Accusation and blame would be futile — this is how the free market works — but to abolish high blood pressure this obstacle has to be recognised from the outset. It's a big obstacle, but by no means insurmountable. Many sections of the food industry are trying to help salt skippers — there is already a niche market. In the end the consumer is the final arbiter. The industry can sell nothing unless we — the consumers — are willing to buy it.

Bringing about change

Change is long overdue. In 2002 the executive director of the American Public Health Association (APHA) told the annual general meeting, 'America is hooked on snacks and foods high in sodium'. The meeting called for a fundamental shift in the nutrient composition of processed foods, along with a change in consumer behaviour. The new APHA policy called for a 50 per cent reduction in the sodium content of processed foods over the next ten years, educating consumers to choose lower sodium foods, and making prevention and control of high blood pressure a higher priority throughout the United States.

Twenty-five years earlier, however, a US Senate Select Committee (the McGovern Committee) had recommended the same 50 per cent reduction in salt intake for the same reasons. In 1977 Mark

Hegsted, professor of nutrition at Harvard University, told the committee that the American diet was not planned — it was just an accidental mix-up of affluence, farm productivity and food technology. He said: 'Heart disease, cancer, diabetes and hypertension are the diseases that kill us. They are epidemic in our population ... We have an obligation ... to assist the public in making the correct food choices'.[5]

Companies with vested interests in fat, salt and sugar have strongly resisted much health reform suggested by state and federal governments and non-government health agencies in the US and other industrialised societies. They have successfully preserved a stalemate for a quarter of a century. The fat message has been given the most lip service, while salt has been the Cinderella, the most neglected and the least understood health message.

Somebody must do something, but the question is — Who? And what should be done? The Salt Institute, its medical advisory board and other sceptics demand that a randomised controlled trial be carried out to show the efficacy of a low salt diet. Meanwhile they try to ensure that the general public receives as little advice as possible about salt intake.[6]

A large randomised controlled trial

The sceptics agree that it is worth avoiding salt if you have high blood pressure. The central issue of the salt debate is *whether everybody else should skip salt to **prevent** high blood pressure before it develops*. High blood pressure is usually symptomless, and sceptics in the salt debate want proof that skipping salt will prevent strokes, heart attacks and kidney failure. They also want proof of the safety of a lower salt intake ('the benefit must outweigh the risk'). They insist that large, long-term, randomised controlled trials would be feasible and affordable.

The Framingham study followed 6000 people for twenty years searching for causes of coronary heart disease.[7] A salt trial would need a diet group and a control group. The diet group would skip salt while the control group continued the usual Australian rate of salt intake. A study with two samples would observe 12 000 people for twenty years. A randomised trial would mean that volunteers would have to take part without knowing beforehand if *for the next twenty years* they would skip salt or not. When they knew they might decide to withdraw, or perform badly. Both actions would make the study yet another inconclusive trial of *effectiveness* rather than efficacy (a very important distinction explained in Chapter 16).

A long-term *efficacy* trial (the efficacy of genuinely skipping salt) would have to provide the food (just as the DASH–Sodium study did), which would explode the budget with the cost of all the food eaten by 12 000 people for twenty years. Free meals for twenty years might help recruitment, but only a country like the United States could afford such a trial. When a workshop set up by the National Heart, Lung and Blood Institute discussed the feasibility of such a trial, it regarded the cost as prohibitive, even without feeding 12 000 people for twenty years.[8]

The ethical problems are even more formidable. There is an assumption that everybody would join the trial with a normal blood pressure and many would show the usual increase in blood pressure with age, especially in the control group, where some people would develop high blood pressure. There is a further assumption that the control group would eventually have more heart attacks and strokes than the diet group. However, for ethical reasons all members of the control group who developed high blood pressure would have to be treated, and even the sceptics would agree that they must skip salt now — but that means they are now in the control group in name only. Members of the control group — the main candidates for strokes and heart attacks — would have adopted the same diet and lifestyle as the diet group, destroying the difference between the two groups.

Moreover, such a study would not be funded unless it followed the latest US guidelines, which recommend that people with prehypertension skip salt too.[9] This would create further problems:

- People whose blood pressure was above 120/80 would be excluded (they have prehypertension and need treatment with a diet and lifestyle that would make them unsuitable for the control group).
- A study confined to people entering with such low blood pressure would need an even larger sample and longer duration.
- When blood pressure rose to 120/80 or above in members of the control group, they would move to a low salt diet. As a control group it would gradually be destroyed.

It is not surprising that none of the salt sceptics has ever put forward a practical proposal for such a randomised trial. Devil's advocates have published no convincing evidence of health risks resulting from skipping salt, so we still have no grounds for warning anybody against skipping salt. This is reassuring but hardly surprising (when we remember that skipping salt is simply returning to the salt intake on which humans evolved, and on which about twenty tribal societies still thrive).

It would be a great pity to succeed in preventing high blood pressure without any data to confirm that crowning achievement. An effect should be measurable in national health statistics. A *region with a low salt cuisine* could provide local statistics. It would be a happy hunting ground for epidemiologists to link salt intake with health outcomes, and for sceptics to go on looking for any adverse effects. Although the main aim of skipping salt is to prevent high blood pressure, the evidence that 'the benefits outweigh the harm' should take full account of the great benefit to all the other health problems linked with salt that were presented in Chapter 13.

Changing public health policy

There are two main approaches to introducing changes in public health policy:
- to promote gradual change in the whole population (population approach), or
- to concentrate on the radical change needed by those who are at high risk or already sick (high risk approach).

The two methods can be carried out side by side. Both could be applied in a national campaign or at greater intensity in a local region. The high risk approach looks dramatic when sick people make radical changes. They realise how well they might have been if they had adopted this diet and lifestyle earlier — they might never have been sick in the first place. A paradox of public health, however, is that the population approach alters the national death rates sooner, because the high risk group is too small to alter the average rates very much. In the population approach small differences in the average blood pressure of the whole population can make surprising differences in national death rates from stroke and heart attack.[10,11] Public ignorance creates the catch-22 problem that supply depends on demand, yet there is no demand before the product is on the shelf.

The public needs to learn that processed foods supply 75 per cent of the salt they eat. Next, they need to learn that taste is not a guide to salt content in food — checking the food label is crucial. Some sections of the food industry lobbied strenuously to prevent Australia and New Zealand from introducing mandatory nutrition information panels on food labels, even though they knew the panel could hardly be described as self-explanatory. Although they are here at last, shoppers often overlook nutrition information panels — they are of little value until consumers know how to read and understand them. An education program is necessary.

Learning to read food labels

Motivated salt skippers (sick people in the high risk approach) can learn to read food labels quite easily. They find Australian food labels user-friendly. The Menzies Clinic collects packets and tins of some of the main low salt foods to show people what they are looking for, along with examples of a few very salty ones for comparison. In more than ten years, only two patients have left without being able to read food labels accurately for sodium. One patient had early dementia and the other was semi-literate, but came along with a partner who could read the labels without difficulty.

Salt skippers don't need to look at serving sizes and try to add up the day's sodium intake — that is too much work, and too inaccurate. Rather, they just *choose foods low in salt*. At a sodium figure below 120 mg/100 g the food is low in salt. Salt skippers who choose the right foods are not on a diet — they eat as much or as little as they like, limited only by appetite and common sense.

However, there are sections of the food industry with a vested interest in high salt products and thus a vested interest in public ignorance, who strongly object to publication of simple details that would let consumers make an informed choice. These organisations are so influential that we may never see labels telling shoppers in plain language if the food is *high*, *medium* or *low* in energy, protein, fat, carbohydrate or salt.

There is a dilemma with salt, however, and that is that explicit information might go either way with the general public — the population approach. Many shoppers believe (because their palates tell them) that salt is essential for flavour, and would buy 'normal' foods in preference to low salt foods. Palates adapted to foods preserved with salt need education and time to adapt to low salt foods. The same applies to fat, and for this reason the National Heart Foundations of Australia and New Zealand have tried to educate consumers with their 'Pick the Tick' program, based on gradual change. The Heart Foundation has found it difficult to go all the way with the Australian dietary guideline on salt, for a variety of reasons discussed below. One is that both fat and salt affect current perceptions of palatability, and in the event of a compromise the Heart Foundation's first priority is fat.

'Pick the Tick' program

A single 'Tick' identifies the foods that are a healthier choice. It sounds ideal. Shoppers benefit from better foods, modified to comply with the Heart Foundation criteria, and the 'Tick' identifies these foods at a glance at the point of sale. The food industry joins willingly, expecting the Heart Foundation's endorsement to increase sales and profits. It has been an extremely worthwhile experiment, and its track record has shown more advantages than disadvantages.

Inevitably a diet acceptable to everybody (the population approach) is a compromise between the ideal and the feasible. The best possible diet for a speedy recovery from heart disease or high blood pressure would be ideal, but the general public wouldn't buy it because there is too wide a gap between the ideal and the fare that is currently popular. Thus the 'Tick' designed for everybody has bread with a sodium content up to 450 mg/100 g and this is no use to salt skippers.

Bread and cheese, two major food items, create their own special problems. When reduced salt bread was included in the 'Tick' program, it didn't sell well. A program like the 'Tick' system has to increase profits — it must at least pay the manufacturer's entrance fee to the 'Tick' program and annual royalties that cover the Heart Foundation's overheads, which include the cost of monitoring the composition of every food (with samples bought in the open market and analysed at random intervals at a central laboratory). To make the program work, the Heart Foundation had to raise the sodium criterion for bread from the original upper limit of 345 mg/100 g to 450 mg/100 g. This is so high that it brought it within the Australian range for standard bread (400–725 mg/100 g).

Cheese is no longer recognisable as cheese if it is low in both fat and salt — the dairy industry can make either low fat cheese or low salt cheese. The Salt Skip Program's compromise is Salt Skip *low* salt, *reduced* fat cheddar, while the Heart Foundation gives greater priority to reducing the fat further in cheese, especially saturated fat, and endorsing a low fat cheese, which is impossible to make if the salt is also low.

The Heart Foundation's gradual approach sometimes invites professional accusations of timidity and half-measures. Health professionals may ask why breakfast cereals with a sodium content as high as 400 mg/100 g can carry the 'Tick' when for a decade up to 2003 Australia's best-selling ready-to-eat breakfast cereal (Weet-Bix) has had a sodium content of only 280 mg/100 g.

The Heart Foundation has an answer. One effect of the ceiling of 400 mg/100 g has been to reduce the salt content of very salty cereals. Reducing the sodium content of All Bran (sodium 849 mg/100 g) by 55 per cent to 380 mg/100 g met the criterion for the 'Tick'. In 1997 the Kellogg company alone removed 235 tonnes of salt annually from the Australian food supply and several New Zealand food companies made reductions in bread, breakfast cereals and margarine that removed about 33 tonnes annually from the New Zealand food supply.[12,13]

On the whole the Australian and New Zealand Heart Foundations have done well. They have improved two national diets, and continue to improve them. A major review in 2003 and 2004 reduced the sodium criteria for the 'Tick' in a number of products and withdrew processed cheeses altogether from the 'Tick' list of eligible foods, because with present food technology it is impossible to reduce their very high sodium content.

It is a great disappointment that a staple as important as bread will be a permanent exception for commercial reasons, with a sodium content remaining indefinitely at 450 mg/100 g. Salt (not fat or sugar) is the problem with bread, and a health program allowing a permanently high salt content in bread can never abolish high blood pressure.

One disadvantage of a self-funded program run by a non-government agency is that many eligible companies don't take the financial risk of joining, so many products have no 'Tick', even though they qualify for it. Government funding could rectify these problems and even alter the bread policy. The two 'Tick' programs are working models for government-funded systems. They are already efficient and it would be cheaper and better for the government to subsidise them than to compete with them. Government subsidies would allow all companies with eligible products to apply for the 'Tick' without any entrance fee or annual royalties.

Revenue-neutral taxes and subsidies could improve the demand for low salt bread, giving the patients in the high-risk approach the bread they need. The same fiscal policy could create some turnover for low salt bread in the population approach if it used a low salt bread recipe (patented in Hobart) that is surprisingly palatable to people with salt–adapted palates.

The delicate question of coercion

It's not the customer's fault that so many choices in the supermarket contain too much saturated fat, sugar and salt. People eat what is most profitable for the food industry to sell. When food is contaminated governments can act at once, but they are powerless to help consumers by controlling the sale of foods that provide poor nutrition (because so many voters are fond of them and can't see — and don't want to know — what's wrong with these foods). If consumer pressure eventually changes the politics, health *promotion* can do more. Health *promotion* can include legislation, inspection and enforcement where appropriate, but only when it is politically feasible.[14]

With community support governments can already tax cigarettes. One day a 2-cent tax on high salt foods and a 2-cent subsidy on low salt foods might change patterns of consumption, or could be adjusted until it did. The tax and subsidy could balance one another and be revenue-neutral. People could still buy salty foods, but reduced salt foods would be cheaper (no tax), and low salt foods would be cheaper still (subsidised). Governments won't suggest this — consumers have to. Only strong pressure will persuade a government to act decisively. Governments don't lead public opinion (it is politically safer to follow).

Finland is one country that already uses fiscal pressure in the high risk approach to health policy. The government withholds the subsidy on drugs for high blood pressure unless the doctor certifies that the patient has followed an ideal diet and lifestyle for six months, including skipping salt. If drugs are still needed despite that background, the doctor must also certify that the patient agrees to continue an ideal diet and lifestyle indefinitely (to permit better control at a lower dose).

In Australia, the last Heart Foundation survey showed that 16 per cent of Australians aged twenty to sixty-nine had high blood pressure, therefore the total population in 2003 of over 19 million would provide two million customers (16 per cent of over 12 million people in that age range) for low salt foods for high blood pressure alone.[15] The single drug enalapril, which cost the government $60 million in 1998, is an ACE inhibitor, and works better — and at lower doses — when the patient skips salt.

Even an idea originally as controversial as seatbelt legislation was politically feasible. The Victorian parliament responded to strong pressure from the Australasian College of Surgeons. All Australian states and territories followed suit within twelve months, and seatbelt legislation today saves lives all over the world.

We need community action on salt, from concerned citizens acting on their own initiative. This is not a fanciful idea — it actually happened in Britain in 1996, when a dozen medical specialists with research credentials on salt and high blood pressure founded CASH (Consensus Action on Salt and Health). They adopted the population approach, and CASH organises an annual Salt Awareness Day in the UK to promote reduced salt foods and persuade people to start cutting down their excessively high salt intake. It aims at a gradual and progressive reduction in the salt content of as many processed foods as possible, and works chiefly with major supermarkets. CASH also has a dialogue with government agencies in an effort to improve food labelling.

After an approach from CASH, the UK Food and Drink Federation (the main umbrella organisation for the food and soft drink industries) reported that it would be feasible to reduce the salt content of a whole range of processed foods by as much as 10–25 per cent without loss of safety or palatability. Palatability is a subjective judgement that adapts to the customary salt intake, both upwards and downwards.[16,17] This means that the initial reduction of 10–25 per cent doesn't have to stop there. It can be followed later by further reductions.

In recent years Sainsburys, ASDA and Co-op led a number of UK supermarket chains in reducing the salt content of their own 'home brand' products and telling their suppliers they were interested in stocking products containing less salt. The result in Britain has been an annual reduction of several thousand tonnes of salt from the food supply, across a broad range of processed foods, including many ready-made meals, crisps, sausages and breads.

Encouraged by these successes, CASH is planning to set up World Action on Salt and Health (WASH). Global action is needed to counter the opposition of multinational companies that supply so many of the world's foods and drinks, especially processed meats and soft drinks. One option for Australia would be to join WASH.

Help from the food industry

Some sections of the food industry specialise in high salt foods such as smallgoods and snack foods, and strongly resist change.[18] Nevertheless, many food manufacturing companies deserve full credit for *reducing* the salt content of their products. The sodium content drops sometimes by as much as 50 per cent, occasionally more. Some previously salty foods have already become low salt foods.

Consider the brilliant performance of Kellogg (Australia). The Heart Foundation 'Tick' may have influenced it, but Kellogg went further on its own initiative, reducing the sodium content of the cereal Just Right from 284 to 49 mg/100 g — an 83 per cent reduction — even though the sodium content of 284 mg/100 g had qualified it for the 'Tick' without any reduction.

Kellogg (Australia) reduced salt in products across the board. Some cereals remained too high for the 'Tick' system, but at the other extreme the Kellogg's brand acquired no less than twelve low salt cereals (with sodium levels of 120 mg/100 g or less). A diet of these and other low salt foods would be expected to abolish high blood pressure in a community that controlled the other errors of diet and lifestyle. This company now gives its customers a wide choice.

In 2001 a few people bought the wrong packet when Kellogg

tested the Australian market with the UK recipe for Just Right (sodium 600 mg/100 g). The experiment was short-lived. Since 2002 Australia has had three cereals called Just Right, with three different sodium claims — 49 mg/100 g ('Original'), 112 mg/100 g ('Just Right Just Grains') and 225 mg/100 g ('Just Right Fruit'n'Flakes').

Coles supermarkets have done more than any other Australian food company to help people who wish to avoid salt. They introduced a no-added-salt range in their Farmland groceries in 1983, which had expanded to twenty-three products by 1987. Their initiative proved to their competitors that a market existed. In peanut butter, for example, the Farmland brand now shares the market with two other brands of no-added-salt peanut butter.

Choice magazine (the publication of the Australian Consumers' Association) made an interesting comparison between fourteen standard peanut butters and three no-added-salt peanut butters. The sodium content ranged from 395 to 605 mg/100 g in the standard brands, and from 6 to 10 mg/100 g in the other three. As there were no reduced salt peanut butters this was a contest between the unmodified standard product and a radically different one meant for the high risk approach. The thirty people who tasted them predictably placed the no-added-salt peanut butters at the bottom of the list. However, the peanut butter with 10 mg/100 g came in at fourteenth place, above a standard peanut butter with 580 mg/100 g.[19]

Choice recommended no-added-salt peanut butter for people who 'watch their salt intake'. They also recommended it for *children* (the tasting panel were adapted to salty peanut butter), and advised their readers that *children who didn't ear salted peanut butter wouldn't acquire the taste*.[19]

Another company working to help consumers looking for low salt foods is the small health food company Freedom Foods. It has a relatively high turnover through being well represented on the health food shelves of major supermarket chains. Almost its whole range consists of low salt foods, with the exception of a few products made with ordinary baking powder.

Other companies producing low salt foods include FC Newman and Variety Dash. Most of the horseradish sauce eaten in South Australia is FC Newman's Red Label brand, made without added salt or fat. The same company sells several other foods preserved in vinegar without added salt, including garlic and ginger. Variety Dash is another supermarket brand of garlic and ginger preserved without salt, and made from fresh unsalted ingredients. Shoppers buy these products for the flavour without noticing the sodium content.

These and other friends in the food industry deserve better support — consumers are letting them down. Since the 1980s many excellent new low salt processed foods have been withdrawn within a year or two for lack of a rapidly vigorous sales turnover. ETA, for example, discontinued a very tasty low salt barbecue sauce, and Weston Biscuits discontinued their excellent no-added-salt Ryvita crispbread, which had been very popular with salt skippers.

Catering for low salt lifestyles

Each state could form a support group for people with high blood pressure, or better still for all salt skippers, whatever their reason for skipping salt. The QHA is already a de facto national support group for salt skippers, with members in all Australian states and territories. Many of its most active members skip salt in order to control vertigo.

Every Australian state needs a health resort like the one founded by Maurie and Gwen Rayner in 1985 at Bellbrae, near Bell's Beach in Victoria, a famous mecca for surfers. A holiday venue in each state where residents can attend cookery classes that observe all the Australian dietary guidelines, including the salt guideline, could become the focal point of a low salt district attracting salt skippers from all over the state. Unfortunately, the Bellbrae resort had to close at the height of its popularity, when a building program to expand the accommodation came to an abrupt halt with the collapse of the Victorian Pyramid Building Society in the early 1990s.

Bellbrae followed the Pritikin program in principle but adopted Australia's version (stricter with bread) and provided excellent wholemeal salt-free bread as well as salt-free meals, and used sodium-free baking powder.[20] (The original Pritikin program uses reduced salt bread and only limits sodium intake to 70 mmol/day [1600 mg/day].) The Bellbrae cuisine was inspired by Julie Stafford's cookbook *Taste of Life*.[21] First published in 1983, this low salt cookbook sold over two million copies before going out of print in 2003.

In 1986 quantitative data were collected at Bellbrae, by arrangement with a very cooperative management. Twelve residential guests at the resort (six men and six women) agreed to make 24-hour urine collections over a period of two weeks.[22] The average sodium excretion of the group was 19 mmol/day. One woman provided the lowest sodium result (5 mmol) and another provided the highest (35 mmol). As explained in Appendix 1, diuretics would be unnecessary — and could be dangerous — for people guided by popular cookbooks that can get positive results like this.[22]

Bellbrae had many regular visitors from interstate. Although it was fairly expensive, it gave value for money. Given the demand, a low salt youth hostel, backpackers' hotel, caravan park and camping ground in the same district could cater for all incomes. If all those at high risk in a geographical region began to ask for the food they really needed, restaurants would be able to cater for a large and growing low salt clientele. Eventually a regional low salt cuisine might emerge with multiple ethnic variations, including perhaps several versions of the Mediterranean cuisine such as low salt Italian, Greek, and Lebanese cuisines, and several varieties of low salt Asian cuisine including Chinese, Thai and Vietnamese.

Reasons for serious concern

Cost of high blood pressure

In 1984 the annual cost of cardiovascular disease in Australia was already put at up to $2 billion, and by 1993–94 it had risen to $3.7 billion.[23,24] Cardiovascular disease consists of high blood pressure and the fatal diseases to which it strongly contributes (coronary heart disease, heart failure, stroke and other diseases of the blood vessels such as peripheral vascular disease, which can cause loss of a limb from gangrene). High blood pressure alone cost Australia $0.83 billion in 1993–94 and stroke (which would be very rare in the absence of high blood pressure) cost $0.63 billion.[24] A single drug for high blood pressure (enalapril) cost the government about $60 million a year in 1998.[25] Abolishing high blood pressure would transform the total health budget. Consider also the social cost. The 40 000 strokes that occur each year cause nearly 25 per cent of all chronic disability in Australia.[26]

The size of the international consensus

Since 1993 in the US, the FDA has allowed labels on low salt foods to carry a health claim saying that diets low in sodium may reduce the risk of high blood pressure. Would such a conservative body as the FDA allow health claims on food labels for a decade if there were not international scientific and medical agreement about the value of reducing salt intakes in our diets? The American Public Health Association in 2002 called for a 50 per cent reduction in the salt content of processed foods. Would it go public with such a radical proposal in the absence of an overwhelming consensus? The US government's Joint National Committee on Prevention, Detection, Evaluation and Treatment of High Blood Pressure has issued periodic reports advocating better lifestyle, including low salt intake, for twenty years, and the latest was supported in 2003 by thirty-nine national professional, public and voluntary health organisations and seven federal agencies.[9]

The US is not alone in its consensus that salt matters. The developed nations, including Britain and Australia, support the same consensus.[27,28] The existence of a few noisy sceptics cannot destroy a consensus.

Destroying an industry

The dietary guideline to choose low salt foods threatens to cripple a huge industry. About 90 per cent of the total output of the salt industry is industrial which would be unaffected by a lower consumption of edible salt. Nevertheless, the US alone consumes over a million tonnes of edible salt a year, and might need only 40 per cent of that at the sodium intake of 65 mmol/day recommended by the US national government after the DASH-Sodium study.[29]

The industry will have to diversify to survive, just as the tobacco, sugar and beef industries have done. Consideration could be given to government assistance, with special tax concessions, inducements and compensation for loss of production. A condition of government assistance would be to abandon the campaign of opposition to government promotion of low salt foods in the industry's publications, media releases and web pages.

The US Salt Institute and its counterparts, the UK Salt Manufacturers' Association and European Salt Producers'

Association, are non-profit trade organisations representing the manufacturers. Their purpose is to defend their members with every legal means at their disposal. But any industry that saw its business dwindle to 40 per cent of its former turnover as a direct result of government health policy would surely have a good case for government assistance in return for its huge losses.

Low salt foods should not be negotiable

To curtail the epidemic of high blood pressure the sodium excretion of the whole population should be limited to the 65 mmol/day of the DASH-Sodium study.[30] In routine clinical practice at the Menzies Institute, people who follow the dietary guideline to choose foods low in salt actually have even lower sodium excretion rates — below 50 mmol/day for men and below 40 mmol/day for women. To abolish high blood pressure as thoroughly as in salt-free societies might need a still lower figure[31], which is also a common outcome in the Salt Skip Program.

Meanwhile the DASH-Sodium diet with more fruit and vegetables than usual and less salt (65 mmol/day) would be expected to prevent a great many cases of high blood pressure because it had such a good effect on the upper levels of 'normal' blood pressure (prehypertension). Moreover the American government believes it would be feasible today for the whole population.[29] The DASH-Sodium diet should therefore be the community starting point, with individuals being free to be as strict as they like, choosing for example the Australian dietary guideline on salt if they want even better protection.

The distribution of hypertension and prehypertension in the last Heart Foundation survey indicates that by 2003 Australia had about 5 million people needing low salt foods to treat these two conditions alone (about 2 million with hypertension and at least 3 million with prehypertension).

In a nutshell

This book has set out to show that salt matters for a whole variety of reasons. It matters most of all because health authorities worldwide are unanimous in blaming salt among other things for high blood pressure, and for the rise of blood pressure that occurs in almost everybody in an industrialised society by the time they reach middle age.

Salt also matters for the many other health problems described in Chapter 13. For example, salt matters because about 5 per cent of women aged fifteen to forty-five (about a quarter of a million Australian women) are incapacitated every month by severe PMS, which can be abolished completely, or almost completely, by following the salt guideline of the Dietary Guidelines for Australian Adults. It is foolish to put up with severe PMS without testing the effect of following the salt guideline.

Salt matters because it is the main trigger for vertigo in about 10 000 Australians with Meniere's syndrome, the great majority of whom can abolish the vertigo completely, or almost completely, by following the salt guideline of the Dietary Guidelines for Australian Adults.

Surely the greatest paradox and the greatest challenge for public health in the 21st century, however, is that about twenty salt-free tribal societies can prevent high blood pressure without even trying, while the world's most advanced nations find it easier to visit the moon than to prevent high blood pressure. Don't put this book down without resolving to do something about it yourself, in the one area you could control if you wanted to — your own diet and lifestyle.

If you do improve your diet and lifestyle, remember the message of Appendix 1 — that (unless you are under close medical supervision for heart failure) prescription diuretics are not considered very helpful or very safe for people who conscientiously follow the salt guideline of the Dietary Guidelines for Australian Adults.

Appendixes

Appendix 1
Skipping salt safely

If you are pregnant, ill or taking prescribed medication, or if you have a history of kidney disease, read this appendix carefully. Show it to your doctor before making any changes to your salt intake. The first question to look at is whether you are taking a diuretic.

Talk to your doctor about diuretics ('fluid tablets')

This book recommends first and foremost that you follow your doctor's advice. If your doctor recommends a healthier sodium intake, this book can help.

The modern treatment for a sodium problem is to prescribe drugs that will make the kidneys eliminate sodium faster than normal. These drugs are called diuretics. They are also called 'fluid tablets' because the damage caused by sodium includes fluid retention, and getting rid of the sodium gets rid of the fluid.

Herbal diuretics work differently. They remove some fluid, but without removing sodium; the resulting thirst replaces the fluid. Removing sodium, however, requires a prescription drug. Prescription diuretics are very popular, with many patients taking their high salt intake for granted, and showing no interest in choosing less salty food, that is, in avoiding bacon, ham, pizza, olives, anchovies, mature cheeses, smoked salmon and so on. It's easier to take a pill than to alter the diet that is causing the illness.

All drugs have side-effects, so doctors reserve drugs for situations where the good outweighs the harm. With diuretics doctors limit the long-term side-effects by prescribing low doses. Low doses are less effective, so a reduced sodium intake is also important. Treatment will be far less effective if you eat pizzas and delicatessen-style foods with sodium levels above 1000 mg/100 g.

A drug that drives sodium out could drive too much sodium out. So how low can you go with your sodium intake and still take a diuretic safely? Don Gazzaniga in California faced this question when he was in severe heart failure with fluid retention, and was about to go on the waiting list for a heart transplant. His doctor prescribed a diuretic and Don did his best to help by getting his sodium intake right down to around 500 mg/day (about 20 mmol/day in a 24-hour urine test).

That is a perfectly natural diet. On its own it would not only be safe, it would be ideal, but at that low sodium level a diuretic might have made Don ill at any time with a low blood sodium (hyponatraemia). Treatment is urgent if the blood sodium is low enough to cause symptoms.

Symptoms of low blood sodium

With low blood sodium (hyponatraemia) some people just feel 'awful'. Others may complain of headache, dizziness, nausea, lethargy, dullness and confusion. This could become dangerous — even fatal — in people who were living alone. With nausea putting them off their food, their blood sodium could fall low enough to cause stupor, convulsions and coma. Everything returns rapidly to normal with urgent treatment to replace some of the salt that the diuretic was removing.

Blood tests can detect low blood sodium early, before it causes any symptoms. Knowing exactly what Don was doing, his doctor kept him under close observation with regular blood tests. In time Don improved enough for his doctor to reverse his earlier decision to put him on the waiting list for a heart transplant, and a few years later Don's 20 mmol sodium intake enabled his doctor to go one better and take him off the diuretic. Chapter 5 describes Don's three low salt cookbooks, and Appendix 5 gives his web address.

If salt skippers choose low salt foods (sodium up to 120 mg/100g) they don't have to maintain a vigil of counting the milligrams of sodium per serving in every food they eat. When well-motivated salt skippers choose low salt foods without any mistakes we know from their 24-hour urine results (20–30 mmol/day) that their sodium intake is very similar to Don's.

It's your choice

Before you join the Salt Skip Program we therefore recommend that you make a choice — talk to your doctor and choose either the Salt Skip Program or a diuretic. The combination of the Salt Skip Program and a diuretic requires close medical supervision (which you would get anyway if you had heart failure) and the added risk of taking a diuretic while following the Salt Skip Program needs your doctor's full knowledge and consent.

A word of caution — a so-called 'low salt diet' (sodium below 100 mmol/day) is all that most people can achieve without special help, and is therefore all that most doctors would expect, but the Salt Skip Program (sodium below 50 mmol/day, frequently 20–30 mmol/day) gives very different results. To make this distinction perfectly clear, make sure that your doctor sees this book so that he or she can make a professional judgement of the information given here in Appendix 1.

Diuretics, and tablets containing diuretics

(Correct as at November 2003, but subject to change every three months)

Check this list if you are not sure if you are taking a diuretic. Some items listed here are diuretics and some are tablets combining diuretics with another active drug. Trade names are shown with a capital letter.

Accuretic, Aldactone, amiloride, Amizide, Aprinox, Atacand Plus, Avapro HCT, bendrofluazide, Burinex, chlorthalidone, Coversyl Plus, Dapa-Tabs, Edecril, ethacrynic acid, frusemide, Frusid, Hydrene, hydrochlorothiazide, Hygroton, Indahexal, Insig, Kaluril, Karvezide, Lasix, Lasix-M, Micardis Plus, Midamor, Moduretic, Monoplus, Napamide, Natrilix, Natrilix SR, Renitec Plus, Spiractin 25, Spiractin 100, spironolactone, Teveten Plus, Urex, Urex-Forte, Urex-M.

Other drugs affected by salt intake

Lithium carbonate (a treatment for depression) works better at a lower salt intake. It may even cause side-effects at the dose that was previously suitable at a higher salt intake, so the doctor who is prescribing lithium must know what you are doing and see you more often, to check the dose.

Nearly all drugs prescribed for high blood pressure work noticeably better at a lower salt intake, with the possible exception of the calcium channel blockers. Two classes of drugs for high blood pressure (ACE inhibitors and angiotensin antagonists) are far more effective at a lower salt intake. The dose must often be reduced progressively to avoid over-dosage, and eventually some patients are able to stop their medication altogether.

Wolves in sheep's clothing

With the best of motives (patient convenience) some drug companies incorporate diuretics with other drugs used for treating high blood pressure. If Avapro or Karvea are not controlling the blood pressure, it may be worth adding another drug, and the choice includes a diuretic. To save patients buying two pills (and perhaps forgetting one), the doctor can prescribe Avapro HCT or Karvezide — Avapro or Karvea with a diuretic. *This means you could be taking a diuretic and not even be aware of it.* The full list in November 2003 was: Accupril (changed to Accuretic), Atacand (Atacand Plus), Avapro (Avapro HCT), Karvea (Karvezide), Micardis (Micardis Plus), Monopril (Monoplus), Coversyl (Coversyl Plus), Renitec (Renitec Plus) and Teveten (Teveten Plus).

Pregnancy

Pregnancy is a very important reason for a woman to consult her doctor. Good doctor-patient teamwork with mutual understanding and trust is vital at this time.

Change your salt intake only on medical advice

During pregnancy you should make no change of diet without medical advice and supervision. Stay on your 'normal' (high) salt diet if pregnancy started at that intake, or stay on a low salt intake if you were already following it when pregnancy started.

Pregnancy in the salt-free societies

It is artificial to add salt to the diet — salt was not available as an artificial food additive until bulk manufacture began about 5000 years ago. The Yanomama Indians of South America have the lowest salt intake of any human group.[1] Their total sodium intake has been estimated to be as low as 7–8 mmol (160–185 mg) in a whole day, which is equivalent to the sodium content of a single slice of ordinary bread in an industrialised society.[2,3] Medical expeditions to the Yanomama have confirmed that pregnancy and breastfeeding occur normally on their normal diet with no added salt.[1]

Pregnancy in industrialised societies

By contrast, in developed nations pregnancy usually begins on excessively high salt intakes that can be ten to thirty times greater than the mother's natural requirement. A change made *for the first time* after the onset of pregnancy introduces a slight risk of paradoxical effects (blood pressure may rise and swollen ankles may get worse). Other effects of pre-eclampsia (also called pregnancy toxaemia) may get worse on a diuretic or at a lower salt intake, so it is very important to change your diet *only on medical advice*.

Diseases that increase the need for salt

Temporary illness

Diarrhoea and vomiting — for example in severe gastroenteritis — may cause salt loss that needs to be replaced. Pharmacies sell sachets with measured doses of salt and sugar for Oral Rehydration Therapy (ORT) with full directions for use. Cholera and typhoid are more serious conditions involving loss of salt. Survival may depend on more rapid salt and fluid replacement (a routine part of hospital treatment).

Chronic diseases

A disease is described as chronic if it goes on for a long time. Chronicity has nothing to do with severity (chronic diseases may be mild or severe). One chronic disease that increases the need for salt is Addison's disease, in which the adrenal glands fail to produce their usual hormones that enable the kidneys to retain salt. It is a rare illness, and difficult to diagnose early. An important clue to the diagnosis is an unusual appetite for salt.

Other chronic diseases that increase the need for salt are also rare, and most patients are already undergoing regular medical care by the time they need extra salt, and well aware of it. Advanced kidney failure, for example, will be well known to the patient a long time before it progresses to 'salt-losing nephritis'; patients with burns or weeping eczema that are extensive and severe enough to cause significant salt loss will be in hospital. Cystic fibrosis may cause salt loss through excessively salty sweat, which is highly characteristic. When the sweat is normal (as sometimes happens) salt intake is not affected.

Variable salt loss may occur in bowel conditions such as ulcerative colitis, ileostomy, colostomy and gastrointestinal fistula. The likely need for extra salt is a matter of medical judgement in each case.

Appendix 2
The 24-hour urine collection

The 24-hour urine collection is currently the best way to measure sodium intake, but only when the sample is properly collected, as described in these notes. Fuller details on interpreting the results are given in a handbook for doctors called 'Salt in Medical Practice', available from the QHA.

Measuring salt intake

Salt intake cannot be measured by a blood test. The kidneys keep the level of blood sodium constant within narrow limits, and surplus sodium is found only in the urine.

Everybody would like a quick and easy way of measuring sodium intake, and a few years ago the Ames company produced a paper strip test called Saltex, which measured the concentration of chloride in a urine sample. In practice it was too inaccurate, because people who used potassium chloride as a salt substitute got high chloride readings at low salt intakes, and people who drank a lot of water and soft drinks passed a dilute urine that had low chloride *concentration* even at a high total salt *intake*. The reverse happened when they were not drinking enough to keep up with fluid losses.

Electronic salt meters have also appeared on the market at different times. They again measure the *concentration* of salt in the urine, with the same limitation as mentioned above. 'Spot' urine samples are inaccurate for another reason — sodium excretion has a circadian rhythm, and is misleadingly low in one part of the 24-hour cycle (usually about mid-morning to early afternoon) and is misleadingly high in the other part. There is one time of day (the first morning specimen) when a 'spot' urine sample can give some information (see Appendix 6).

An alternative is to count the milligrams of sodium per serving of the foods eaten, but this is very tedious, and once again the results are surprisingly inaccurate, even in professional hands.

About 90 per cent of the salt we eat ends up in the urine, so it is possible to measure how much is excreted over 24 hours. In practice no allowance is made for the small difference between intake and urinary excretion, and all discussion is based on the reported excretion rate. The next section tells you how to make an accurate 24-hour urine collection, how to understand the result, and how your doctor can choose a suitable laboratory.

How to collect a 24-hour urine sample

The container

The laboratory usually supplies disposable plastic bottles that hold 2 litres. It is best to take two bottles (return the second one empty if you don't use it). People with a very large fluid intake sometimes need three bottles.

Filling the bottle

Some people find it easier to pass urine into a separate container and then transfer it to the 24-hour container. A plastic 2-litre ice-cream container is ideal. The ones with a square shape pour well from one corner like a jug.

Choice of day

Weekday collections are better if meals are different at the weekend (especially if you combine breakfast and lunch at the weekend). If you use an ice-cream container, remember to take it to work if necessary, as well as the bottle for a weekday collection.

Starting time

Most people find it convenient to start when they get up in the morning. If you start on a Tuesday, the collection starts when you get up on Tuesday morning.

the 24-hour urine collection

Start EMPTY

When you get up on Tuesday morning go to the toilet as usual — it is essential to start *EMPTY* (empty bottle and empty bladder). Note the time you went to the toilet and write this on the label as the *starting date and time* (say Tuesday, 7 am and the date, month and year).

Collect the next specimen

The first sample for the bottle will be the next sample of urine that you pass. This may be as late as 10 am, but some of that urine dates back to the last time you emptied your bladder — which is why 7 am counts as the starting time.

Continue to collect every specimen

From then on, collect all the urine that you pass on Tuesday and during Tuesday *night*. If you need to collect urine during the night, place an obstacle in the toilet that will remind you to collect it.

Finishing time

The next morning (in this case Wednesday), collect your last sample exactly twenty-four hours after the starting time — 7 am again. The sample on Wednesday morning completes the collection. On the label record your *name*, the *date* and the *finishing date and time*.

Delivering the collection

Take the container and pathology request form to the laboratory on Wednesday. The lids of these disposable bottles sometimes leak, so be sure to keep the bottles upright. If you take them by car they can be kept upright in a small cardboard box, or in a plastic bag hanging from a door handle in the car.

Common mistakes

1 Failure to discard the first specimen

On the first day it is essential to discard the first urine passed (use the toilet). The 24-hour period starts with an *empty bladder*. People are

appendix 2

often reluctant to discard urine when they have a bottle for collecting it, but on the first morning your first job is to *get rid of yesterday's urine.*

2 Incomplete collection

If at any time during the twenty-four hours you find yourself passing urine into the toilet by mistake, you will have to abandon the collection that day, ask for another container and start again on another day. One way to protect yourself from this mistake is to fasten a large safety-pin to the underclothes in a place where you will find it and be reminded in time.

3 Loss during a bowel movement

When you go to the toilet to have a bowel movement, be careful to collect urine first, otherwise you are likely to empty the bladder accidentally during the bowel movement.

4 Collecting during the premenstrual week

Women retain sodium during the premenstrual week, which in turn causes fluid retention. They should preferably collect a sample during the first week or ten days after their period finishes, especially if they have premenstrual syndrome (PMS).

How to understand the result

The report will tell you how much sodium you passed in twenty-four hours, also potassium if requested. The diagram below shows the results from a survey conducted in 1995 in Hobart with 194 people (87 men and 107 women) who made 24-hour urine collections. Chapter 2 showed these results plotted for sodium and age; here the results are plotted for sodium and potassium.

The more sodium each person passed, the further their dot was placed to the right. The more potassium they passed, the nearer it went to the top of the graph.

Sodium

One man passed nearly 350 mmol of sodium in twenty-four hours, while one woman passed only 27 mmol.

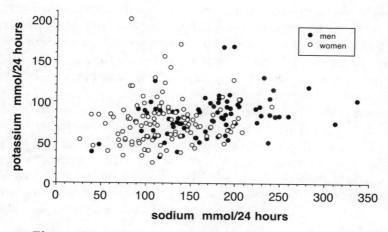

Figure A2.1 24–hour sodium excretion of 194 Hobart people plotted by sex and potassium excretion

Potassium

One woman passed 202 mmol of potassium and another passed only 27 mmol during the 24-hour period. The recommended dietary intake for potassium is 50–140 mmol/day. Most of the people with low potassium intakes (under 50 mmol) are women, who may manage with a little less potassium, especially if they are small or elderly.

Choice of laboratory

Some medical laboratories cannot provide useful information for all salt skippers because their equipment is not sensitive enough at low sodium excretion rates. For example, a laboratory might report that your sodium excretion rate is 'below 67 mmol/24 hours'. If you are trying to control the vertigo of Meniere's syndrome you need to know if your sodium excretion rate is below 50 mmol/day for a man or 40 mmol/day for a woman. A more accurate result from another laboratory using more sensitive equipment would answer that question.

A laboratory works out your 24-hour excretion by measuring the concentration of sodium per litre and multiplying that by the volume of the collection in litres, so this problem shows up mainly in collections of dilute urine with a volume of over 3 litres, and people with a large fluid intake could get over the problem by simply restricting their fluids for twenty-four to forty-eight hours before making the collection. A more satisfactory solution is to use a laboratory that has suitable equipment. Your doctor can ask the laboratory whether they can measure sodium concentrations below 20 mmol/L, and may need to see this note.

Some laboratories measure down to 5 mmol/L, which is ideal, and some measure down to 10 mmol/L, which is the minimum for a useful answer in a urine sample of low sodium content and high volume. Every laboratory can obtain an accurate result by sending the sample elsewhere (no single laboratory can do every test that is now available). It is a normal part of their daily routine to send samples needing specialised information to a laboratory that has suitable equipment.

The reference range

After the 24-hour urine result some doctors tell their patients they are not getting enough salt! If this happens to you, your doctor will need to see this part of the book. Laboratory reports print the reference range beside the result. This is the range of values that covers 95 per cent of the normal population. Results outside the reference range get special attention.

Some healthy people have results *outside the reference range*, especially the range for blood cholesterol in a sick society like ours.[1] Blood cholesterol below the reference range indicates a low risk of heart disease. Likewise the reference range is inappropriate in our society for sodium excretion.[2] Results below the reference range can safely abolish the vertigo of Meniere's syndrome.

When printing the report, the computer automatically uses bold type to draw the doctor's attention to any values that fall outside the reference range. With sodium results this can be very misleading for doctors who have not previously helped people to monitor the good urine results they can get with the Salt Skip Program.

Measuring 24-hour urinary calcium excretion

Some patients need to measure both calcium and sodium excretion. For example, a calcium stone in the urinary tract is usually due to high urinary calcium excretion, which usually drops to normal at sodium excretion rates below 80 mmol/day (see Chapter 13).

Most laboratories require two urine collections and provide two different containers (a plain bottle for sodium and another containing hydrochloric acid for calcium). The acid keeps the calcium in solution, and stops it forming an insoluble precipitate on cooling, but the sodium analysis can only be done on a plain specimen.

To avoid the inconvenience of making two separate 24-hour urine collections, the laboratory may be willing to compromise after a discussion with your doctor. One Hobart laboratory allows patients to collect urine in a plain bottle and the lab reports the volume, sodium, potassium and creatinine. The lab then acidifies the rest of the sample and performs the calcium analysis a day later.

Six quick conversions

grams to milligrams — multiply by 1000

grams to millimoles — multiply by 17.1

mg/100 g to mmol/kg — divide by 2.3

500 mg diet — 22 mmol

1000 mg diet — 43 mmol

1500 mg diet — 65 mmol

Appendix 3
Weights and measures

Many people find it confusing that urine results give sodium in millimoles and food labels give it in milligrams. This happens because food labels preserve the chaos of the old metric system. Australia shows sodium in milligrams per 100 grams and per serving; Europe uses grams per 100 grams and per serving; and the US uses only milligrams per serving.

This is a small residue of far greater chaos that existed within living memory. Children had to learn how many feet there were in a rod, pole or perch, and medicine used the Apothecaries' System of Weights and Measures, in which the dose of morphia was one-eighth to one-third of a grain.

One-eighth is less than one-third, but that is easy. The Apothecaries' System gave pharmacists a lot of arithmetic to do. Apothecaries' grains and imperial grains were the same size, but the Apothecaries' ounce had 480 grains, while the imperial ounce had only 437 and a half grains. The Apothecaries' System had no pounds, so pharmacists placed bulk orders in imperial pounds (16 imperial ounces or exactly 7000 grains — 16 times 437.5 is 7000), which came to 14 Apothecaries' ounces plus 280 grains when dispensed.

A large class of mature students at a public health course at the Berkeley campus, University of California, was asked in 1967 how many ounces there were in a gallon. Nobody knew and nobody could even work it out. The answer was 128 in California, and 160 in Britain and Australia (both imperial and US gallons were 8 pints, but the imperial pint was 20 ounces and the US pint was 16 ounces).

Because it is simpler to work with, science uses the metric system, updated in the 20th century to the International System of Weights and Measures (known as the SI, an abbreviation of its French title —

Système International de Poids et Mesures). Most countries, including the United States, have legislated for metric conversion to the SI, which establishes one appropriate unit for each physical quantity, thereby replacing the duplications and ambiguities of the traditional metric system with a self-consistent and universal language of simplified terminology.

Australian medical laboratories adopted the SI in 1974. In that year the 30th World Assembly of the WHO strongly recommended that health authorities worldwide convert to the SI without delay, to avoid dangerous confusion between two systems. Unfortunately, this has not yet happened universally, even in the health field. Australian medicine has finished converting, but nutritionists (and the Commonwealth government) still use milligrams for sodium, potassium and calcium a quarter of a century after medical laboratories converted to millimoles, so it is not surprising that food labels also lag behind.

Countries that finish implementing their own legislation (to adopt the SI) will show sodium on food labels in millimoles per kilogram (mmol/kg). Kilograms are a familiar weight to most people — everybody buys bags of flour, sugar and potatoes in kilos or multiples of a kilo. Small, sedentary women eat about a kilo of food every day and large men with manual jobs eat about 2 kilos. A food with a sodium content of 1600 mmol/kg would give small women a 24-hour sodium excretion rate of about 1600 mmol if they lived on nothing else, and large manual workers would excrete about 3200 mmol. Salted anchovies and several other foods preserved with salt contain even more than 1600 mmol/kg.

Food labels will be easier to understand when sodium is shown in mmol/kg. You can then look at the sodium figure on a food label and know what it might do to your urine result if you ate nothing else. It will be a great help when world governments finish implementing the legislation they enacted in the 1970s and convert to the SI.

The origin of millimoles

We shall always need kilograms, grams, milligrams, litres and millilitres to measure the mass or volume of a substance, and the SI includes them, but the SI specifies *molar units* for elements and compounds of known atomic or molecular weight.

The scientific advantage of the mole (mol), and derivatives such as the millimole (mmol), for measuring an 'amount of substance' is fairly technical. Chemists need it because chemical reactions depend on the *numbers* of atoms or molecules involved (not the weight). Appendix 6 adds further technical comments on SI units, but conversion tables will serve to illustrate the practical relationship between teaspoons of salt, grams of salt, milligrams of sodium and millimoles of salt and sodium.

Sodium in mmol/kg in food labels

For mathematical reasons (explained in Appendix 6) the three tables that follow show a sodium content in logarithmic progression, with each value rising 1.4 times higher than the previous value, so that each second value doubles. The first table rises from the level of low salt foods to the level found in the bloodstream. Even this first table reaches a sodium content that causes chimpanzees to develop high blood pressure when consumed in food.[1]

Sodium (mmol/kg)	Sodium (mg/100 g)	Comments
50	115	Low salt foods allowed up to 52 mmol/kg (120 mg/100 g)
70	160	Some breakfast cereals
100	230	Gives zoo chimpanzees high blood pressure
140	320	Normal sodium level in the blood

Foods in the next two tables have a higher sodium concentration than the blood level. They make us thirsty, and the extra water dilutes the salt and makes it easier to excrete.

Sodium (mmol/kg)	Sodium (mg/100 g)	Comments
200	460	Some breads
280	640	Some breads, some cheeses
400	920	Some cheeses
560	1280	Seawater (1068), ham, salami, corned beef

Foods in the third table are saltier than seawater, with some brands of soy sauce up to nine times saltier than seawater.

Sodium (mmol/kg)	Sodium (mg/100 g)	Comments
800	1840	Fried bacon, some mayonnaises
1120	2560	Stuffed olives
1600	3680	Vegemite, other yeast extracts, meat extracts
2240	5120	Salted anchovies
3200	7360	Soy sauce

Converting daily intake in teaspoons and grams of salt to millimoles

The table below shows approximate equivalents. On a laboratory scale, 1 level metric teaspoonful (5 mL) of salt weighs 5.4 g (92.3 mmol, or in round figures 90 mmol).

weights and measures

Salt (tsp)	Salt (g)	Sodium/salt (mmol) (accurate)	Sodium/salt (mmol) (rounded)	Comments
	1	17.1	17	
	2	34.2	35	
	3	51.3	50	
	4	68.4	70	
1	5	85.5	85	
	6	102.6	100	
	7	119.7	120	Average/day (Female)
	8	136.8	135	
	9	153.9	155	
2	10	171.0	170	Average/day (Male)

European food labels give sodium in grams per 100 grams (g/100g) to one decimal place, which translates into mmol/kg like this:

Sodium (g/100 g)	Sodium (mmol/kg)	Comments
0.1	43	Low salt foods up to 52 mmol/kg
0.2	87	
	100	High blood pressure in chimpanzees
0.3	130	
	135–145	Normal blood level
0.4	174	Upper limit for soup
0.5	217	Lower limit for biscuits
0.6	261	Some breads
0.7	304	Some breads, some cheeses
0.8	348	Some cheeses
0.9	391	Some cheeses
1.0	435	Seawater (approximate)

Suggested boundaries for low, medium and high salt foods

To abolish high blood pressure altogether it may be necessary to eat low salt foods exclusively.[2] In any case people who want to 'cut down' but not exclude other foods should remember that high salt foods and very high salt foods keep the palate adapted to salt and limit the enjoyment of low salt foods.[3,4]

Conversion to SI units would provide an opportunity to bring the present definition of low salt foods slightly lower, from 52 to 50 mmol/kg, a slightly safer distance from the sodium level that gives chimpanzees high blood pressure. The other boundaries are obtained by multiplying 50 mmol by an arbitrary constant of 3.0.

mmol/kg	mg/100 g	Comments
		LOW SALT FOODS
50	115	*Boundary* (Food Standards Code 120 mg)
		MEDIUM SALT FOODS
150	345	*Boundary* (upper blood level)
		HIGH SALT FOODS
450	1035	*Boundary* (seawater)
		VERY HIGH SALT FOODS

By coincidence this brings the second boundary of 150 mmol to the approximate upper limit of the range for normal blood sodium (135–145 mmol/L, depending on the laboratory, and roughly the same per kilogram). Most people would agree that foods that induce thirst by being saltier than the blood plasma are high salt foods.

The third boundary coincides with the sodium content of seawater, and few people would disagree that foods saltier than seawater are very high salt foods.

One of the problems with take-away foods is their heavy reliance on high salt and very high salt ingredients that induce thirst. This is often attributed to a deliberate policy to increase sales of soft drinks from the same outlet.[5] A Canberra man who spent a weekend in Sydney living exclusively on take-away foods made a 24-hour urine collection on return. With normal values for potassium and creatinine he passed 578 mmol of sodium.[6]

Appendix 4
Sodium-free baking powder

Salt is especially harmful for high blood pressure, but all sodium compounds are equally harmful for salt skippers who are trying to control fluid retention or the vertigo of Meniere's syndrome. They need sodium-free self-raising flour, because ordinary self-raising flour (consisting of flour plus ordinary baking powder) has a sodium content of about 700 mg/100 g. Owing to the lack of demand for sodium-free self-raising flour, salt skippers at present have to make their own with plain flour and sodium-free baking powder. This is available as Salt Skip Baking Powder in health food shops and by mail order.

Using Salt Skip Baking Powder

Salt Skip Baking Powder has excellent performance, flavour and keeping properties, and needs no 'use-by' date. Carbon dioxide gas is released in an evenly controlled way:
- 2 minutes after mixing, the first 15 per cent of gas is released
- for 10–15 minutes after mixing, the next 35 per cent is released
- during baking the remaining 50 per cent is released.

Because of this controlled rise there is no special hurry to cook the cake or batter mixture all at once — you have a quarter of an hour for bench handling time. The 50 per cent reserve of gas released during baking should save most cakes from dropping in the middle.

Appendix 5 provides details of availability for Salt Skip Baking Powder. As soon as the seal on the plastic bag is broken, transfer the contents to a small airtight container. This is especially important with Salt Skip Potassium Bicarbonate also.

Ingredients in Salt Skip Baking Powder

Calcium phosphate (additive 341)

Calcium phosphate forms 40 per cent of the mixture. The brand used in Salt Skip Baking Powder was first introduced to the baking industry and home cooks in 1939, and is in wide use throughout the world. Commercial baking powders usually combine it with sodium bicarbonate and cornflour (an anti-caking agent) to make a free-flowing powder. In that form this brand of calcium phosphate is in common use in prepared cake mixes, pancake mixes, self-raising flours, waffle mixes, cornmeal mixes and baking powder.

Potassium bicarbonate (additive 501)

Potassium bicarbonate has been used in sodium-free baking powders for over a century. Note that people with kidney failure are warned to avoid extra potassium in any form. Pharmacies sell potassium bicarbonate over the counter without a prescription. Delicatessens sometimes stock it, but Salt Skip Potassium Bicarbonate is usually cheaper. Recipes for Anzac biscuits use extra sodium bicarbonate (baking soda) to produce an alkaline dough that will go brown when cooked. Salt skippers can replace sodium bicarbonate with potassium bicarbonate, using the same amount, teaspoon for teaspoon. The amount is not critical. The pharmaceutical grade sold in pharmacies is fairly expensive but the food grade (Salt Skip Potassium Bicarbonate) costs very little more than ordinary baking soda. It attracts moisture from the air and sets hard in the packet, hence the advantage of a very airtight container. Increasing demand in future would make it possible to import an American free-flowing alternative called Flow-K.

Calcium carbonate (additive 170)

Calcium carbonate is used to balance the phosphorus content. It is also an anti-caking agent and removes the need for cornflour. The absence of cereal guarantees that it is gluten free. Calcium carbonate is the usual form of calcium sold in pharmacies over the counter to prevent osteoporosis. When the UK rationed milk and cheese during the Second World War, calcium carbonate was blended in bulk with the National Flour, to give the whole UK population of 50 million people a calcium supplement. Some UK loaves still contain added calcium carbonate.

How much baking powder to use?

Self-raising flour

For a recipe using self-raising flour, mix 2–3 level metric teaspoons (10–15 mL) Salt Skip Baking Powder with 1 metric cup (250 mL) plain flour, then sift it several times through a flour sifter. Most people use 2 teaspoons but you may need another quarter or half teaspoon to match self-raising flour very precisely.

Cake shops don't use self-raising flour, because it never has exactly the right amount of baking powder for any given recipe, and in some parts of America home cooks refuse to use it for the same reason. In the UK, Mrs Beeton's classic cookery book says 'self-raising flour is more expensive than plain flour, but it has an appeal for the amateur'.

With 3 tsp per cup of flour, Salt Skip Baking Powder gives a slightly greater rise than most brands of self-raising flour. However, some recipes will need 3 tsp, and on rare occasions you may even find a recipe that needs a bit more.

Adjusting baking powder quantities

A recipe requiring 2 teaspoons of ordinary baking powder will need 2 teaspoons of Salt Skip Baking Powder, plus another quarter of a teaspoon — but it may depend on the recipe. The right amount of baking powder for one recipe is often too much or too little for another. A prize-winning sponge cake needs no baking powder at all, while at the other extreme some recipes don't rise well even with self-raising flour — they need extra baking powder.

The plainer the mixture (the less eggs and/or less fat), the greater the need for baking powder. Wholemeal flour is heavier than white flour and needs a little more baking powder. There is no health reason to limit the amount of Salt Skip Baking Powder in a recipe except when kidney failure severely limits tolerance for potassium. On the other hand, too much baking powder can be one of the half-dozen reasons for fruit to sink to the bottom of a fruit cake.

Advantages of using Salt Skip Baking Powder

Salt Skip Baking Powder is sodium free. Ordinary baking powders use sodium bicarbonate, which brings the sodium content of ordinary self-raising flours to between 650 and 750 mg/100 g. Because it contains no cereal products, Salt Skip Baking Powder is also ideal for gluten-free diets.[1]

It contains much more calcium and less phosphorus than most baking powders. Calcium helps to prevent osteoporosis, while excess dietary phosphorus (one source of which is the high phosphorus content of other phosphate baking powders) has been linked with the development of osteoporosis. Like bone and breast milk, Salt Skip Baking Powder contains more calcium than phosphorus in international molar (SI) units.

Unlike many other baking powders, Salt Skip Baking Powder is completely free from aluminium. Although small amounts of aluminium are believed to be harmless to adults with normal kidney function, the WHO has set a strict upper limit for the aluminium content of baking powders, as some brands add significant amounts of aluminium to the diet.

Like cream of tartar (potassium bitartrate), Salt Skip Baking Powder helps to remedy the low potassium content of most processed foods. For the same gas output, ordinary cream of tartar baking powders have the same potassium content as Salt Skip Baking Powder (along with a high sodium content from sodium bicarbonate that salt skippers need to avoid).

Brown spots with Salt Skip Baking Powder

The particle size of food grade potassium bicarbonate is occasionally large enough to produce tiny brown spots in the finished cake or scone. Although no larger than a sesame seed, they may show up in white scones. These spots are harmless — it's as if there are tiny bits of Anzac biscuit in the scone. If wholemeal flour rather than ordinary flour is used, the tiny brown spots are not noticeable; wholemeal flour has more fibre, more vitamins, more flavour and three times more potassium than white.

Appendix 5
Useful addresses

Salt skipping

The author

Dr Trevor Beard, Senior Research Fellow at the Menzies Research Institute, is a retired general practitioner who also sees patients by referral. He runs the Salt Skip Program at the Menzies Institute and writes and updates the materials of the Salt Skip Program. He welcomes questions about the Salt Skip Program and related issues.

Dr Trevor Beard
Salt Skip Program, Menzies Research Institute, Private Bag 23,
GPO Hobart, Tas. 7001
Phone (03) 6226 7708 (International 61 3 6226 7708)
Fax (03) 6226 7704 (International 61 3 6226 7704)
email salt.matters@utas.edu.au

The Salt Skip Program

The Salt Skip Program has two addresses, the academic address for all discussion about the program, and the business address for joining the program or buying the publications.

Academic address: Menzies Research Institute, Hobart (same as the author's address shown above)

Business address: Queensland Hypertension Association Inc (address shown below)

Menzies Research Institute

This academic research institute (affiliated with the University of Tasmania) was founded in 1988 by the present director, Professor

Terry Dwyer. It takes advantage of the opportunities for epidemiology in a relatively stable island population of just under half a million with families that can trace their origins to early European settlers for up to six generations. The Menzies Institute has a major interest in genetics, and is a WHO Collaborating Centre for Population Based Cardiovascular Disease Prevention Programs, which is where the Menzies Salt Skip Program fits.

Queensland Hypertension Association Inc

Established in Brisbane in 1981 by grateful patients of Professor Richard Gordon, the Queensland Hypertension Association Inc (QHA) is Australia's only support group for patients with high blood pressure. Since adopting the Salt Skip Program in 1998, QHA has gained members in all Australian states and territories; the national membership now outnumbers the Queensland membership.

QHA is a voluntary, non-profit organisation incorporated in Queensland. The membership fee pays for a regular newsletter and a copy of this book to be sent to all new members (replacing and updating an extensive literature of booklets and leaflets). New members are also entitled to two copies of 'Salt in Medical Practice' (one for their doctor).

'Salt in Medical Practice' is a 78-page outline of the medical management of the Salt Skip Program, written by Dr Trevor Beard and Dr Michael Stowasser. It is written for general practitioners and other health professionals (nurses, pharmacists, dietitians and others). Many patients also find 'Salt in Medical Practice' interesting as it gives them a useful understanding of the science behind the dietary guidelines, and why it can be so beneficial to skip salt.

QHA has meetings every two months in Brisbane addressed by experts in all the practical aspects of living with high blood pressure. After each meeting, the next issue of *The BP Monitor* (the QHA newsletter) summarises the talk for the benefit of members who were unable to attend, and to give all members a permanent record. It also incorporates *Salt Skip News*, the newsletter of the Salt Skip Program, with notes on new low salt products, warnings on labelling errors, misinformation in the media and how to spot it, and new recipes.

Although QHA has developed into a de facto support group for all Australians with high blood pressure or any other reason for skipping salt, it has no current plans to expand further into a national role with a larger membership, but would welcome the appearance of a new group with that ambition. Salt skipping affects more people than diabetes, and offers scope for an organisation even larger than the Australian Diabetes Association, which has about 80 000 members. Australia has about 2 million patients with high blood pressure, over 3 million with prehypertension (blood pressure between 120/80 and 140/90) and up to a million with other salt-related illness, of whom an estimated quarter of a million have severe PMS and would feel much better if they skipped salt seriously. QHA would be happy to see a larger national organisation conceived, and to assist at its birth. Meanwhile QHA (staffed by volunteers and one part-time paid staff member) serves as the business address of the Salt Skip Program.

Queensland Hypertension Association Inc, PO Box 193,
Holland Park, Qld 4121
Phone (07) 3899 1659 (International 61 7 3899 1659)
Fax (07) 3394 7815 (International 61 7 3394 7815)
Email armstrongr@gph.ramsayhealth.com.au

Note that the website of the New South Wales Meniere's Support Group contains their attractive and well-designed Leaflet 8 (the Salt Skip Program for Meniere's disease), which is an outline of using the Salt Skip Program to control the vertigo of Meniere's Disease:
<http://hinet.net.au/nswmsg/~SaltSkip.htm>

Suppliers of low salt products

Ancient Distributors
PO Box 1081, Dandenong, Vic. 3175
Toll-free phone 1800 033 868
Fax (03) 9794 0833
Email ancdist@bigpond.com.au

Ancient Distributors supply several products that are low in salt; we especially recommend their Mayvers Low Salt Mayonnaise, made with canola oil. In a large supermarket look for it on the health food shelves (not among the mayonnaises). If you can't find it, your local health food shop can order it, or you can order it yourself by direct mail.

This company has developed a recipe for an extremely palatable yeast extract. Whereas Natex (see Chapter 11) resembles Marmite and has a sodium content of 400 mg/100 g, this yeast extract resembles Vegemite and has less than 120 mg/100 g (about 80 mg in a recent batch). Bulk manufacture would require a substantial investment, but this might be feasible if enough interested backers approached the company to form a business consortium. The contact is Trevor Mayhew at the above address or by direct email <trevor@ancient.com.au>.

Basic Ingredients and Homebread

Shop 2/9, Northlink Place (corner of Toombul Road),
Virginia, Qld 4014
(There are also outlets at Buderim on the Sunshine Coast and Nerang on the Gold Coast.)
Phone (07) 3260 7655
Nationwide order line 1300 720 037
Fax (07) 3260 7122
Email info@basicingredients.com.au
Email for Roland Bok rolandbok@powerup.com.au
Website www.basicingredients.com.au or
www.homebread.com.au

Basic Ingredients are dedicated to helping customers get the most out of their bread machine. Staff, headed by Roland Bok, call themselves 'The Homebread Team'. All the ingredients you need for making bread are available by mail order, including white, wholemeal, gourmet, spelt and gluten-free flours, and a dough improver. At present all the premixes are presalted, including the gluten-free premixes, but the company has an excellent recipe for salt-free bread. Home delivery is available to Sydney residents at 'local freight charges'.

You can register for a free email newsletter, and interact with them by phone and fax, mail, email and by one of their web addresses (both of which take you to the same website).

Carol Bates's Simply No Knead Breadmaking

SNK Breadmaking, 5 Cumberland Drive, Seaford, Vic. 3198
Phone (03) 9786 0266
Fax (03) 9786 1123
Email info@snk.com.au
Website www.snk.com.au

Ken and Carol Bates run popular courses on bread-making in Melbourne, stressing the 'No Knead' principle, where a liquid batter is stirred instead of kneading the dough by hand. This is not only convenient but happens to be ideal for salt skippers, because a solid dough without salt in the recipe becomes inconveniently sticky for kneading by hand. Bread machines work on this principle, and Ken and Carol Bates' courses are a mecca for people who want to know more about bread machines and how to use them.

SNK supplies by mail order everything you need for bread-making, including many different varieties of bread flour, and a dough improver that you can buy retail locally if you give your local health food store the postal address and other contact details.

DS Trading

75 Albert Road, Moonah, Tas. 7008
Phone (03) 6278 2866
Fax (03) 6226 7704
Email admin@dstrading.com.au

DS Trading specialise in imported Italian foods, and also supply Salt Skip Low Salt Reduced Fat Cheddar Cheese and Lactos No-Added-Salt Fruit Cheese.

Eumarrah Wholefoods

30 Pearl Street, Derwent Park, Tas. 7009
Phone (03) 6273 9511
Fax (03) 6273 9936
Email eumarrah@trump.net.au

Eumarrah Wholefoods take mail orders for Salt Skip Baking Powder, Salt Skip Potassium Bicarbonate and Salt Skip Stock Powders.

Freedom Foods (Aust) Pty Ltd
Unit 11A, 56 Keys Road, Cheltenham, Vic. 3192
Phone (03) 9553 5155
Fax (03) 9553 5133
Email info@freedomfoods.com.au
Website www.freedomfoods.com.au

Freedom Foods produce a comprehensive range of products that
are low in salt (sodium under 120 mg/100 g), low in saturated fat
and low in total fat (under 3 per cent), except where otherwise stated
in the price list. The website has the current price list and the firm
will also supply an up-to-date price list on application.

The Freedom Foods range is available in health food shops and in
the health food section of most of large supermarkets. Although you
are unlikely to find the whole range in one shop, the whole range
can be obtained direct by mail order. For delivery anywhere in
Australia, place orders for weights up to 3 kilograms with a surcharge
to cover the cost of postage and packing.

Garnisha Products Pty Ltd
44 Hatch Road, Boreen Point, Qld 4565
Phone (07) 5485 3386
Email garnisha@bigpond.com

Garnisha make about a dozen curry pastes. All are low salt, except
for two containing fish sauce and two containing prawn paste. They
are sold in gourmet food outlets in the capital cities. If you have any
difficulty finding them you can ask the company for details.

Indian Bread Company
23 Burke Avenue, Berala, NSW 2141
Phone (02) 9649 8454

This company produces salt-free chapati.

Lactos Tasmania
Old Surrey Road, Burnie, Tas. 7320
Phone (03) 6431 3386
Toll-free phone 1800 030 333
Fax (03) 6431 2647

Lactos are the well-known makers of a prize-winning salt-free fruit cheese (see Chapter 11). Lactos cheese is distributed by an affiliate called Lactos Fresh, but the company suggests that first enquiries could be made on their toll-free number.

Newman's Red Label products
BJ Meakins P/L
Lake Plains Road, Langhorne Creek, SA 5255
Phone (08) 8537 3086
Fax (08) 8537 3220
Email horseradish@oils.net.au

BJ Meakins produce a range of no–added–salt products: American Mustard, Crushed Chilli–Garlic, Crushed Garlic, Crushed Ginger, French Mustard, Hot English Mustard, Prepared Horseradish (a horseradish sauce ready to serve) and Seeded Mustard.

Osborne Olives
PO Box 87, Yackandandah, Vic. 3749
Phone (02) 6027 1503
Fax (02) 6027 1969

Osborne Olives supply no–added–salt dried olives.

Spice World
Bank Arcade, Liverpool Street, Hobart, Tas. 7000
Phone (03) 6231 6270
Mobile 0418 136 625
Fax 6267 2654
Email spiceworld@iprimus.com.au

Spice World takes mail orders for about 300 spices, including thirteen different no–added–salt curry powders, a herb blend (with or without cayenne), and Salt Skip Flavour Booster. A product and price list is available on application.

Related websites

megaheart.com
Don Gazzaniga publishes new recipes in a monthly Internet newsletter called *MegaHeart News*. He uses no salt at all in cooking or in any of the ingredients. Chapter 5 mentions his three cookbooks and Appendix 1 refers to the medical history that inspired them. He

interacts with low salt enthusiasts around the world by email <don@megaheart.com> and has many Australian correspondents.

All his recipes would do well for the Salt Skip Program, although he does occasionally use salt-free butter for patients whose doctors don't mind if they use butter (the Salt Skip Program follows the Australian dietary guideline to limit saturated fat).

A computer program enables him to work out the sodium content of all his ingredients, and he often gives the sodium in each ingredient and each recipe to two decimal places of a milligram. The sodium content is always under 120 mg/100 g and salt skippers don't need to do any of this arithmetic if they measure their progress with 24-hour urine collections. Don Gazzaniga's 500 mg diet corresponds to a 24-hour sodium excretion rate of about 20 mmol/day. His website makes it easy to achieve that with flair and flavour, and is well worth visiting regularly.

www.healthyheartmarket.com

Peter Eiden at Healthy Heart Market in Minnesota has a large selection of low salt groceries that can be ordered by mail order — a sort of Sears Roebuck for low salt foods.

Note that American food regulations allow soy sauce with a sodium content over 3000 mg/100 g to be described as 'low salt', which leads Healthy Heart Market to stock it. Salt skippers with disappointing urine results can often attribute them to errors of this kind.

Peter Eiden's email is <peiden@healthy heartmarket.com>. Ask to be put on the email address list for his latest offerings and recipes. His recipes are usually salt free and ideal for salt skippers, like those from MegaHeart.

Although freight to Australia is expensive, Healthy Heart Market does take Australian orders.

Appendix 6
Some technical comments

The comments collected here are technical points that may interest health professionals and serious salt skippers.

'Equal steps' in drug doses and tasting tests

A stepwise increase in taste perception requires a logarithmic increase in salt concentration.[1] The reason is mathematical. In a set of metric drills ranging in size from 1.0 mm to 10 mm in steps of 0.5 mm, the second drill is 50 per cent larger than the first, but the last is only 5.3 per cent larger than the one below it. Added constants gradually become imperceptible, while subtracted constants become giant snowballs. Stepwise changes in drug doses and tasting tests need logarithmic progression such as doubling or halving. The dose at each step is multiplied or divided by a constant.

Arithmetic progression (snowball effect) gave the downward steps of the DASH–Sodium study powerful validation. Food was supplied at three target levels of sodium intake (143, 104 and 65 mmol) at equal arithmetic intervals of 39 mmol and mean sodium excretion rates were remarkably close to this (142, 107 and 67 mmol/day), yet the lower interval had more effect on blood pressure than the first.[2] Admittedly the difference in sodium excretion was 40 mmol at the second step, and this was 14 per cent larger than the first (35 mmol) but equal effects would only be expected from starting at 166 mmol and dividing by a constant of 1.6, as shown overleaf.

Biological phenomena including salt taste require logarithmic progression for stepwise effects. The reason is mathematical (not biological) and the other figures in this appendix will display sodium data on a log scale.

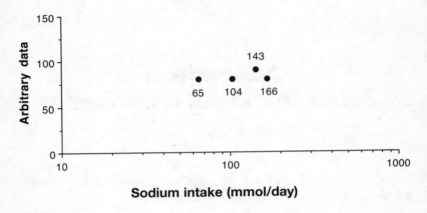

Figure A6.1 This figure plots the DASH–Sodium targets on a log scale against arbitrary data chosen to display the arithmetic steps (143, 104 and 65 mmol) in a slight curve and corresponding logarithmic steps (166, 104 and 65 mmol) in a straight line

Significant differences in blood pressure at such close intervals in the DASH–Sodium data confirmed the strength of an efficacy study that supplied all the food. The larger difference in blood pressure between the target intakes of 104 and 65 mmol may have been a chance result. As it is exactly what would be expected, it is more likely to be an example of the clinical precision of an efficacy study. Results from an efficacy study of a wider log series like 40, 80 and 160 would no doubt be very impressive.

It's alarming to find a few people a whole step higher than 160 mmol (320 mmol), but it's wrong to think that all Australians have too much salt. [3] In the Hobart survey ten people, mostly women, were already at or below the DASH–Sodium upper limit of 65 mmol on the day of the survey, as shown in the next figure.

On a 'normal' diet sodium excretion varies widely from day to day; this means the under-65 mmol region is visited by more people than the ones identified in one day — some in that region on the day would change places afterwards with some who had been above it.[4] However, ten out of 194 adults (5.2 per cent) were at or below the DASH–Sodium level on the day of the survey without even trying — and without even knowing — and a similar proportion of all

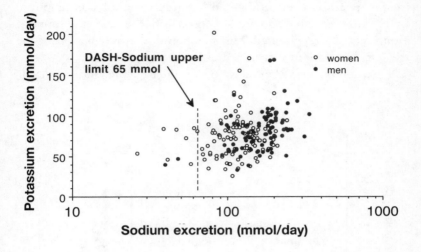

Figure A6.2 Ten people (5.2 per cent of this
Hobart sample) were at or below the DASH-Sodium
upper limit of 65 mmol/day. Most were women.

Australian adults would come to over half a million people who
might find themselves unwittingly at the DASH-Sodium level on
any given day.

It is therefore tempting to speculate that perhaps half a million
Australians would enjoy the DASH-Sodium diet at once without
having to re-educate their palates. They might buy meals based on
the DASH-Sodium diet if they were available ready-prepared at an
attractive price. These are ordinary people in addition to the two
million Australians with high blood pressure and over three million
with prehypertension who actually need the DASH-Sodium diet as
a prescribed medical treatment (unless they go further and adopt the
salt guideline of the Dietary Guidelines for Australian Adults).

The Intersalt study

The Intersalt study examined the distribution of sodium excretion
rates and blood pressure in 10 079 subjects from fifty-two centres in
thirty-two countries, with standardisation of clinical and laboratory
procedures and analysis of three confounding variables — over-

weight, potassium excretion and reported alcohol consumption. Each centre recruited about 200 people, with the sexes and four age groups equally represented. This plot shows the distribution of the raw data from the fifty-two centres.[5]

Hypertension was rare below 65 mmol/day (the lowest DASH-

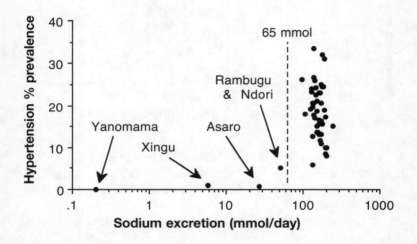

Figure A6.3 Distribution of the 52 Intersalt centres by their median sodium excretion rate and prevalence of hypertension. Four societies had median sodium excretion rates below 65 mmol/day.

Sodium level), except in two villages in Kenya (Rambugu and Ndori) with 5.0 per cent prevalence of hypertension. This was surprisingly high at a median sodium excretion rate of 51 mmol/day, but these two societies had a potassium-deficient diet. The prevalence of hypertension in the three salt-free societies was 1 per cent (Xingu, Brazil), 0.8 per cent (Asaro, Papua New Guinea) and zero in the Yanomama (Brazil).

Above 96 mmol/day the association with median blood pressure and prevalence of high blood pressure was surprisingly weak, suggesting that many confounders other than weight, potassium and alcohol have yet to be identified. It is a pity that different ethnic groups cannot yet be compared for their genetic predisposition to high blood pressure. Nevertheless, the equal representation of four different age groups in the population samples enabled the data analysis to calculate the *slope of the rise of blood pressure with age*, and the link with salt was stronger, and significant both within each centre and across all centres.

With systolic blood pressure the annual rise varied between 0.052 mm of mercury for the Xingu (Brazil) and 1.326 mm for the Cartaxo villagers (rural Portugal), which means that every ten years the Xingu and Yanomama (South America) could expect a rise of about 0.5 mm and 0.7 mm respectively, while the Cartaxo villagers (Portugal) could expect a rise of 13 mm. The median sodium excretion rate was 6 mmol/day for the Xingu and 175 mmol/day in Cartaxo.

The estimated Yanomama sodium *intake* may be up to 7–8 mmol/day.[6] They owe their extremely low excretion rate of 0.2 mmol/day to the fact that their kidneys recycle most of the dietary sodium. This is normal in many terrestrial mammals.[7] Urinary sodium excretion approaches intake only when there is dietary excess, and it reflects about 90 per cent of human intake in the industrialised societies.

Six levels of human salt intake

If an intake of 6 mmol/day is multiplied by a constant of 2.5 it takes only six steps to reach 1600 mmol/day. The evidence on salt that has been accumulating for over a century can be classified according to its place in these six intervals.

sodium (mmol/day)	salt level	habitat	attitude to salt
1600-			
	6	experimental trials	excessive thirst
625-			
	5	Akita (Japan), rural Portugal	strongest preference
250-			
	4	industrial societies	strong preference
100-			
	3	recommended dietary intake	preference
40-			
	2	'salt free' animal husbandry	AVERSION
16-			
	1	'salt free' hunting & gathering	AVERSION
6-			
	0	animals in continental pastures	salt hunger (some habitats)

Reproduced with permission of the Dieticians Association
of Australia from: Beard TC. The bread of the 21st century:
The First Jo Rogers memorial oration. Australian Journal
of Nutrition and Dietetics 1997;54(4):198–203.

Level 6 is experimental. At 1200–1600 mmol/day each of fourteen volunteers showed a rise of blood pressure within three days.[8]

At Level 5 in Akita (Japan), and in rural Portugal, stroke has been the most common cause of death.

Level 4 is where nearly all the hypertension occurred in the Intersalt data.

Level 3 (40–100 mmol/day) has been the Australian RDI for sodium, but is currently under revision.

Levels 1 and 2 are found in the salt-free societies, all of whom strongly dislike the taste of salt until they get used to it. Serious salt skippers with urine results below 40 mmol/day also develop an increasing dislike for salty foods, but it remains less intense than the aversion displayed in societies unacquainted with salt.

Level 0 (non-human) occurs in herbivores in certain habitats, and is included to illustrate salt hunger.

How milligrams can fool you

A food label on a can of tomato juice showing a sodium content of 160 mg/100 g and potassium 183 mg/100 g would give the impression that the sodium was more than balanced by a generous excess of potassium. That would be quite wrong and illustrates why chemists and biochemists use molar units.

The SI (International System) needs molar units because chemical reactions depend on the *numbers* of atoms or molecules involved (not the weight). As in football, where a fair game gives each team an equal number of players (not an equal weight or volume of players), chemical reactions depend on the numbers of atoms combining, not their weight. Molar units therefore take account of the atomic weight of elements (or molecular weight of compounds), so the SI converts milligrams of sodium to millimoles by dividing by 23 (atomic weight of sodium), or 39 (atomic weight of potassium) in the case of potassium. Thus 10 mmol of sodium weigh 230 mg and 10 mmol of potassium weigh 390 mg, but each amount contains the same number of atoms, which is what matters in chemistry — and also what matters to a kidney when called upon to excrete these electrolytes. In the SI, molar units are correct for sodium and potassium and other electrolytes. No other unit is correct.

On the can of tomato juice the label using milligrams shows 160 mg for sodium and 183 mg for potassium, and yet that tomato juice makes the kidney handle 50 per cent more sodium atoms than potassium atoms. Sodium at 160 mg/100 g is 70 mmol/kg, while potassium at 183 mg/100 g is only 47 mmol/kg. This is the basic science behind the SI molar units. Appendix 3 mentions other practical advantages of updating food labels with SI units in mmol/kg.

The simplest definition of the mole is that it is the gram–molecular weight, or the gram–atomic weight, in other words the amount of substance having a mass in grams equal to its molecular or atomic weight. Moles (mol) and millimoles (mmol) have replaced the *equivalent* (Eq) and *milliequivalent* (mEq), which are obsolete because the equivalence of a substance varies with the chemical reaction — the equivalence of an acid donating hydrogen atoms may be different from its equivalence based on its oxygen requirement during complete oxidation.

Some notes on potassium

Inadequate potassium intake is historically recent. It is an artefact of industrialised societies, and unknown among hunter–gatherer societies and terrestrial wildlife, because potassium is the principal intracellular cation (positively charged electrolyte) abundant in all living cells.[9] Nearly all biological materials — including fresh foods before they are processed in kitchens or factories — contain more potassium than sodium, the only common exceptions being eggs and kidneys (unfertilised eggs have no cellular structure, and kidneys are unique — intracellular sodium is abundant because the renal tubules recycle it).

Sodium/potassium (Na/K) ratio

The optimum dietary Na/K ratio has not been established, but chimpanzees have a molar Na/K between 0.01 and 0.22 on their usual diet of fruit and vegetables, and become hypertensive when the ratio is raised by salt to between 1.17 and 2.25, with a full remission on return to the ratio of the control group.[10]

The food tables show that the net molar Na/K ratio of a natural diet with no added sodium would be around 0.25, with a range between about 0.005 and 0.5. This is the physiological range of the diet on which the human body evolved. Breast milk has Na/K 0.46 (cow's milk 0.63), and adults in the three salt-free societies in the Intersalt study (the Yanomama, the Xingu and the Asaro) excreted urine with mean Na/K ratios (±SD) of 0.01 (±0.04), 0.20 (±0.47) and 0.62 (±0.57) respectively.[5] As a result of potassium deficiency, the Rambugu and Ndori had Na/K 1.78 in spite of their low sodium excretion of 51 mmol/day.

Industrialised societies add enough salt to invert the dietary Na/K ratio after weaning to between about 2 and 8. The molar Na/K ratios of a few common foods before and after processing can be calculated from the food tables:

Food	Fresh	Processed
Wholemeal flour/bread	0.03	3.0
Pork/ham	0.31	9.9
Peas (fresh/canned)	0.01	3.3
Cow's milk/cheddar cheese	0.55	15.2

The molar Na/K ratio in morning urine

There is a consensus that the 24-hour urinary molar Na/K ratio should be less than 1.0.[11] Although the ratio could be measured in casual urine collections ('spot' urine samples), it is unfortunately of no value because circadian rhythms in sodium and potassium excretion are out of phase with one another, making 'spot' urine samples generally useless as a guide to the 24-hour ratio. At one easily identifiable time of day, however, (the early morning urine sample passed on arising), the Na/K ratio is fairly close to the 24-hour ratio, with a tendency to be slightly higher. This makes a good ratio (less than 1.0) in the early morning urine a fairly reliable index of a 24-hour ratio less than 1.0.[12]

At present even this information is of limited value because clinical medicine usually needs greater precision, and in community surveys a ratio less than 1.0 would be rare in an industrialised society. It could be a useful alternative to 24-hour collections in large-scale community interventions where a safe ratio was a dietary goal.

The recommended dietary intake (RDI) for potassium

The RDI for potassium (50–140 mmol/day) is currently being reviewed. For potassium the significant figure in the RDI is the *minimum* of 50 mmol; around 90 per cent of urban Australians achieved this in the Hobart survey.[3] Under-collection may cause low 24-hour urinary excretion, which needs to be kept in mind. Otherwise excretion rates below the RDI for potassium may be due to low intake, or excess faecal loss.

Low intakes occur in starvation, during dieting for weight loss and with poor diets. African Americans and the urban poor may have a marginal potassium deficiency through excessive reliance on processed foods and a lack of fresh fruit and vegetables. One of the health hazards of excluding fresh foods from the diet is that the natural electrolyte balance of the raw materials is grossly distorted in processed foods.

Faecal losses occur in chronic diarrhoea and the abuse of purgatives. The muscle metabolism of marathon runners, both amateur and professional, can lead to increased plasma levels and urinary loss of potassium that requires dietary replacement.

Excess urinary loss (kaluresis) may be due to high salt diets, thiazide diuretics or medication with steroids. It can give the impression that intake is adequate unless blood potassium is also measured.

Potassium wasted during food preparation

Commercial processing not only adds sodium but also removes potassium from foods. Food tables show that even the thirty-four potassium compounds permitted as food additives seldom compensate for these losses.

Food (content mg/100g)	Fresh		Processed		Potassium losses
	Sodium (Na)	Potassium (K)	Sodium (Na)	Potassium (K)	
Pork/ham	65	355	1580	270	**24%**
Peas (fresh/canned)	2	250	230	120	**52%**
Milk/cheddar cheese	51	158	655	73	**54%**
Wheat/white bread	5	315	450	110	**65%**

Asian diets that depend on polished rice are especially deficient in potassium. Brown rice loses 70 per cent of its potassium when milled to make polished white rice, making white rice unsuitable even for famine relief.[13] Chinese centres in the Intersalt study showed no individuals with Na/K less than 1.0, and very few with Na/K less than 3.0.[14] Mainland Chinese centres all had mean Na/K ratios greater than 6.0, which helps to explain why stroke became the most common cause of death at a time when the masses had scant acquaintance with obesity, lack of exercise or abuse of alcohol.[14-16] Many home kitchens also waste the natural potassium content of fresh foods. For example, unpeeled potatoes lose potassium when boiled in salted water, and up to 50 per cent when peeled, depending on the size of the potato, cooking time and salt concentration.[17] Peeled potatoes take up almost half the salt concentration in the water, but steaming removes only 3–6 per cent of the potassium and adds no sodium. The same happens with carrots, beans and peas.[17]

Steaming, roasting, microwave cooking and stir-frying conserve potassium and flavour.

When washed, fresh fruit and raw salad vegetables keep all their potassium intact, but water leaches potassium from any plant material immersed after being broken up or shredded (store it in plastic wrap in the fridge instead).

The NHMRC Working Party on Sodium in the Australian Diet (1984) recommended that the food industry give the public a double benefit (less sodium and more potassium) by replacing some of the salt in processed foods with potassium chloride.[18] The food regulations were amended to permit it, and both reduced salt and low salt cheese and reduced salt bread were marketed successfully with added potassium chloride. Only a few people detect this partial substitution and object to it.

Any of the thirty-four potassium compounds permitted as food additives could replace their sodium counterparts without detection — only the chloride makes much difference to the flavour. The baking industry already replaces sodium bicarbonate with potassium bicarbonate or ammonium bicarbonate in some products. Baking powder containing sodium could be discontinued if a government subsidy removed the slight difference in cost. However, only two countries — Germany and USA — export potassium, and world supplies could replace only a fraction of all the sodium compounds in use.

The danger of excess potassium

Potassium is more difficult to excrete than sodium because of its low concentration in plasma and glomerular filtrate. The tubules have to excrete it actively, which is slow even with normal renal function.

Potassium is released at a manageable rate from food, and people with normal kidneys are in no danger of an overdose of potassium from natural sources.[19] Some vegetarian cultures excrete up to 200 mmol/day. More may be unsafe. The Papua New Guinea tribesmen who make 'salt' out of vegetable ash can tolerate up to 400 mmol/day, but only as a result of an acquired tolerance.[20]

Like all ionised salts, potassium chloride can be fatal in overdose. (Fatal accidents have also occurred with salt in an infant formula, and when given as an emetic, if the salt is retained instead of being vomited.) One advantage of potassium chloride is that only safe doses are palatable.

Kidney failure

Patients with kidney failure *must* avoid potassium supplements, and even limit many ordinary foods that have a high natural potassium content. They must also avoid potassium-sparing diuretics, even those that incorporate a thiazide.

These patients need full warning if potassium is added to processed foods, as the special danger in kidney failure is that the first symptom of a high blood level of potassium may be fatal cardiac arrest. Until now the waste of potassium in food processing has protected kidney patients. They already look out for potassium chloride (additive 508), but could hardly be expected to check labels for all the thirty-four potassium compounds permitted as food additives. They need a clear statement that there is 'added potassium', which could be mandatory except where the net potassium content remains below that of the raw materials (as it usually does at present).

Natural foods that are high in salt

Nearly all natural foods are low in salt. The most important exceptions are the invertebrate seafoods — shellfish, shrimps, crayfish, prawns and squid. In these foods sodium content may exceed 300 mg/100 g. Even when these invertebrates are alive, their defences against the high salt content of seawater are not as well developed as in fish that have a backbone, so an oyster freshly collected and rinsed in plain water will still taste salty. There is further postmortem absorption of salt if they are stored too long in refrigerated seawater after they are caught.

The flesh of sea fish and freshwater fish, red meat and poultry are all similar in sodium content (between 50 and 100 mg/100 g). This applies to fresh fish, although tuna or sardines canned with no added salt may still have a higher sodium content from storage in refrigerated seawater in the hold of a ship that has remained at sea for several weeks.

Two other natural foods above the limit for low salt foods are eggs and kidneys (133 and about 160–200 mg/100 g respectively, with differences between beef, veal and lamb kidneys). Plants that belong to the beet family such as beetroot and silverbeet may absorb salt when grown under irrigation with estuary water or bore water. The beet family are related to salt-tolerant plants that grow in sand dunes, and they can be grown commercially in districts too salty for anything else. If grown at home they are low salt foods like other vegetables.

The exceptions mentioned above can usually be ignored in a diet otherwise consisting of low salt foods. The sodium content of fruit, unprocessed cereals and most other fresh, unsalted plant products is usually well below 50 mg/100 g. People who choose low salt foods to prevent the vertigo of Meniere's syndrome will probably decide to avoid invertebrate seafood.

Salt in the Pritikin diet

Nathan Pritikin (1915–1985) was an engineer and inventor, but also an avid student of medical journals from an early age. When he developed angina in 1955 he was dismayed to find that treatment was far from satisfactory. His own interpretation of the published evidence persuaded him that coronary heart disease could probably be prevented by diet and exercise, perhaps even cured.

He found articles on the health of the Tarahumara Indians of northern Mexico, and their complete freedom from heart disease. Their active lifestyle and simple diet also seemed to protect them from overweight, diabetes and high blood pressure, and gave the men surplus energy for extraordinary ball games in which they ran for up to 150 kilometres a day. Pritikin wrote, 'I began to imitate their dietary and exercise habits, and my recovery was under way'.[21]

The diet gave him a striking clinical remission. His life was cut short at sixty-nine by cancer (malignant lymphoma), at present unpreventable.[22] At postmortem examination his coronary arteries were soft and pliable, and completely free from atherosclerosis.[22] Coronary occlusion with cholesterol deposits is reversible by diet as well as drugs and there is no reason to question Pritikin's original diagnosis.[23]

The Tarahumara diet was acceptable to Western palates partly because of its moderate use of salt, and the Pritikin program limited sodium intake but allowed a notional maximum of 70 mmol/day (1600 mg)— a level vindicated after his death by the 65 mmol (1500 mg) of the DASH–Sodium study. It avoided salty foods such as crackers, pretzels, smoked meats and fish, along with table salt, but allowed 'less salt' soy sauce (sodium over 3000 mg/100 g) in cooking.

Results from a Tarahumara group that joined the Intersalt study were published after Pritikin's death and are shown in the figure below.

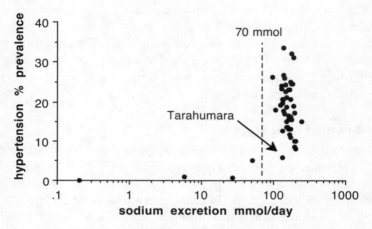

Figure A6.4 Position of the Tarahumara among the 52 Intersalt centres, showing their median sodium excretion rate (135 mmol/day) and prevalence of high blood pressure (5.9 percent)

In spite of their average (median) sodium excretion rate of 135 mmol/day the prevalence of hypertension was only 5.9 per cent, far lower than that of any other group with a sodium excretion rate between 70 and 135 mmol/day. The mean sodium excretion rate (±SD) was 144 mmol/day (±84.0).

There is no reason to doubt that the Pritikin diet and lifestyle when correctly followed might be as effective as the DASH–Sodium diet for treating high blood pressure, but the Intersalt data show a higher sodium excretion rate for the Tarahumara that came to approximately double the Pritikin level. In spite of a diet and lifestyle that was otherwise apparently ideal, this relatively high salt intake was still associated with high blood pressure at a prevalence of 5.9 per cent — more than one person in 20. This would hardly make the Tarahumara a suitable model for abolishing high blood pressure.

Acknowledgements

First I must thank Janet Coburn of Woden College of Technical and Further Education in Canberra for coming up with such a positive word for avoiding salt — 'skipping' it — and Elisabeth Marchant, founder and elected president of a highly successful consumer group for Canberra salt skippers (NoSal Incorporated, later renamed Salt Skip Incorporated).

I am especially grateful to Professor Terry Dwyer, founding director of the Menzies Research Institute in Hobart, for allowing me to join him as part-time senior research fellow and to explore the feasibility of the ultimate randomised controlled trial in the primary prevention of hypertension, and to Professor Richard Heller from the Faculty of Medicine, University of Newcastle, for joining me as co-author of a paper about it.

Emeritus Professor Dick Gordon, at the Department of Medicine, University of Queensland, has given me constant encouragement in developing the Salt Skip Program, and Associate Professor Michael Stowasser, from the same department and director of the Hypertension Unit, has followed up with regular help and advice, especially as technical editor of this book. My thanks also to the second technical editor, Associate Professor Malcolm Riley of the Nutrition and Dietetics Section, Department of Medicine, Monash University, with whom I have had a close and stimulating working relationship for many years.

Philip Moore (Hobart otolaryngologist) conceived the idea that the Salt Skip Program might spare his patients the long-term side-effects of diuretics as a treatment for the vertigo of Meniere's syndrome. It has proved to be a very effective treatment, much appreciated by patients, for over a decade.

From 1988 to 1998 the management committee of Salt Skip Incorporated met monthly, with Joanne McKim as the able secretary of an enthusiastic membership including Allan Clarke, Pam Hamilton, Dot and Ron Lord, Lindsay Morris and Kevin

Richmond, joined for some of the time by Fay Brown, Cynthia Lohrey, Rosemary Nicholls and Elaine Speakman. In 1998 Queensland Hypertension Association Incorporated agreed to take over as the business address of Salt Skip Program.

Over the years my rudimentary education in nutrition has been updated by Vicki Deakin of Canberra University and the Australian Institute of Sport; the late Jo Rogers, Royal Prince Alfred Hospital, Sydney; Professor Mark Wahlqvist, Department of Medicine, Monash University; Emeritus Professor Stewart Truswell, Sydney University; dietitians Rosemary Stanton and Catherine Saxelby; and others too numerous to name individually. Over many years I am also greatly indebted to Professor Graham MacGregor of St George's Hospital, London, for help and encouragement and for agreeing to write the Foreword to this book.

Several people have given special help with sections of this book: Dr Brigitte Cox and Dr Keith Richardson, Food Science Australia (CSIRO); Dr Alison Venn, cohort epidemiologist, Menzies Research Institute; Dr Guy Burgess, Tasmanian Thyroid Advisory Committee; Alun Stevens, Thyroid Australia; Professor Cres Eastman, Australian Centre for Control of Iodine Deficiency Disorders (ACCIDD); Dr John Brotherhood, School of Exercise and Sport Science, Sydney University; Dr Paul McCartney, Hobart ophthalmologist; Associate Professor Caryl Nowson, Nutrition and Dietetics, Deakin University; Clare Rawcliffe, cardiology dietitian, St Vincent's Hospital, Sydney; and Jane Brown, home economist, Salt Skip Program, Hobart. I would also like to thank the many salt skippers who have generously contributed tips and recipes, some of which are reproduced in *Salt Matters*, to the monthly Salt Skip Program newsletter.

I have had invaluable assistance from friends and relatives — some chosen as expert laypersons and some as novices — who have helped to remove obscurities and ambiguities. These were John Gardner, Joan, Conrad and Sarah Krapf, Joanne and John McKim, and my daughter Jane Parris and her husband Bill. As one of Australia's leading salt skippers, Rick Keam deserves special mention.

I am grateful to Lothian Books for accepting the manuscript for publication and in particular for all the help I have had from publisher Averill Chase and editor Jean Kingett.

Finally my greatest debt of gratitude is to my wife Joan Beard (née Frankau) for being my main inspiration and support for most of my adult life, and at the same time my severest and yet my most supportive critic.

Notes

1 Why salt matters

1. Select Committee on GRAS Substances. GRAS evaluation of the health aspects of sodium chloride and potassium chloride as food ingredients. Bethesda, Maryland: Life Sciences Research Office; 1979:4.
2. Morris S, Mackley L. The spice ingredients cookbook. London: Lorenz Books; 1997:70.
3. Tobian L. Dietary salt (sodium) and hypertension. American Journal of Clinical Nutrition 1979;32(Suppl):2659–62.
4. Sinnett PF, Whyte HM. Epidemiological studies in a total highland population, Tukisenta, New Guinea. Journal of Chronic Disease 1973;26:265–90.
5. National Health & Medical Research Council. Dietary Guidelines for Australian Adults. Canberra: Australian Government Publishing Service; 2003.
6. Ambard L, Beaujard E. Causes de l'hypertension artérielle. Archives Generales de Médecine 1904;1:520–33.
7. Vasan RS, Beiser A, Seshadri S, Larson MG, Kannel WB, D'Agostino RB, et al. Residual lifetime risk for developing hypertension in middle-aged women and men: the Framingham Heart Study. Journal of the American Medical Association 2002;287:1003–10.
8. WHO/ISH Statement Committee. Prevention of hypertension and associated cardio-vascular disease: a 1995 statement. Clinical and Experimental Hypertension—Theory and Practice 1995;18(3&4):581–93.
9. Godlee F. The food industry fights for salt. British Medical Journal 1996;312:1239–40.
10. Denton D. The hunger for salt. Berlin: Springer-Verlag; 1984:86.
11. Stefansson V. My life with the Eskimos (revised edition). London: George G Harrap; 1924:46.
12. Trowell HC, Burkitt DP. Western diseases: their emergence and prevention. London: Edward Arnold; 1981:161.
13. Oliver WJ, Cohen EL, Neel JV. Blood pressure, sodium intake, and sodium related hormones in the Yanomamo Indians, a 'no-salt' culture. Circulation 1975;52:146–51.
14. Denton D. The hunger for salt. Berlin: Springer-Verlag; 1984:577.
15. Chagnon NA. Yanomamö: the fierce people: Holt, Rinehart & Wilson; 1983:63.
16. National Health & Medical Research Council. Report of the working party on sodium in the Australian diet. Canberra: Australian Government Publishing Service; 1984:20.
17. Thaler BI, Paulin JM, Phelan EL, Simpson FO. A pilot study to test the feasibility of salt restriction in a community. New Zealand Medical Journal 1982;95:839–42.
18. MacGregor GA, Markandu ND, Best F, Elder DM, Cam J, Sagnella GA, et al. Double-blind randomised controlled trial of moderate sodium restriction in essential hypertension. Lancet 1982;1:351–5.
19. Beard TC, Cooke HM, Gray WR, Barge R. Randomised controlled trial of a no-added-sodium diet for mild hypertension. Lancet 1982;2:455–8.
20. Denton D. The hunger for salt. Berlin: Springer-Verlag; 1984:12.

21. Bertino M, Beauchamp GK, Engelman K. Long-term reduction in dietary sodium alters the taste of salt. American Journal of Clinical Nutrition 1982;36:1134–44.

2 The salt shaker is not the problem
1. Beard TC, Woodward DR, Ball PJ, Hornsby H, von Witt RJ, Dwyer T. The Hobart Salt Study 1995: few meet national sodium intake target. Medical Journal of Australia 1997;166:404–7.
2. James WPT, Ralph A, Sanchez-Castillo CP. The dominance of salt in manufactured food in the sodium intake of affluent societies. Lancet 1987;1:426–9.
3. Woodward DR, Beard TC, Ball PJ, Hornsby H, von Witt RJ, Dwyer T. Should the male and female RDI for sodium be the same? [abstract]. In: 16th Dietitians' Association of Australia National Conference; 1997 14–17 May; Hobart, Tasmania; 1997.
4. Pritikin N, Leonard JN, Hofer JL. Live longer now. New York: Grosset & Dunlap; 1974.
5. Tobian L. Dietary salt (sodium) and hypertension. American Journal of Clinical Nutrition 1979;32(Suppl):2659–62.

3 Achieving independence from salt
1. Rose G. Sick individuals and sick populations. International Journal of Epidemiology 1985;14:32–8.
2. National Health & Medical Research Council. Dietary Guidelines for Australian Adults. Canberra: Australian Government Publishing Service; 2003.
3. Trowell HC, Burkitt DP. (editors): Western diseases: their emergence and prevention. London: Edward Arnold; 1981.
4. Beard TC, Cooke HM, Gray WR, Barge R. Randomised controlled trial of a no-added-sodium diet for mild hypertension. Lancet 1982;2:455–8.
5. Bertino M, Beauchamp GK, Engelman K. Long-term reduction in dietary sodium alters the taste of salt. American Journal of Clinical Nutrition 1982;36:1134–44.
6. Bertino M, Beauchamp GK, Engelman K. Increasing dietary salt alters salt taste preference. Physiology & Behavior 1986;38:203–13.
7. Bragg PC, Bragg P. Salt free health sauerkraut cookbook. Santa Barbara, CA: Health Science; 1979.
8. Joint National Committee. The seventh report of the Joint National Committee on Prevention, Detection, Evaluation, and Treatment of High Blood Pressure. Journal of the American Medical Association 2003;289:2560–72.

4 Flavouring food without salt
1. Brenner E. Gourmet cooking without salt. Garden City, NY: Doubleday & Co; 1981.
2. Claiborne C, Franey P. Craig Claiborne's gourmet diet. New York: Times Books; 1980.
3. Meneely GR, Battarbee HD. High sodium–low potassium environment and hypertension. American Journal of Cardiology 1976;38:768–85.
4. National Health & Medical Research Council. Report of the working party on sodium in the Australian diet. Canberra: Australian Government Publishing Service; 1984:4.
5. Yang WH, Drouin MA, Herbert M, Yang M, Karsh J. The monosodium glutamate complex: assessment in a double-blind placebo-controlled study. Journal of Allergy and Clinical Immunology 1997;99:757–62.
6. Ball PJ, Woodward DR, Beard TC, Shoobridge A, Ferrier M. Calcium diglutamate improves taste characteristics of lower-salt soup. European Journal of Clinical Nutrition 2002;56:519–23.
7. Murphy PA. Phytoestrogen content of processed soybean products. Food Technology 1982;36:60–4.
8. Dahl LK, Heine M. Effects of chronic excess salt feeding: Enhanced hypertensinogenic effect of sea salt over sodium chloride. Journal of Experimental Medicine 1961;113:1067–76.

9. Manfield C. Spice. Ringwood, Victoria: Penguin Books, Australia Ltd; 1999:16.
10. Bharadwaj M. The Indian pantry. London: Kyle Cathie Limited; 1996:73.
11. Beard TC, von Witt RJ. Wrong messages about black salt. Nutrition and Dietetics 2002;59: 232–3.
12. Sacks FM, Svetkey LP, Vollmer WM, Appel LJ, Bray GA, Harsha D, et al. Effects on blood pressure of reduced dietary sodium and the Dietary Approaches to Stop Hypertension (DASH) diet. New England Journal of Medicine 2001;344:3–10.
13. Page LB, Damon A, Moellering RC. Antecedents of cardiovascular disease in six Solomon Islands Societies. Circulation 1974;49:1132–46.
14. de Wardener HE, Kaplan NM. On the assertion that a moderate restriction of sodium may have adverse health effects. American Journal of Hypertension 1993;6:810–14.
15. Korhonen MH, Järvinen RMK, Sarkkinen ES, Uusitupa MIJ. Effects of a salt-restricted diet on the intake of other nutrients. American Journal of Clinical Nutrition 2000;72:414–20.
16. Bertino M, Beauchamp GK, Engelman K. Long-term reduction in dietary sodium alters the taste of salt. American Journal of Clinical Nutrition 1982;36:1134–44.
17. Bertino M, Beauchamp GK, Engelman K. Increasing dietary salt alters salt taste preference. Physiology & Behavior 1986;38:203–13.
18. Brewer C. Axis restaurant at the National Museum. Canberra Times 2001;Friday (6 April):6.
19. National Health & Medical Research Council. Dietary Guidelines for Australian Adults. Canberra: Australian Government Publishing Service; 2003.

5 Cooking to conserve flavour

1. Henningsen NC, Larsson L, Nelson D. Hypertension, potassium and the kitchen. Lancet 1976;1:133.
2. Harben P. The grammar of cookery. Harmondsworth, UK Penguin Books; 1965.
3. Anon. Women's Weekly microwave cookbook. Sydney: Australian Consolidated Press; n.d.:5.
4. Dealler SF, Lacey RW. Superficial microwave heating. Nature 1990;344:496.
5. Perlman A. Hazards of a microwave oven. New England Journal of Medicine 1980;302:970–1.
6. Pritikin N, Leonard JN, Hofer JL. Live longer now. New York: Grosset & Dunlap; 1974.
7. Pritikin N. The Pritikin promise. New York: Bantam Books; 1985.
8. MacGregor GA, MacGregor C. The low-salt diet book. 2nd edn. London: Macdonald & Co; 1991.
9. Gazzaniga D. The no-salt, lowest-sodium cookbook. New York: St Martin's Press; 2001.
10. Gazzaniga D. The no-salt, lowest-sodium baking book. New York: St Martin's Press; 2003.
11. Anderson DC, Anderson TD. The no-salt cookbook. Avon, MA: Adams Media Corporation; 2001.
12. Claiborne C, Franey P. Craig Claiborne's gourmet diet. New York: Times Books; 1980.
13. Brenner E. Gourmet cooking without salt. Garden City, NY: Doubleday & Co; 1981.
14. Medical Research Council. The rice diet in the treatment of hypertension. Lancet 1950; 2: 509–13.
14. Stafford J. Taste of life. Melbourne: Viking O'Neill; 1991.
15. O'Sullivan M. Mustards, pickles and chutneys. North Ryde, NSW: Angus & Robertson; 1991.

6 The overriding importance of bread

1. English R, Lewis J. Nutritional values of Australian foods. Canberra: Australia New Zealand Food Authority; 2000.
2. Beard TC. Sodium update. In: Truswell AS, Dreosti IE, English RM et al; eds. Recommended nutrient intakes: Australian papers. Sydney: Australian Professional Publications; 1990:182–90.

3.   www.nhlbi.nih.gov/new/press/may17-00.htm (accessed 14 July 2003).
4.   Sacks FM, Svetkey LP,Vollmer WM, Appel LJ, Bray GA, Harsha D, et al. Effects on
      blood pressure of reduced dietary sodium and the Dietary Approaches to Stop
      Hypertension (DASH) diet. New England Journal of Medicine 2001;344:3–10.
5.   Obarzanek E. Division of Epidemiology & Clinical Applications, NHLBI, Bethesda,
      MD. Personal communication 2003.
6.   Pritikin N, Leonard JN, Hofer JL. Live longer now. New York: Grosset & Dunlap;
      1974.
7.   Beard TC. The bread of the 21st century: the first Jo Rogers memorial oration.
      Australian Journal of Nutrition and Dietetics 1997;54:198–203.
8.   Margan F. The grape and I. London: Paul Hamlyn; 1969:92.
9.   Symons M. One continuous picnic: a history of eating in Australia. Ringwood,
      Victoria: Penguin Books; 1984:7.
10.   Romer E. The Tuscan year: life and food in an Italian valley. London: Hodder &
      Stoughton; 1985:9–10.

7 Low salt recipes

1.   Sacks FM, Svetkey LP,Vollmer WM, Appel LJ, Bray GA, Harsha D, et al. Effects on
      blood pressure of reduced dietary sodium and the Dietary Approaches to Stop
      Hypertension (DASH) diet. New England Journal of Medicine 2001;344:3–10.
2.   Baghurst KI, Crawford D,Worsley Aea, Syrette JA, Record SJ, Baghurst PA. The
      Victorian nutrition survey: a profile of the energy, macronutrient and sodium intakes
      of the population. Community Health Studies 1988;12:42–54.
3.   Gazzaniga D. The no-salt, lowest-sodium cookbook. New York: St Martin's Press; 2001.

9 Getting enough iodine

1.   Gillum RF. Will persons on low sodium diets become iodine deficient? American
      Heart Journal 1982;103:1084–5.
2.   Simpson FO,Thaler BI, Paulin JM, Phelan EL, Cooper GJS. Iodide excretion in a
      salt-restriction trial. New Zealand Medical Journal 1986;97:890–3.
3.   Gunton JE, Hams G, Fiegert M, McElduff A. Iodine deficiency in ambulatory partici-
      pants at a Sydney teaching hospital: is Australia truly iodine replete? Medical Journal
      of Australia 1999;171:467–470.
4.   McDonnell CM, Harris M, Zacharin MR. Iodine deficiency and goitre in school-
      children in Melbourne, 2001. Medical Journal of Australia 2003;178:159–62.
5.   Guttikonda K, Burgess JR, Hynes K, Boyages S, Byth K, Parameswaran V. Recurrent
      iodine deficiency in Tasmania, Australia: a salutary lesson in sustainable iodine pro-
      phylaxis and its monitoring.Journal of Clinical Endocrinology and Metabolism
      2002;87:2809–15.
6.   Beard TC,Woodward DR, Ball PJ, Hornsby H, von Witt RJ, Dwyer T. The Hobart
      Salt Study 1995: few meet national sodium intake target. Medical Journal of Australia
      1997;166:404–7.
7.   Richards PAC. Iodine nutrition in two Tasmanian cultures. Medical Journal of
      Australia 1995;163:628–30.
8.   Giovannucci E, Stampfer MJ, Colditz GA, Hunter DJ, Fuchs C, Rosner BA, et al.
      Multivitamin use, folate, and colon cancer in women in the nurses' health study.
      Annals of Internal Medicine 1998;129:517–24.

10 Shopping within the dietary guidelines

1.   National Health & Medical Research Council. Dietary Guidelines for Australian
      Adults. Canberra: Australian Government Publishing Service; 2003.
2.   Trowell HC, Burkitt DP, eds. Western diseases: their emergence and prevention.
      London: Edward Arnold; 1981.

11 Low salt shopping

1.   Simpson FO, Currie IJ. Licorice consumption amongst high school students. New
      Zealand Medical Journal 1982;95:31–3.

12 Salt and high blood pressure

1. Risk Factor Prevalence Study Management Committee. Risk factor prevalence study: Survey No. 3—1989. Canberra: National Heart Foundation of Australia and Australian Institute of Health; 1990.

2. National Center for Health Statistics. NCHS Advance Data, No 84. Vital and health statistics of the National Center for Health Statistics. Washington DC: US Department of Health & Human Services; 1982.

3. Vasan RS, Beiser A, Seshadri S, Larson MG, Kannel WB, D'Agostino RB, et al. Residual lifetime risk for developing hypertension in middle-aged women and men: the Framingham Heart Study. Journal of the American Medical Association 2002;287:1003–10.

4. Kannel W, Gordon T, eds. The Framingham study. An epidemiological investigation of cardiovascular disease. Section 26: 16-year followup. Washington DC: US Government Printing Office; 1970.

5. Joint National Committee. The seventh report of the Joint National Committee on Prevention, Detection, Evaluation, and Treatment of High Blood Pressure. Journal of the American Medical Association 2003;289:2560–72.

6. Trowell HC, Burkitt DP, eds. Western diseases: their emergence and prevention. London: Edward Arnold; 1981.

7. WHO/ISH Statement Committee. Prevention of hypertension and associated cardiovascular disease: a 1995 statement. Clinical and Experimental Hypertension—Theory and Practice 1995;18(3&4):581–93.

8. Hollenberg NK, Martinez G, McCullough M, Meinking T, Passan D, Preston M, et al. Aging, acculturation, salt intake, and hypertension in the Kuna of Panama. Hypertension 1997;29(part 2):171–6.

9. Tobian L. Dietary salt (sodium) and hypertension. American Journal of Clinical Nutrition 1979;32(Suppl):2659–62.

10. He FJ, Ogden LG, Vupputuri S, Bazzano LA, Loria C, Whelton PK. Dietary sodium intake and subsequent risk of cardiovascular disease in overweight adults. Journal of the American Medical Association 1999;282:2027–34.

11. Leibel RL, Hirsch J. Diminished energy requirements in reduced-obese patients. Metabolism 1984;33:164–70.

12. Weigle DS, Sande KJ, Iverius PH, Monsen ER, Brunzell JD. Weight loss leads to a marked decrease in non-resting energy expenditure in ambulatory human subjects. Metabolism 1988;37:930–6.

13. Leibel RL, Rosenbaum M, Hirsch J. Changes in energy expenditure resulting from altered body weight. New England Journal of Medicine 1995;332:621–8 [Erratum New England Journal of Medicine 1995;333:399].

14. Jennings G, Nelson L, Nestel P, Esler M, Korner P, Burton D, et al. The effects of changes in physical activity on major cardiovascular risk factors, hemodynamics, sympathetic function, and glucose utilization in man: a controlled study of four levels of activity. Circulation 1986;73:30–40.

15. Puddey IB, Beilin LJ, Vandongen R, Rouse I, Rogers P. Evidence for a direct effect of alcohol consumption on blood pressure in normotensive man: a randomised controlled trial. Hypertension 1985;7:707–13.

16. Meneely GR, Battarbee HD. High sodium–low potassium environment and hypertension. American Journal of Cardiology 1976;38:768–85.

17. Intersalt Cooperative Research Group. Intersalt: an international study of electrolyte excretion and blood pressure. Results for 24 hour urinary sodium and potassium excretion. British Medical Journal 1988;297:319–28.

18. He FJ, MacGregor GA. Beneficial effects of potassium. British Medical Journal 2001;323:497–501.

19. Henry JP, Stephens PM, Santisteban GA. A model of psychosocial hypertension showing reversibility and cardiovascular complications. Circulation Research 1975;36:156–64.

20.   Michell AR. The clinical biology of sodium. Oxford: Elsevier Science; 1995:108.

21.   Lindquist TL, Beilin LJ, Knuiman MW. Influence of lifestyle, coping, and job stress on blood pressure of men and women. Hypertension 1997;29:1–7.

22.   Freis ED, Wanko A, Wilson IM, Parrish AE. Treatment of essential hypertension with chlorothiazide (Diuril). Journal of the American Medical Association 1958;166: 137–40.

23.   Guyton AC. The surprising kidney-fluid mechanism for pressure control—its infinite gain! Hypertension 1990;16:725–30.

24.   Bianchi G, Fox U, Di Francesco GF, Giovanetti AM, Pagetti D. Blood pressure changes produced by kidney cross-transplantation between spontaneously hypertensive rats and normotensive rats. Clinical Science and Molecular Medicine 1974;47: 435–48.

25.   Woolfson RG, de Wardener HE. Primary renal abnormalities in hereditary hypertension. Kidney International 1996;50:717–31.

26.   Denton D, Weisinger R, Mundy NI, Wickings EJ, Dixson A, Moisson P, et al. The effect of increased salt intake on blood pressure of chimpanzees. Nature Medicine 1995;1:1009–16.

27.   Beard TC. The bread of the 21st century: the first Jo Rogers memorial oration. Australian Journal of Nutrition and Dietetics 1997;54:198–203.

28.   Robertson JIS. Dietary salt and hypertension: a scientific issue or a matter of faith? Journal of Evaluation in Clinical Practice 2003;9:1–22.

29.   Beard TC, Liu S, Wang TY, Wang YG, Dwyer T, Liang LQ. Is it feasible to prevent hypertension and stroke in China? Australian Journal of Nutrition and Dietetics 1993;50:146–51.

30.   Liu LS. Epidemiology of hypertension and cardiovascular disease: China experience. Clinical and Experimental Hypertension—Theory and Practice 1990;A12(5):831–44.

31.   Smith SJ, Markandu ND, Rotellar C, Elder DM, MacGregor C. A new or old Chinese restaurant syndrome? British Medical Journal 1982;285:1205.

32.   Rikimaru T, Fujita Y, Okuda T, Kajiwara N, Miyatani S, Alpers MP, et al. Responses of sodium balance, blood pressure, and other variables to sodium loading in Papua New Guinea highlanders. American Journal of Clinical Nutrition 1988;47:502–8.

33.   Luft FC, Rankin LI, Bloch R, Weyman AE, Willis LR, Murray RH, et al. Cardiovascular and humoral responses to extremes of sodium intake in normal black and white men. Circulation 1979;60:697–706.

34.   Simpson FO, Currie IJ. Licorice consumption amongst high school students. New Zealand Medical Journal 1982;95:31–3.

35.   MacGregor GA, Markandu ND, Singer DRJ, Cappuccio FP, Shore AC, Sagnella GA. Moderate sodium restriction with angiotensin converting enzyme inhibitor in essential hypertension: a double-blind study. British Medical Journal 1987;294:531–34.

36.   Dahl LK. Effects of chronic excess salt feeding. Induction of self-sustained hypertension in rats. Journal of Experimental Medicine 1961;114:231–6.

37.   Beard TC, Cooke HM, Gray WR, Barge R. Randomised controlled trial of a no-added-sodium diet for mild hypertension. Lancet 1982;2:455–8.

38.   Law MR, Frost CD, Wald NJ. By how much does dietary salt reduction lower blood pressure? I—Analysis of observational data among populations. British Medical Journal 1991;302:811–15.

39.   Dyer AR, Stamler R, Elliott P, Stamler J. Dietary salt and blood pressure. Nature Medicine 1995;1:994–6.

40.   Mattes RD, Falkner B. Salt-sensitivity classification in normotensive adults. Clinical Science 1999;96:449–59.

41.   Weinberger MH, Fineberg NS. Sodium and volume sensitivity of blood pressure: age and pressure change over time. Hypertension 1991;18:67–71.

42.   Appel LJ, Moore TJ, Obarzanek E, Vollmer WM, Svetkey LP, Sacks FM, et al. A clinical trial of the effects of dietary patterns on blood pressure. New England Journal of Medicine 1997;336:1117–24.

43. Sacks FM, Svetkey LP, Vollmer WM, Appel LJ, Bray GA, Harsha D, et al. Effects on blood pressure of reduced dietary sodium and the Dietary Approaches to Stop Hypertension (DASH) diet. New England Journal of Medicine 2001;344:3–10.

44. www.nhlbi.nih.gov/new/press/may17-00.htm (accessed 14 July 2003).

13 Salt and other health problems

1. He FJ, Markandu ND, Sagnella GA, MacGregor GA. Effect of salt intake on renal excretion of water in humans. Hypertension 2001;38:317–20.

2. Freis ED. Salt, volume and the prevention of hypertension. Circulation 1976;53: 561–63.

3. Murphy RJF. The effect of 'rice diet' on plasma volume and extracellular space in hypertensive subjects. Journal of Clinical Investigation 1950;29:912–16.

4. MacGregor GA, Tasker P, de Wardener HE. Diuretic-induced oedema. Lancet 1975;1:489–92.

5. MacGregor GA, Markandu ND, Roulston JE, Jones JC, de Wardener HE. Is 'idiopathic' oedema idiopathic? Lancet 1979;1:397–400.

6. Furstenberg AC, Lashmet FH, Lathrop F. Ménière's symptom complex: medical treatment. Annals of Otology, Rhinology and Laryngology 1934;43:1035–46.

7. Boles R, Rice DH, Hybels R, Work WP. Conservative management of Ménière's disease: Furstenberg regimen revisited. Annals of Otology 1975;84:513–17.

8. Harrison MS, Naftalin L. Meniere's disease: mechanism and management. Springfield, ILL: Charles C Thomas; 1968:85–101.

9. Gibson WPR. Royal Prince Alfred Hospital, Sydney. Personal communication 1999.

10. Derebery J. Allergic management of Meniere's disease: an outcome study. Otolaryngology and Head and Neck Surgery 2000;122:174–82.

11. Rose G. Sick individuals and sick populations. International Journal of Epidemiology 1985;14:32–8.

12. Davies J. Recipes for health: PMS. Over 100 recipes for overcoming premenstrual syndrome. London: Thorsons; 1995.

13. Goulding A. Fasting urinary sodium/creatinine in elation to calcium/creatinine and hydroxyproline/creatinine in a general population of women. New Zealand Medical Journal 1981;93:294–7.

14. Trowell HC, Burkitt DP, eds. Western diseases: their emergence and prevention. London: Edward Arnold; 1981.

15. Muldowney FP, Freaney R, Moloney MF. Importance of dietary sodium in the hypercalciuric syndrome. Kidney International 1982;22:292–6.

16. Borghi L, Schianchi T, Meschi T, Guerra A, Allegri F, Maggiore U, et al. Comparison of two diets for the prevention of recurrent stones in idiopathic hypercalciuria. New England Journal of Medicine 2002;346:77–84.

17. Bushinsky DA. Recurrent hypercalciuric nephrolithiasis—does diet help? New England Journal of Medicine 2002;346:124–5.

18. Kwok RHM. Chinese restaurant syndrome. New England Journal of Medicine 1968;278:796.

19. Yang WH, Drouin MA, Herbert M, Yang M, Karsh J. The monosodium glutamate complex: assessment in a double-blind, placebo-controlled study. Journal of Allergy and Clinical Immunology 1997;99:757–62.

20. Smith SJ, Markandu ND, Rotellar C, Elder DM, MacGregor C. A new or old Chinese restaurant syndrome? British Medical Journal 1982;285:1205.

21. Hofman A, Hazebroek A, Valkenburg HA. A randomised trial of sodium intake and blood pressure in newborn infants. Journal of the American Medical Association 1983;250:370–3.

22. Geleijnse JM. Erasmus University Medical School, Rotterdam, personal communication 1999.

23. Geleijnse JM, Hofman A, Witteman JCM, Hazebroek AAJM, Valkenburg HA. Long-term effects of neonatal sodium restriction on blood pressure. Hypertension 1997;29:913–17.

24. Nazario CM, Szklo M, Diamond E, Román-Franco A, Climent C, Suarez E, et al. Salt and gastric cancer: a case-control study in Puerto Rico. International Journal of Epidemiology 1993;22:790–7.

25. Takahashi M, Nishikawa A, Furukawa F, Enami T, Hasegawa T, Hayashi Y. Dose-dependent promoting effects of sodium chloride (NaCl) on rat glandular stomach carcinogenesis initiated with N-methyl-N'-nitro-N-nitroguanidine. Carcinogenesis 1994;15:1429–32.

26. Schmieder RE. Salt intake is related to the process of myocardial hypertrophy in essential hypertension. Journal of the American Medical Association 1989;262: 1187–8.

27. Avolio AP, Chen SG, Wang RP, Zhang CL, Li MF, O'Rourke MF. Effects of aging on changing arterial compliance and left ventricular load in a northern Chinese urban community. Circulation 1983;68:50–8.

28. Avolio AP, Clyde KM, Beard TC, Cooke HM, Ho KKL, O'Rourke MF. Improved arterial distensibility in normotensive subjects on a low-salt diet. Arteriosclerosis 1986;6:166–9.

29. Burney PGJ, Britton JR, Chinn S, Tattersfield AE, Platt HS, Papacosta AO, et al. Response to inhaled histamine and 24 hour sodium excretion. British Medical Journal 1986;292:1483–6.

30. Carey OJ, Locke C, Cookson JB. Effect of alterations of dietary sodium on the severity of asthma in men. Thorax 1993;48:714–18.

31. Burney PGJ. The causes of asthma—does salt potentiate bronchial reactivity? Journal of the Royal Society of Medicine 1987;80:364–7.

32. Middleton E. Calcium antagonists and asthma. Journal of Allergy and Clinical Immunology 1985;76:341–6.

33. Heeg JZE, de Jong PE, van De Hem GK, de Zeeuw D. Efficacy and variability of the antiproteinuric effect of ACE inhibition by lisinopril. Kidney International 1989;36: 272–9.

34. Bakris GL, Smith A. Effects of sodium intake in patients with diabetic nephropathy treated with long-acting calcium antagonists. Annals of Internal Medicine 1996;125: 201–4.

35. Fourlanos S, Greenberg P. Managing drug-induced hyponatraemia in adults. Australian Prescriber 2003;26:114–17.

36. Adrogue HJ, Madias NE. Hyponatremia. New England Journal of Medicine 2000;342:1581–9.

37. Hartung TK, Schofield E, Short AI, Parr MJ, Henry JA. Hyponatraemic states following 3,4-methylenedioxymethamphetamine (MDMA, 'ecstasy') ingestion. Quarterly Journal of Medicine 2002;95:431–7.

38. Seidel S, Kreutzer R, Smith D, McNeel S, Gilliss D. Assessment of commercial laboratories performing hair mineral analysis. Journal of the American Medical Association 2001;285:67–72.

14 Hot weather, sport and cramp

1. Beard TC, Cooke HM, Gray WR, Ellem DP. Spontaneous remission and its significance for trials in primary prevention of hypertension. Annals of Clinical Research 1984;16 (Suppl 43):132–5.

2. National Health & Medical Research Council. Report of the working party on sodium in the Australian diet. Canberra: Australian Government Publishing Service; 1984:20.

3. Bloomfield J, Fricker PA, Fitch KD. Science and medicine in sport. 2nd edn. Carlton, Victoria: Blackwell Science; 1995:111.

4. Summerton C, Shetty P, Sandle LN, Watt S. In: Haslett C, Chilvers ER, Boon NA, Colledge NR, Hunter JAA, eds. Davidson's principles and practice of medicine. Edinburgh: Churchill Livingstone; 2002:330–1.

5. Noakes TD. Advice to overdrink may cause fatal hyponatraemic encephalopathy. British Medical Journal 2003;327:113–14.

6.   Weiner IH, Weiner HL. Nocturnal leg muscle cramps. Journal of the American Medical Association 1980;244:2332–3.
7.   Oliver WJ. Professor of Pediatrics, Ann Arbor, MI, personal communication 1991.
8.   Beard TC, Cooke HM, Gray WR, Barge R. Randomised controlled trial of a no-added-sodium diet for mild hypertension. Lancet 1982;2:455–8.
9.   MacGregor GA, Markandu ND, Best F, Elder DM, Cam J, Sagnella GA, et al. Double-blind randomised controlled trial of moderate sodium restriction in essential hypertension. Lancet 1982;1:351–5.
10. Thaler BI, Paulin JM, Phelan EL, Simpson FO. A pilot study to test the feasibility of salt restriction in a community. New Zealand Medical Journal 1982;95:839–42.
11. Beard TC, Liu S, Wang TY, Wang YG, Dwyer T, Liang LQ. Is it feasible to prevent hypertension and stroke in China? Australian Journal of Nutrition and Dietetics 1993;50:146–51.
12. Liu K, J S. Assessment of sodium intake in epidemiological studies on blood pressure. Annals of Clinical Research 1984;16(Suppl43):49–54.
13. Black JS. Night cramps. Australian Family Physician 1988;17:941.

15 Sodium in water and in the pharmacy

1.   National Health & Medical Research Council. Report of the working party on sodium in the Australian diet. Canberra: Australian Government Publishing Service; 1984.
2.   National Health & Medical Research Council. Dietary Guidelines for Older Australians. Canberra: Australian Government Publishing Service; 1999:91.
3.   Beard TC. Low sodium prescribing. Australian Prescriber 1992;15(2):44–6.
4.   Beard TC, Wilkinson SJ, Vial JH. Hazards of urinary alkalising agents [letter]. Medical Journal of Australia 1988;149:723.

16 The problem of what to believe

1.   Nestlé M. Food politics: how the food industry influences nutrition and health. Berkeley, CA: University of California Press; 2002.
2.   Walker C, Cannon G. The food scandal. London: Century Publishing; 1984.
3.   Trowell HC, Burkitt DP, eds. Western diseases: their emergence and prevention. London: Edward Arnold; 1981.
4.   de Langre J. Sea salt's hidden powers. Magalia, CA: Happiness Press; 1994.
5.   Davis H. Sea change. The Age 'Good Weekend' 2002 (2 March):54.
6.   Dahl LK, Heine M. Effects of chronic excess salt feeding: Enhanced hypertensino-genic effect of sea salt over sodium chloride. Journal of Experimental Medicine 1961;113:1067–76.
7.   Page LB, Damon A, Moellering RC. Antecedents of cardiovascular disease in six Solomon Islands Societies. Circulation 1974;49:1132–46.
8.   Tomlinson M. Iodine idiocy. The Age 2003 (18 February):letters.
9.   www.celtic-seasalt.com/saltoflife/celseasalan.html
10. De Costa CM. 'The contagiousness of childbed fever': a short history of puerperal sepsis and its treatment. Medical Journal of Australia 2002;177:668–71.
11. Management Committee. Untreated mild hypertension: a report of the Management Committee of the Australian therapeutic trial in mild hypertension. Lancet 1982;1: 185–91.
12. Baron JH. James Lind would not have approved. Lancet 1982;1:1313.
13. Puddey IB, Beilin LJ, Vandongen R, Rouse I, Rogers P. Evidence for a direct effect of alcohol consumption on blood pressure in normotensive man: a randomised controlled trial. Hypertension 1985;7:707–13.
14. Anon. Scientists' statement regarding data on the sodium-hypertension relationship and sodium health claims on food labelling. Nutrition Reviews 1997;55:172–5.
15. MacGregor GA, de Wardener HE. Salt, diet and health. Neptune's poisoned chalice: the origins of high blood pressure. Cambridge: Cambridge University Press; 1998:193–217.

16. Taubes G. The (political) science of salt. Science 1998;281:898–907.
17. Fletcher RH, Fletcher SW, Wagner EH. Clinical epidemiology: the essentials. 2nd edn. Baltimore: Williams & Wilkins; 1988:132–3.
18. Sacks FM, Svetkey LP, Vollmer WM, Appel LJ, Bray GA, Harsha D, et al. Effects on blood pressure of reduced dietary sodium and the Dietary Approaches to Stop Hypertension (DASH) diet. New England Journal of Medicine 2001;344:3–10.
19. www.nhlbi.nih.gov/new/press/may17-00.htm accessed 14 July 2003.
20. Alderman MH. Dietary sodium and blood pressure [letter]. New England Journal of Medicine 2001;344:1716.
21. Rothman KJ. Conflict of interest: the new McCarthyism in science. Journal of the American Medical Association 1993;269:2782–4.
22. Doll R, Peto R. Mortality in relation to smoking: 20 years' observations on male British doctors. British Medical Journal 1976;2:1525–36.
23. Chalmers I, Enkin M, Kierse M. Effective care in pregnancy and childbirth. New York: Oxford University Press; 1991.
24. Naylor CD. Grey zones of clinical practice: some limits to evidence-based medicine. Lancet 1995;345:840–2.
25. Anon. Research update: low-salt diets feel the pinch. Australian Medicine 2003; 15:16.
26. Anon. Low salt diet benefits are marginal. Health Reader 2003;April:9.
27. Anon. Evidence salt is OK. The Mercury 2003;28 January:33.
28. Jürgens G, Graudal NA. Effects of a low sodium diet versus high sodium diet on blood pressure, renin, aldosterone, catecholamines, cholesterols, and triglyceride (Cochrane Review). In: The Cochrane Library, Issue 1. Oxford: Update Software; 2003.
29. Law MR, Frost CD, Wald NJ. By how much does dietary salt reduction lower blood pressure? III—Analysis of data from trials of salt reduction. British Medical Journal 1991;302:819–24.
30. Whelton PK, Cohen JD, Applegate WB. Dietary sodium and blood pressure [letter]. Journal of the American Medical Association 1996;276:1467–8.
31. He FJ, MacGregor GA. Effect of modest salt reduction on blood pressure: a meta-analysis of randomized trials. Implications for public health. Journal of Human Hypertension 2002;16:761–70.
32. Perry IJ. Salt, science and politics. Journal of Human Hypertension 2003;17:1–3.
33. Hooper L, Bartlett C, Davey Smith G, Ebrahim S. Reduced dietary salt for prevention of cardiovascular disease (Cochrane Review), In: The Cochrane Library, Issue 1, 2003. Oxford: Update Software. Oxford: Update Software; 2003.
34. Godlee F. The food industry fights for salt. British Medical Journal 1996;312: 1239–40.
35. Beard TC, Stowasser M. Cochrane and the salt debate. Lancet 2003;362:403.
36. Wright JM. Cochrane and the salt debate. Lancet 2003;362:403.
37. Last JM. A dictionary of epidemiolog. 3rd edn. Oxford: Oxford University Press; 1995:52.
38. Cochrane AL. Effectiveness and efficiency: random reflections on health services. London: The Nuffield Provincial Hospitals Trust; 1972:2.
39. Whalley H. Salt and hypertension: consensus or controversy? Lancet 1997;350:1686.

17 Can we abolish high blood pressure?

1. Ambard L, Beaujard E. Causes de l'hypertension artérielle. Archives Generales de Médecine 1904;1:520–33.
2. Tobian L. Dietary salt (sodium) and hypertension. American Journal of Clinical Nutrition 1979;32(Suppl):2659–62.
3. Intersalt Cooperative Research Group. Intersalt: an international study of electrolyte excretion and blood pressure. Results for 24 hour urinary sodium and potassium excretion. British Medical Journal 1988;297:319–28.

4. Boseley S. WHO infiltrated by food industry. The Guardian 2003;9 January 2003.

5. Walker C, Cannon G. The food scandal. London: Century Publishing; 1984:xvi–xvii.

6. Kincaid-Smith P, Alderman MH. Universal recommendations for sodium intake should be avoided. Medical Journal of Australia 1999;170:174–5.

7. Dawber TR. The Framingham Study: the epidemiology of atherosclerotic disease. Cambridge, MA: Commonwealth Fund; 1980:18.

8. Chobanian AV, Hill M. National Heart, Lung, and Blood Institute Workshop on sodium and blood pressure: a critical review of current scientific evidence. Hypertension 2000;35:858–63.

9. Joint National Committee. The seventh report of the Joint National Committee on Prevention, Detection, Evaluation, and Treatment of High Blood Pressure. Journal of the American Medical Association 2003;289:2560–72.

10. Rose G. Sick individuals and sick populations. International Journal of Epidemiology 1985;14:32–8.

11. Law MR, Frost CD, Wald NJ. By how much does dietary salt reduction lower blood pressure? III—Analysis of data from trials of salt reduction. British Medical Journal 1991;302:819–24.

12. Williams P, McMahon A, Boustead R. A case study of sodium reduction in breakfast cereals and the impact of the Pick the Tick food information program in Australia. Health Promotion International 2003;18:51–6.

13. Young L, Swinburn B. Impact of the Pick the Tick food information programme on the salt content of food in New Zealand. Health Promotion International 2002;17: 13–19.

14. Green LW. National policy in the promotion of health. International Journal of Health Education 1979;22:161–8.

15. National Heart Foundation of Australia. Risk factor prevalence study: survey no. 3— 1989. Canberra: National Heart Foundation; 1990:44.

16. Bertino M, Beauchamp GK, Engelman K. Increasing dietary salt alters salt taste preference. Physiology & Behavior 1986;38:203–13.

17. Bertino M, Beauchamp GK, Engelman K. Long-term reduction in dietary sodium alters the taste of salt. American Journal of Clinical Nutrition 1982;36:1134–44.

18. Godlee F. The food industry fights for salt. British Medical Journal 1996;312: 1239–40.

19. Anon. A better peanut butter. Choice 2003;June:22–3.

20. Pritikin N, McGrady PM. The Pritikin program for diet and exercise. New York: Grosset & Dunlap; 1979.

21. Stafford J. Taste of life. Melbourne: Viking O'Neill; 1993.

22. Beard TC, Farrance I. Danger of over-medication with no-added-salt diets. [letter]. Medical Journal of Australia 1987;147:46–7.

23. Anon. Health for all Australians. Report of the Health Targets and Implementation (Health for All) Committee to Australian Health Ministers. Canberra: Australian Government Publishing Service; 1988:37.

24. Australian Institute of Health and Welfare. Heart, stroke and vascular diseases— Australian facts 2001. AIHW Cat. No. CVD 13. Canberra: AIHW, National Heart Foundation of Australia, National Stroke Foundation of Australia; 2001:80.

25. Anon. Top 10 drugs. Australian Prescriber 1999;22(5):119.

26. National Health & Medical Research Council. Clinical practice guidelines: prevention of stroke—the role of anticoagulants, antiplatelet agents and carotid endoarterectomy. Canberra: Australian Government Publishing Service; 1997.

27. Scientific Advisory Committee on Nutrition. Salt and health. London: H.M. Stationery Office; 2003.

28. National Health & Medical Research Council. Dietary Guidelines for Australian Adults. Canberra: Australian Government Publishing Service; 2003.

29. www.nhlbi.nih.gov/new/press/may17-00.htm (accessed 14 July 2003).

30. Sacks FM, Svetkey LP, Vollmer WM, Appel LJ, Bray GA, Harsha D, et al. Effects on blood pressure of reduced dietary sodium and the Dietary Approaches to Stop Hypertension (DASH) diet. New England Journal of Medicine 2001;344:3–10.
31. Alderman MH. Salt, blood pressure and health: a cautionary tale. International Journal of Epidemiology 2002;31:311–15.
32. Freis ED. Salt, volume and the prevention of hypertension. Circulation 1976;53: 561–63.

Appendix 1: Skipping salt safely

1. Oliver WJ, Neel JV, Grekin RJ, Cohen EL. Hormonal adaptation to the stresses imposed upon sodium balance by pregnancy and lactation in the Yanomama Indians, a culture without salt. Circulation 1981;63:110–16.
2. Denton D. The hunger for salt. Berlin: Springer-Verlag; 1984:577.
3. Beard TC. The bread of the 21st century: the first Jo Rogers memorial oration. Australian Journal of Nutrition and Dietetics 1997;54:198–203.

Appendix 2: The 24-hour urine collection

1. Rose G. Sick individuals and sick populations. International Journal of Epidemiology 1985;14:32–8.
2. Beard TC. An alternative to the 'reference range' for reporting urinary sodium and potassium and blood lipids. Pathology 2000;32:158.

Appendix 3: Weights and measures

1. Denton D, Weisinger R, Mundy NI, Wickings EJ, Dixson A, Moisson P, et al. The effect of increased salt intake on blood pressure of chimpanzees. Nature Medicine 1995;1:1009–16.
2. Freis ED. Salt, volume and the prevention of hypertension. Circulation 1976;53: 561–3.
3. Bertino M, Beauchamp GK, Engelman K. Long-term reduction in dietary sodium alters the taste of salt. American Journal of Clinical Nutrition 1982;36:1134–44.
4. Bertino M, Beauchamp GK, Engelman K. Increasing dietary salt alters salt taste preference. Physiology & Behavior 1986;38:203–13.
5. MacGregor GA, de Wardener HE. Salt, diet and health. Neptune's poisoned chalice: the origins of high blood pressure. Cambridge: Cambridge University Press; 1998:193–217.
6. Beard TC, Cooke HM, Gray WR, Barge R. Randomised controlled trial of a no-added-sodium diet for mild hypertension. Lancet 1982;2:455–8.

Appendix 4: Sodium-free baking powder

1. Beard TC. Baking powders to meet the demand for better nutrition. What's New in Food Technology & Manufacturing 1998;March/April:48–9.

Appendix 6: Some technical comments

1. Meiselman HL. Adaptation and cross-adaptation of the four gustatory qualities. Perception & Psychophysics 1968;4:368–72.
2. Sacks FM, Svetkey LP, Vollmer WM, Appel LJ, Bray GA, Harsha D, et al. Effects on blood pressure of reduced dietary sodium and the Dietary Approaches to Stop Hypertension (DASH) diet. New England Journal of Medicine 2001;344:3–10.
3. Beard TC, Woodward DR, Ball PJ, Hornsby H, von Witt RJ, Dwyer T. The Hobart Salt Study 1995: few meet national sodium intake target. Medical Journal of Australia 1997;166:404–7.
4. Liu K, Cooper R, McKeever J, et al. Assessment of the association between habitual salt intake and high blood pressure: methodological problems. American Journal of Epidemiology 1979;110:219–26.
5. Intersalt Cooperative Research Group. Intersalt: an international study of electrolyte excretion and blood pressure. Results for 24 hour urinary sodium and potassium excretion. British Medical Journal 1988;297:319–28.

6. Denton D. The hunger for salt. Berlin: Springer-Verlag; 1984:577.

7. Michell AR. The clinical biology of sodium. Oxford: Elsevier Science; 1995:62–3.

8. Luft FC, Rankin LI, Bloch R, Weyman AE, Willis LR, Murray RH, et al. Cardiovascular and humoral responses to extremes of sodium intake in normal black and white men. Circulation 1979;60:697–706.

9. Meneely GR, Battarbee HD. High sodium–low potassium environment and hypertension. American Journal of Cardiology 1976;38:768–85.

10. Denton D, Weisinger R, Mundy NI, Wickings EJ, Dixson A, Moisson P, et al. The effect of increased salt intake on blood pressure of chimpanzees. Nature Medicine 1995;1:1009–16.

11. National Health & Medical Research Council. Dietary Guidelines for Australians Canberra: Australian Government Publishing Service; 1991:77.

12. Mensink RP, Beard TC. Unpublished data, Woden Valley Hospital, Canberra. 1984.

13. Michaelsen KF, Clausen T. Inadequate supplies of potassium and magnesium in relief food—implications and countermeasures. Lancet 1987;1:1421–3.

14. Nichols R. St Marys Hospital, London. Personal communication 1992.

15. Liu LS. Epidemiology of hypertension and cardiovascular disease: China experience. Clin and Exper Hypertension—Theory and Practice 1990;A12(5):831–44.

16. Beard TC, Liu S, Wang TY, Wang YG, Dwyer T, Liang LQ. Is it feasible to prevent hypertension and stroke in China? Australian Journal of Nutrition and Dietetics 1993;50:146–51.

17. Henningsen NC, Larsson L, Nelson D. Hypertension, potassium and the kitchen. Lancet 1976;1:133.

18. National Health & Medical Research Council. Report of the working party on sodium in the Australian diet. Canberra: Australian Government Publishing Service; 1984:4.

19. Meneely GR. Toxic effects of dietary sodium chloride and the protective efects of potassium. In: Committee on Food Protection. Toxicants occurring naturally in foods. Washington DC: National Academy of Sciences; 1973:26–42.

20. Anon. Potassium [editorial response to letter]. Australian Prescriber 1987;9:28.

21. Pritikin N. The Pritikin promise. New York: Bantam Books; 1985:x.

22. Hubbard JD, Inkeles S, Barnard RJ. Nathan Pritikin's heart. New England Journal of Medicine 1985;313:52.

23. Ornish D, Brown SE, Scherwitz LW, Billings JH, Armstrong WT, Ports TA, et al. Can lifestyle changes reverse coronary heart disease? Lancet 1990;336:129–33.

Index

Page references to figures in *italic*;
page references to tables in **bold**

index